GOVERNING HABITS

EXPERTISE

CULTURES AND
TECHNOLOGIES
OF KNOWLEDGE

EDITED BY DOMINIC BOYER

A list of titles in this series is available at www.cornellpress.cornell.edu.

Governing Habits

Treating Alcoholism in the Post-Soviet Clinic

Eugene Raikhel

Cornell University Press

Ithaca and London

First published 2016 by Cornell University Press
First printing, Cornell Paperbacks, 2016

Printed in the United States of America

Library of Congress Cataloging-in-Publication Data

Names: Raikhel, Eugene A., 1975– author.
Title: Governing habits : treating alcoholism in the post-Soviet clinic / Eugene Raikhel.
Description: Ithaca : Cornell University Press, 2016. | Includes bibliographical references and index.
Identifiers: LCCN 2016026223 | ISBN 9781501703126 (cloth : alk. paper) | ISBN 9781501703133 (pbk. : alk. paper)
Subjects: LCSH: Alcoholics—Institutional care—Russia (Federation)— Saint Petersburg. | Alcoholism—Hospitals—Russia (Federation)— Saint Petersburg. | Alcoholism—Treatment—Russia (Federation)— Saint Petersburg. | Post-communism—Health aspects—Russia (Federation)—Saint Petersburg. | Medical anthropology—Russia (Federation)—Saint Petersburg.
Classification: LCC HV5283.R92 P4873 2016 | DDC 616.86/106094709045—dc23
LC record available at https://lccn.loc.gov/2016026223

Cornell University Press strives to use environmentally responsible suppliers and materials to the fullest extent possible in the publishing of its books. Such materials include vegetable-based, low-VOC inks and acid-free papers that are recycled, totally chlorine-free, or partly composed of nonwood fibers. For further information, visit our website at www.cornellpress.cornell.edu.

Cloth printing   10 9 8 7 6 5 4 3 2 1
Paperback printing   10 9 8 7 6 5 4 3 2 1

To Iris, Eli, and Agnes

CONTENTS

Acknowledgments

This book has taken a long journey to completion. While the travel has been by no means smooth, it would never have been completed without the help of many people along the way. My deepest thanks go to all the patients and physicians in St. Petersburg who shared their time and stories with me. They include clinicians, staff, and patients at the hospital and district outpatient clinics of the St. Petersburg Municipal Addiction Treatment Service, the House of Hope on the Hill, the Bekhterev Psychoneurological Institute, and several other institutions. Several people were instrumental in helping to foster the contacts that allowed me to work in these institutions: Evgenii Bychkov, Natalia Fedorova, Tamara Metelkina, Peter Meylakhs, Vladimir Mikhailov, Valentina Shabalina, Alexander Sofronov, Victor Styazhkin, Dmitri Shagin, and Vladimir Teplitskii. I owe a great deal to Eugene Zubkov, both for his insights into the state of contemporary Russian narcology and to his generosity with his many contacts. I also thank the entire staff of the House of Hope on the Hill for putting up both with my questions and with the inconvenience that my presence surely caused them. To the patient who asked me one summer afternoon over lunch before a group therapy session, "What are you going to do with our words?," I hope that the book I have written represents your words at least somewhat adequately.

Over the course of many trips to Russia, the staff at the Nevsky Institute for Language and Culture provided key logistical support. I am particularly grateful to Vyacheslav Evseev for everything he has taught me about Russian language and society over the years. The European University at St. Petersburg provided a much-needed academic home away from home during the course of fieldwork.

My family and friends in St. Petersburg were an enormous support in the field. Thanks to Boris and Lyudmilla Raikhel, Valentina Kovaleva, the extended Lapshin family (Volodya, Larisa, Alexey, Sveta, and Illia), and Zhenya and Dina Zelikina. Irina Raikhel and Ilya Skovorodkin made living in St. Petersburg all the more enjoyable. On occasional weekday afternoons, my grandmother Valentina Raikhel fed me platefuls of soy protein, nutritional wisdom, and memories of a life lived in the hardest of times. Unfortunately she did not live to see the completion of this project.

I would like to express my deep gratitude to John Borneman, Carol Greenhouse, Joao Biehl, and Stephen Kotkin at Princeton for their wisdom, patience, and support; each helped to shape this project in distinctive ways. I am also tremendously grateful to the many mentors, colleagues, friends, and students who have shaped this book in countless ways with their generous readings, the inspiring example of their own scholarship, and their friendship: Dominique Behague, Nancy Campbell, Summerson Carr, Suparna Choudhury, Elizabeth Davis, Joe Dumit, Judith Farquhar, Itamar Francez, Ari Gandsman, Angela Garcia, William Garriott, Chris Garces, Cristiana Giordano, Richard Keller, Hanna Kienzler, Heiko Henkel, Laurence Kirmayer, Junko Kitanaka, Eduardo Kohn, Daniel Lende, Stephanie Lloyd, Margaret Lock, Anne Lovell, Zhiying Ma, Tomas Matza, Seth Messinger, Todd Meyers, Kavita Misra, Michael Oldani, Jamie Saris, Aaron Seaman, Lisa Stevenson, Tobias Rees, Michele Rivkin-Fish, Elizabeth Roberts, Na'ama Rokem, Ian Whitmarsh, Matthew Wolf-Meyer, Allan Young, Alexei Yurchak, Natasha Zaretsky, and Li Zhang. Profound thanks to my colleagues in the Department of Comparative Human Development at the University of Chicago, who have supported this project in many ways: Jennifer Cole, Susan Goldin-Meadow, Guanglei Hong,

Micere Keels, John Lucy, Dario Maestripieri, Jill Mateo, Anna Mueller, Lindsey Richland, Rick Shweder, Margaret Beale Spencer, and Richard Taub.

Portions of this book have been presented at a number of workshops, conferences, and seminar series hosted by the Social Science Research Council (SSRC); the Max Planck Institute for Social Anthropology; the École des Hautes Études en Sciences Sociales (EHESS); the Foundation for Psychocultural Research (FPR); the Departments of Anthropology at the University of California-Berkeley, the University of Wisconsin-Milwaukee, and Stanford University; the Department of Medical History and Bioethics at the University of Wisconsin-Madison; and the University of Chicago's Center for East European and Russian/Eurasian Studies. I want to thank the many colleagues at these and other events who have enriched this work with their generous readings and engagements. Portions of chapter 4 appeared as "Post-Soviet Placebos: Epistemology and Authority in Russian Treatments for Alcoholism," *Culture, Medicine and Psychiatry* 34(1): 132 68, and as "Placebos or Prostheses for the Will? Trajectories of Alcoholism Treatment in Russia," in *Addiction Trajectories*, ed. Eugene Raikhel and William Garriott (Durham, NC: Duke University Press, 2013); portions of the introduction and of chapters 3 and 5 appeared as "Institutional Encounters: Identification and Anonymity in Russian Addiction Treatment (and Ethnography)," in *Being There: The Fieldwork Encounter and the Making of Truth*, ed. John Borneman and Abdellah Hammoudi (Berkeley: University of California Press, 2009).

This project could not have been completed without the financial support of several fellowships and institutions. Trips to Russia, as well as periods of writing, have been supported by the Woodrow Wilson Society of Fellows at Princeton University, the Harriman Institution at Columbia University, the Canadian Institutes for Health Research, and the University of Chicago. Fieldwork was also funded by a Fulbright-Hays Doctoral Dissertation Research Abroad Fellowship.

I could not have hoped for a better home for this book than Cornell University Press. I want to thank Dominic Boyer, the editor of the Expertise series; Jim Lance, the acquisitions editor; and everyone at the press who has supported this book and helped it along its way. This book has benefited from the work of several excellent research assistants: Judith Mazdra, Elle Nurmi, and Annie Heffernan. Lissa McCullough and Kim

Greenwell both provided key editorial help. Kenneth Remitz generously offered his home as a writing retreat at a crucial moment.

Thanks also to my favorite parents-in-law, Neriel and Eva Bernblum; to Jonathan Bernblum; and to my aunt Tanya Vinnikova. I owe a great deal to my grandmother Alexandra Vinnikova, who kept me speaking in Russian throughout my childhood. My brother Vincent has always been a great friend and listening ear.

I thank my parents, Alexander and Natasha Raikhel, for teaching me the curiosity that brought me to anthropology and for supporting me in all my endeavors. Without their support this book would not have been completed. Iris Bernblum has had the patience to help me through the most difficult times and to listen to my grumbling, and has always sustained me with her humor, friendship, and love. Thank you for all of it. Eli and Agnes came along once this project was well under way and reminded me just how joyful life beyond the book could be.

GOVERNING HABITS

INTRODUCTION

The central building of St. Petersburg's Municipal Narcological (or Addiction) Hospital stands on a tree-lined street of nineteenth-century buildings on Vasilievsky Island. The area was one of the first parts of the city to be laid out; the succession of parallel numbered streets, called "lines," suggests the Enlightenment ideals of order that Peter I and his city planners sought to impose as they constructed St. Petersburg in the eighteenth century (Lincoln 2001, 24). With the upsurge in the real estate market in the early 2000s, this district in the historical center of the city regained its status as a desirable place to live. While some of the old housing stock still contained Soviet-era communal apartments in the first decade of the twenty-first century, many buildings have been converted back into elite homes for the wealthy and for new professionals. St. Petersburg University lies several streets to the east of the hospital; to the west, an avenue has been converted into a pedestrian walkway lined with boutiques, cafés, beer halls, and the occasional sushi bar.

In the midst of so much recent change, the cracked walls of the narcological hospital initially struck me as signs of deterioration or stasis when I first visited in early 2003. Like many of the city's prerevolutionary structures, the building bears visible marks of its transformation from private residence for the elite to municipal hospital. Just inside the entrance, past the landing, an enormous metal gate stretches across what was presumably once the main vestibule; an attendant sits in an adjoining wooden booth, controlling traffic into and out of the clinical section of the hospital. To the right, near the hospital's administrative offices, prospective patients and their family members wait on low benches for admission. Many of the wards are accessible only by way of the building's muddy, pitted, and overgrown courtyard, where, during the summer months, patients and nurses stand by entrances to staircases, smoking and chatting. In the nineteenth and early twentieth centuries, these "black entrances" and stairwells opening onto courtyards were meant for use by servants; the bard Bulat Okudzhava's "Song about a Black Cat" described these entrances as redolent of the fear, mutual suspicion and collective inaction of Soviet communal life (cf. Boym 1994, 141). At the hospital, the staircases are narrow and spare—concrete steps with unornamented metal railings. Doorways on each floor lead directly to the wards. The first time I walked up the staircase, a sign hanging above the entrance to Ward Six caught my eye. It was an off-white plastic box designed to light up from the inside, with the words "Quiet: Hypnosis in Progress" printed across its face in slightly faded text.

My initial impressions of the hospital building as a relic or an object of decay or near ruin were not surprising, as they had been shaped by everything I had read about alcohol and substance dependence treatment in Russia—that is, by accounts of what went on inside this hospital and others like it. Since the Soviet anti-alcohol campaign of the mid-1980s, and especially since the turbulent post-Soviet years of the mid-1990s, there had been widespread discussion—both inside and outside Russia—about the effects of alcohol consumption and alcoholism on mortality rates in Russia. During the years of the most dramatic social and political economic changes—between 1990 and 1994—male life expectancy in Russia plummeted from 63.8 to 57.7 years, a drop that one group of health statisticians called "beyond the peacetime experience of industrialized countries" (Notzon et al. 1998, 793). Many public health researchers agreed that these figures were in some way linked to both the experience of stress and alcohol consumption or the harms associated with it, although the specific causal mechanisms continue to be debated.

Motivated in part by these concerns, increasing numbers of public health workers, clinicians, psychologists, counselors, and other specialists in addiction from North America and Western Europe began to visit the clinical institutions in Russia that addressed substance abuse, often as consultants to various internationally funded public health programs. Their reports almost all described narcology—as addiction medicine is called in Russia—as "backward," stuck in "the dark ages" (Fleming, Meyroyan, and Klimova 1994, 360), and otherwise having failed to advance along with contemporary global medicine. Writing in the mid-1990s, a team made up of British and Russian addiction researchers exclaimed, "Current therapeutic practice is still based on people's ignorance, and a neglect by specialists of their professional duty" (ibid.). And while there was certainly a period of the 1990s during which nearly any form of expertise developed under state socialism was widely understood as inherently inferior to its counterparts in the liberal democratic world (if not worthless), such assessments of narcology have continued to the present day.

Nor have such arguments been limited to visiting specialists. For example, Vladimir D. Mendelevich (2004), a professor at Kazan State Medical University and an outspoken critic of what he calls "official narcology," has argued that many of the basic assumptions underlying the specialty of narcology are faulty and out of sync with addiction medicine throughout the world: "Many principles of Russian narcology contradict healthy reason and diverge from the agreed-upon foundations of the worldwide professional community. The entire world criticizes the practice of compulsory treatment for addicts; we are for it. Everyone is working to introduce 'harm reduction' programs; we are against them. Everyone condemns paternalistic and manipulative methods in narcology; we support them." Here Mendelevich points to three specific issues that have been central to critiques of Russian narcology. "Compulsory treatment for addicts" refers to the legal measures requiring drug addicts (but not alcoholics) to receive treatment but also to the frequent calls for the revival of "compulsory treatment" for alcoholics, which was central to the Soviet narcological system. The paucity of "harm reduction" programs in Russia—and in particular, the official stance against opiate-substitution therapy (OST), employing either methadone or buprenorphine—has been a particularly contentious issue in international public health circles, where such methods are widely accepted as methods demonstrated to reduce the transmission of blood-borne infections such as HIV and hepatitis among injection drug users. Finally, by "paternalistic and manipulative methods" Mendelevich refers to a popular and widely available set of closely related therapeutic techniques for alcoholism (sometimes also offered for opiate and behavioral addictions), which largely rely on hypnotic suggestion and are often collectively referred to as "coding" (*kodirovanie*). Many critics have pointed to what they see as these treatments' disregard for a normative model of patient autonomy; instead of treating patients as autonomous, rational, and potentially self-knowing individuals, these methods are described as relying on people's "ignorance" and "belief" to frighten them into sobriety (Finn 2005; Parfitt 2006).

The criticisms of Mendelevich and others take aim at the central tenets of narcology as a domain of knowledge, ethics, and intervention. They do so in a way that—not surprisingly—links the bioethical principles of consent and patient autonomy and the epistemic practices of evidence-based medicine (EBM) with medical modernity and that characterizes narcology's failure to properly enact these ethical principles and epistemic practices not simply as paternalistic or outdated but as a sign of backwardness and its distance from the global biomedical ecumene. Moreover, both these critiques and the defenses of Russia narcology often written in response to them are often interpreted by the participants in debates as indexing much broader and well-worn arguments about Russia's relationship to "modernity," to "liberalism," to "the West."

All of these were criticisms I had read before starting my fieldwork, and at first, accepting their underlying assumptions made it easy to think that it was not only the crumbling plaster walls of the hospital's examination rooms that had not been renovated since the Soviet days. Indeed, the practices that went on inside the hospital's walls and the concepts that underpinned them—the protocols and therapeutics, the conceptualizations of disease and disorder, and the enactments of care and of ethical clinical practice—all seemed like relics as well.

However, with time it became increasingly clear to me that whatever their ethical and political merits, critiques that cast Russian narcology as backward or even authoritarian ultimately obscured more than they revealed about the epistemic assumptions, clinical practices, and embodied experiences that make up the everyday encounters between narcologists and patients in St. Petersburg. Such critiques had little to say, for example, about what the clinical practices central to narcology meant to clinicians or patients. Why were methods such as kodirovanie so popular with patients and their family members? How did they make sense to clinicians? And beyond a general sense of the supposed inertia and dead weight of Soviet history, such critiques typically had little to say about how these practices had come to be or why they had persisted—and even whether *persistence* was the most useful way of conceiving of their contemporary existence. Moreover, what could these debates over appropriate treatments for alcoholism tell us about broader questions: the authorization of expert knowledge or the transformations of health and social citizenship in contemporary Russia?

In what follows, I train an ethnographic eye on the clinical treatment of alcoholism in St. Petersburg, Russia, and seek to understand it as a changing domain of knowledge and expertise, as a circulation of changing medical technologies, and as a site where distinct forms of personhood are enabled. Rather than interpreting narcology as a Soviet survival or a local clinical "world on the wane" in the face of globalizing evidence-based medicine, I examine the political-economic, epistemic, and clinical changes that have transformed the medical management of alcoholism in Russia over the past twenty years. Drawing on ethnographic and historical research carried out on Russian narcology since 2003, I pay particular attention to the ways in which clinicians and patients have engaged with a range of therapeutic technologies for alcoholism, and how, in doing so, they instantiate specific ideas about illness, clinical authority, and patienthood.

This book may interest distinct groups of readers for different reasons. To some readers, whose interest in the topic stems from their own involvement in substance abuse treatment, global health practice or advocacy, psychiatry, psychology, or other engaged work with people experiencing distress, the world of narcologists and patients in St. Petersburg may be of interest in itself. I want to note at the outset to these readers that the book is neither a critique nor a defense of the practices prevalent in Russian narcology per se. As an anthropologist I am more concerned with complicating the very terms in which the debate takes place, tracing the gray zones of epistemic and ethical ambivalence and uncertainty and ultimately coming to some understanding of these social worlds that is adequate to the complexities of lived experience of my interlocutors. And while the interpretation and analysis contained in this book emerge from my own field experiences and bear the traces of my own history, my research interests, as well as my ethical and political disposition (which I try, whenever necessary, to make explicit), I have made an effort to present the ethnography in a way that would allow for readings against the grain of my own interpretations.

Other readers may be primarily interested in how this book contributes to discussions more specific to the anthropology of medicine and knowledge, to the social science of alcoholism and addiction treatment, and to the study of psychiatry as a social institution. I have for the most part clustered the engagements with such specialist literatures here in the introduction, in notes throughout the text, and in the conclusion. For this reason, it is particularly important to present a brief overview of the arguments that I make in this book.

First of all, as a contribution to the anthropology of medicine, psychiatry, and addiction therapeutics, this book makes an argument about the changing grounds of clinical authority and the conditions for effective therapy during a time of profound social transformation. It contributes to a wave of studies in medical anthropology that question the dominant narrative of medicalization, understood as the subsumption of human problems under the specialist authority of the medical profession, so central to much critical social science of medicine since the 1970s (Conrad 1992; Zola 1972). More recent studies do not deny the significance of medicalization as much as they query its social and institutional sources, shed a more nuanced light on its potential consequences, and raise questions about its ethical and political significance (Biehl 2005; Kitanaka 2012; Lakoff 2006; Schull 2012). Accounts of medicine in socialist and postsocialist states are particularly important to this conversation because, as many scholars have argued, medicalization took on a different shape in these settings than it did in Western European and North American states (Brotherton 2012; Farquhar 2002; Koch 2013; Matza 2012; Petryna 2002; Philips 2010; Rivkin-Fish 2005; Zigon 2011). Rather than being underwritten by the professional autonomy of physicians, medical authority in socialist states was closely entwined with state or bureaucratic power, a set of conditions with important consequences for physicians' enactments of their expertise and for patients' experiences of care (Rivkin-Fish 2005).

As a medical specialty that was created by decree during the 1970s, the ethos and organization of Soviet narcology were much more closely aligned with the security and policing organs of the Soviet party-state than were those of other medical specialties. Moreover, legal provisions for involuntary treatment allowed narcologists to wield the threat of coercion with recalcitrant patients. I posit that during the 1990s and later, narcology experienced a crisis of authority as the legal means for involuntary treatment were removed, funding levels dropped, and new competitors emerged in the domain of alcoholism treatment. As older kinds of bureaucratic authority fell away or became more tenuous, the forms of charismatic authority that narcologists had long been exercising in the clinic became increasingly important. In tracing the consequences of this shift, I draw attention to the ways in which arguments about the political and ethical meanings of distinct interventions methods come to constitute what I call "therapeutic legitimacy."

This book also contributes to work in anthropology on therapeutics, self-fashioning, and subjectivity. Mariana Valverde has proposed that "questions of addiction have been and continue to be important sites upon which the complex dialectic of personal freedom and control/self-control has worked itself out historically" (1998, 5). In this book I suggest that these convergences are particularly salient in Russia, where changes in the discursive, material, and social contours of alcoholism over the past two decades have all broadly coincided with a project of transforming political institutions and subjectivities. As I discuss throughout the book, themes of agency and responsibility, framed in opposing terms of dependence versus autonomy, underlie many debates about treatments for alcoholism in Russia. More broadly, I examine the clinical relationship between physicians and patients in the context of the complex Russian political and social order under Putin, in which responsibility, initiative, and personal sovereignty are affirmed as necessary traits within certain spheres, even as relationships of beneficence and obligation are valorized in others (Bernstein 2013; Rivkin-Fish 2005; Matza 2009, 2012).

Clinical Authority in Crisis

Grigorii, a 12-step counselor and stage actor in his previous life, once told me that he had added up the total length of time he had spent in psychiatric hospitals and had come to the conclusion that it amounted to something like four years. All these commitments had occurred at the end of alcoholic binges; in some cases Grigorii was admitted in a state of alcoholic psychosis. He described the profound sense of bewilderment and distrust he had felt toward the physicians in these institutions: "None of my attempts to leave the madhouse early worked. There was simply no trust or understanding from the physician: you were always under this gaze, examining how you were behaving. I never knew how to behave; I didn't understand why I was there." While many facets of Grigorii's experience shaped his memory of the psychiatric hospital, it was the relationship with the physician—the iconic "clinical encounter"—that seemed to encapsulate his predicament in a way that was both metaphorical and concretely remembered and felt. Grigorii's evocation of the encounter between psychiatrist and patient strikingly echoes an argument that Michel Foucault made in many of his works—but that he stated with particular succinctness in his lectures titled "Psychiatric Power": "Why is it that one cannot leave the asylum? One cannot leave the asylum, not because the exit is far away, but because the entrance is too near. One never stops entering the asylum, and every encounter, every confrontation between the doctor and the patient begins again and indefinitely repeats this founding initial act by which madness will exist as reality and the psychiatrist will exist as doctor" (2006, 269). By now this argument—or some version of it—has been so widely discussed and disputed among historians and social scientists of psychiatry that it may sound either too shopworn or too self-evident to mention. The idea is that the existence of madness as an epistemic object—and psychiatry's claim to reveal the truth of that object—not only undergirds psychiatry's legitimacy as a medical profession but is also intimately linked to the psychiatrist's exercise of clinical authority over the patient.[1] And yet it is precisely the differences in how the authority of physicians as specialists was underwritten in the Soviet Union—as opposed to the liberal European settings on which Foucault founded his argument—that make this notion worth revisiting.

Social scientists and historians of medicine in the Soviet Union and other socialist states have traced the close entwinement of medical authority and state or bureaucratic power in these settings—examining the consequences of this relationship for physicians' enactments of their expertise and for patients' experiences of care (Brotherton 2012; Koch 2013; Rivkin-Fish 2005). As Michele Rivkin-Fish (2005) has argued, medicalization, understood as a particular mode of knowledge and intervention underpinned by the specialist authority of the medical profession, took on a different shape in the Soviet Union than in liberal Western European and North American states, where it was underwritten by the professional autonomy of physicians. On the one hand, the claim to provide universal and free health care was a central means by which the party-state sought to legitimate itself—and throughout the Soviet period, the specialist power of medicine was celebrated. Yet any potential bases for physicians' corporate power or collective autonomy were undercut soon after the revolution, as professional associations were dissolved and physicians became employees of state agencies (Field 1991). As has often been noted, the Physician's Oath of the Soviet Union affirmed a doctor's responsibility not only to his or her patients but also to "the principles of communist morality" and "the Soviet state" (Bloch and Chodoff 1991, 519). Moreover, any claim to a class- or status-based differentiation was curtailed through the scaling of medical wages 70 to 80 percent below those of industrial workers (Rivkin-Fish 2005, 25; Ryan 1990, 22). This simultaneous constraint of physicians' political and economic power and promotion of their disciplinary power created a situation in which the setting of the clinic took on added importance as a key site for their exercise of professional authority (Field 1991, 53). Within the walls of the clinic the physician's authority was meant to be unquestioned, with no patients' rights movements or legal means to challenge their "symbolic power of expertise" (Rivkin-Fish 2005, 26).

As Rivkin-Fish argues, patients' perceptions of Soviet medicine as a highly bureaucratized system in which care was often provided in an uncaring or indifferent way led to an important constraint on the power of physicians' expertise. "It was the association between expertise and bureaucratic power that rendered medical authority and professional domination highly suspect" in a way that endured in post-Soviet Russia (2005, 27). Patients managed this dilemma by personalizing their relationships with particular physicians through informal exchanges of goods and favors mediated by networks of acquaintances (*blat*)—a moral economy understood as distinct from the exchange of money for services. Unlike bribes (*vziatki*), such exchanges were described as motivated by a desire for medical care that was personalized and not delivered by a physician fulfilling his professional obligation as a civil servant (Salmi 2003; Rivkin-Fish 2005).

The relationship between physicians' clinical authority and their relationship to the state was even more freighted and ambivalent in the case of narcology, which was more a product of the Soviet party-state than other medical specialties. Indeed, the professional designation of "psychiatrist-narcologist" was not created until 1975, when the narcological system was established and when the Ministry of Health funded the establishment of departments of narcology at medical schools throughout the country (Babayan and Gonopolsky 1985; Galkin 2004). As I discuss in chapter 2, the narcological system included not only institutions (like hospitals) under the aegis of the Ministry of Health but also explicitly penal ones run by the Ministry of Internal Affairs (Beliaev and Lezhepetsova 1977; Babayan and Gonopolsky 1985; Segal 1990). In other words, narcologists' clinical expertise was authorized as much by the legal provisions for compulsory treatment and by the intermeshing of medical and juridical organizations in the Soviet narcological service as by their medical credentials.

These close institutional links to the state created a paradoxical set of conditions for Soviet narcologists. While their ability to call on the state's means of coercion gave them a certain means to manage patients, it also undermined physicians' legitimacy with many patients. Many narcologists who had practiced during the Soviet period with patients undergoing compulsory treatment described the deleterious effect that such perceptions had on their attempts to establish trust with patients. Other physicians wistfully recalled the Soviet period as a time when their work formed part of a coherent system of surveillance and social control over alcoholics, which they argued had provided care superior to that under the current arrangement.

By the time of my first visit to the Municipal Addiction Hospital in 2003, certain elements of the narcological system had changed profoundly, while others reflected a striking continuity with those in the Soviet period. Shortly after the fall of the Soviet Union, the Russian Federation had moved to dismantle the explicitly punitive elements of the system, outlawing involuntary hospitalization for noncriminal alcoholics. Indeed, patients at the Municipal Addiction Hospital generally needed only to inform their physicians in writing to end their treatment and be discharged.

Physicians at the hospital recounted how, through the 1990s and early 2000s, they had struggled to manage the increasing numbers of alcoholic patients, as well as the sudden rise of injected heroin, which was accompanied by a rapid spread of HIV infection (Leon et al. 2007). As I discuss in chapter 4, these efforts were made all the more difficult by the severe budgetary cutbacks the system experienced in connection with the dismantling of the Soviet-administered economy generally and the restructuring of the healthcare sector in particular. This meant that while basic treatment remained free of charge, the hospital had begun to charge for various additional services. Shortages of medications and staff were also common. Physicians often complained about having to spend more than half their time on paperwork because they lacked computers or administrative support.

At the same time, narcology had offered physicians opportunities for profit during the period of intense economic depression. Narcologists in the state service were paid more than many of their colleagues in other specialties—this was meant to be official remuneration for the difficulty of their work—while the potential for profit in commercial narcology (or unofficial services in the state sector) was significant. For physicians or medical researchers whose small salaries were often delinquent or delayed for months at a time, the promise of a specialty with even a modestly higher pay scale was clearly attractive.

A final change that swept narcology during the 1990s was the loss of the near monopoly over the clinical knowledge and treatment of addiction that it had held during the Soviet period. Narcologists now found themselves competing with a number of methods and movements, some imported, such as Alcoholics Anonymous (AA) and Scientology, and others home-grown, such as the Orthodox Church (Critchlow 2000a; Lindquist 2005; Zigon 2010). Many nonbiomedical practitioners borrowed heavily from narcological therapies, hybridizing them, while others, like some proponents of AA, were either only grudgingly tolerant of the state-run service or, like the Scientologists, devoted to an explicitly antipsychiatric and antinarcological agenda.

Many people active in the sphere of addiction treatment in St. Petersburg interpreted the result of these shifts as a transformation in the basis of narcologists' clinical authority. According to this argument, the most important point of rupture was the collapse of the Soviet party-state and the administered economy, which ushered in a move from state-licensed authority on the part of narcologists to ways of bringing patients into a relationship of dependency that were facilitated and encouraged by the market. As one psychiatrist who was highly critical of narcology put it, "Under the conditions of the market, the job of the doctor is to attach the patient to himself [*priviazat' k sebe bol'nogo*], to make the patient dependent on him." Now narcologists sought to consolidate their clinical authority through other forms of persuasion in their relationships with patients, which often meant an enactment of charismatic authority in the clinical encounter.

In tracing the consequences of this shift, I focus on the discursive and institutional practices through which clinicians and other practitioners enact and affirm what I call "therapeutic legitimacy." This idea builds on a claim that has been central to medical anthropology for decades—namely, that while "[m]astering biomedical technologies requires self-fashioning, . . . practitioner-selves . . . draw their power from the social relations that recognize their efficacy" (Lock and Nguyen 2010, 291). Focusing on therapeutic legitimacy requires us to look beyond the formal criteria of training and credentialing and instead to focus on the much more diffuse, informal, everyday processes through which efficacious healing is enacted, affirmed, and challenged. Medical anthropologists have often drawn attention to the ways in which practitioners legitimize their claims and their practices by linking them to traditional, bureaucratic, and charismatic forms of authority. While such analyses imply that medical claims to legitimacy index a relatively stable referent—such as "the state" or "medicine"—I argue that precisely this stability often remains unclear and is up for grabs. Thus throughout the book I trace how therapeutic legitimacy is performed in specific interactions between clinicians and patients, in debates on the pages of medical journals and newspapers, and in arguments made to this ethnographer. In theorizing therapeutic legitimacy, I link up long-standing anthropological literatures on "symbolic efficacy" and "medical pluralism" with contemporary discussions about the performance of expertise (Boyer 2005; Carr 2010).

Addiction, Knowledge, and Politics

It has long been an assumption of the humanistic social sciences that the ways in which we act in the world (including those experienced as distressful or deemed pathological) cannot be meaningfully disentangled from our knowledge of the world. As Gregory Bateson put it in his influential article on Alcoholics Anonymous, "In the natural history of the living human being ontology and epistemology cannot be separated" (1972, 314). A distinguishing feature of life today, however, is that the "net of epistemological and ontological premises" within which the contemporary human is "bound" (ibid.) often originates in the domain of expertise. Over the past two decades, anthropologists and social scientists concerned with psychiatry and other areas of medicine have addressed this issue by asking how expert and specialized forms of knowledge shape the conditions of possibility for subjectivity in the context of broad institutional, social, and political-economic transformations. However, unlike the theories of labeling or social control favored during the 1960s, '70s and '80s, which understood particular kinds of expert knowledge and their institutional forms as inherently constraining and oppressive, recent research has depicted a more complex and nuanced relationship between clinical expertise and its human subjects. Instead of a unidirectional process, the production, enactment, and materialization of knowledge are seen as interactive or recursive, emphasizing how the actions of individuals and groups come to shape the ways in which the categories they occupy are later revised or reinvented (Hacking 1986, 1995, 2007).

These general insights have informed much recent anthropological work on addiction treatment, which highlights how the social worlds where substances circulate are rarely extricable from epistemic, therapeutic, and punitive interventions, which are, in turn, thoroughly shaped by various forms of specialist knowledge or practical expertise. Such a perspective draws long-standing anthropological literatures on cultures of substance use and drug markets into closer conversation with work on scientific knowledge (Lock and Nguyen 2010), the production and enactment of expertise (Boyer 2005; Carr 2010), and governance.

Recent literature on global psychiatry and addiction treatment has emphasized not only the biologization of psychiatry but its recasting as a "clinical neuroscience discipline" (Insel and Quirion 2005). Coinciding as it has with the neoliberal transformation of health care in many countries and a consequent search for cost-effective therapies, this cardinal shift in psychiatry has also facilitated a growing emphasis on pharmaceutical interventions for mental illnesses (Healy 1997; Luhrmann 2000). While alcoholism and drug addiction have been somewhat more resistant to such biomedicalization (when compared with mental illness), developments in neurobiology and the emergence of potential pharmaceutical therapies suggest that this may be rapidly changing, with addiction increasingly understood by laypeople in North America as a "chronic, relapsing brain disease" (Leshner 1997).[2] Surveying these developments, several social scientists have argued that as neurobiological ways of thinking about and acting upon human beings diffuse beyond the laboratory, a somatic understanding of the self is increasingly displacing—or at least supplementing—the psychological or identity-based subject of the twentieth century (Rose 2007; Vrecko 2006).

This book joins other ethnographic accounts of psychiatry and addiction therapeutics that productively engage with these arguments yet also call into question their epochal and universalizing elements (e.g., Biehl 2005; Carr 2011; Garcia 2010; Kitanaka 2012; Lakoff 2006; Lovell 2006, 2013; Meyers 2013; Schüll 2012). The narrative of Russian narcology is particularly significant to these debates because it so clearly calls into question a number of distinctions that prevail in North American clinical practice as well as in much of the social science literature: not only the distinction between pharmacology and psychotherapy but also that between the biological and the psychological and between autonomy and collectivity. Whereas psychoanalysis, psychosocial approaches, and mutual/self-help programs were prominent in North American and British psychiatry and addiction treatment throughout the post–World War II period, Soviet psychiatry was much more biological in its foundations. In chapter 4 I argue that the ascendancy of Pavlov's theory of reflex action in Soviet psychiatry led to a conceptualization of the human body as dialectically related to both the mind and the environment, which in turn facilitated a particular physiological interpretation of "chronic alcoholism" as well as the popularity of therapies employing hypnotic suggestion.

Therapy and Self-Fashioning

This book also contributes to recent work on self-formation and -transformation in contemporary Russia and other postsocialist states. A number of scholars have examined the projects of subject formation that have accompanied the postsocialist transformations, many of them drawing on a much broader anthropological and sociological literature on the neoliberal subject and the disciplines of the mind and brain (Martin 1996; Rose 1996). Thus several scholars have traced how various human technologies, ranging from labor training to psychotherapy to drug rehabilitation, help to encourage a relationship to self-governance that has an elective affinity to the neoliberal devolution of social support from states to market-based mechanisms, families, and individuals (Dunn 2004; Matza 2012; Zigon 2010). In other words, these therapies or technologies seek to teach people to take on responsibility for the management of their own susceptibilities and desires, engage with risk, and generally relate to themselves as the "proprietor of his or her self as a portfolio" or a business (Martin 2000, 582; Gershon 2011).

However, if the political and economic policies enacted during the early 1990s under the rubric of "shock therapy"—namely, the liberalization of prices and elimination of subsidies, monetary reforms, and the privatization of numerous state assets—were justified as part of a project of neoliberalism, it is more difficult to characterize Russian politics in the Putin era in such terms (Collier 2011; Matza 2009). Indeed, during the first decade of the 2000s—the period of time during which the majority of the fieldwork for this book was conducted—countervailing processes were clear: some industries were being renationalized, and a broader project of consolidating the political authority of the federal Russian state was well under way. And yet, as I show in chapter 3, any attempts by state agencies to regulate the commercial narcology market were partial and incomplete. Tomas Matza shows how a similar set of "market forces and state priorities"—which he calls a "commercial-biopolitical matrix"—articulate with the project of "psychological education" in contemporary Russia. While psychological education for middle-class children "instantiates a form of elite subjectivity similar to the autonomous neoliberal actor primed for competition, success, and instrumental social relations," Matza finds psychologists employing similar therapeutic technologies with working-class children engaged in a project of management "through correction and containment" (2012, 813).

I engage with these questions through an analysis of two distinct forms of long-term therapy: the suggestion-based modes of treatment described above and 12-step programs (such as Alcoholics Anonymous), which were imported to Russia during the 1990s. I compare these modes of self-governance to highlight what recent anthropology's overriding focus on "the neoliberal subject" obscures. On the one hand, I argue in chapter 4 that many patients find narcology's suggestion-based methods of treatment compelling precisely because they function so little like such transformative "technologies of the self" (Foucault 1988). Rather than enjoining patients to work on or be concerned with their selves, these methods work as what I call "prostheses for the will," harnessing patients' preexisting ideas, beliefs, and affects to motivate behaviors such as sobriety. On the other hand, in chapter 5 I interpret AA as what I call an "illness sodality"—a form of sociality and association based on the common identification of members around their experience of suffering. I frame AA in this way in order to focus on the ways that the transformation of subjectivity is tied up with shifts both in forms of sociality in which members engage and in the specific webs of association into which they are drawn. Conceptually, I argue that anthropological studies of subjectivity can pay closer attention to the ways in which distinct therapeutic technologies are assembled from clinical performances and relationships, styles of reasoning and local research traditions, institutional and political economic settings, and the trajectories of individual patients' lives (cf. Raikhel and Garriott 2013).

Clinical Ethnography and Identification

While preparing to depart for St. Petersburg, I was told by a faculty member to conduct my fieldwork with care. My research topic would require that I spend significant amounts of time in institutional settings—clinics, hospitals, rehabilitation centers, and the like. The danger, it was suggested to me, was that such fieldwork might seemingly prove "too easy." This was not simply the idea that a certain level of arduousness is necessary for fieldwork to be experienced as a rite of passage. The concern was that the very things that made conducting research in such a setting potentially attractive—the spatial, temporal, and social structure and stability that institutions supposedly lend to one's otherwise open-ended days—would be too familiar to me, too much like the rhythms of my life at home. I would be lulled into an ethnographic complacency, unreflectingly accept the underlying assumptions of my interlocutors, and thereby lose the productive level of cognitive distance (and dissonance) needed to maintain the visibility of difference.[3]

During a preliminary research trip, I made contact with several physicians at the hospital: a geologist friend of the family put me in touch with Aleksei Vladimirovich,[4] a medical researcher who had served as a physician on several geological field trips to Crimea. Though trained as a narcologist, since the mid-1990s Aleksei Vladimirovich had been working as a researcher in a neurological institute and moonlighting as a lecturer on neurophysiology. However, he knew several narcologists working at the hospital and took me along to visit a ward run by a former classmate, Irina Valentinovna, a warm and personable woman in her early forties. Whereas Aleksei Vladimirovich's difficulty in understanding why my research project required me to speak to physicians and patients ("Can't you just get information about narcology from books and articles?") suggested a set of epistemological assumptions very different from my own, Irina Valentinovna was more open to the idea of fieldwork. "In reality, things don't work the way you'd think they do if you only read texts," she agreed, setting out a tray of cookies and chocolates.

When I returned to St. Petersburg that autumn I again contacted Aleksei Vladimirovich. This time he put me in touch with Grigorii Mikhailovich, a former medical school professor who was now a midlevel administrator at the hospital. Grigorii Mikhailovich allowed me to begin speaking to physicians at the hospital, but he explained that in order to interview patients I would have to have my project approved by the hospital's director, Sergei Tikhomirov. With evident unease at the prospect of an American researcher working in the hospital, he seemed anxious to pass off responsibility for me to his superior.

The process of obtaining permission to speak with patients dragged on for months. It seemed that every time I called him, Grigorii Mikhailovich delayed my next visit to the hospital—once a conference had come up unexpectedly, and the following week everyone was busy filing their annual reports—yet each time he asked me to call back in several days, assuring me that a meeting with Tikhomirov was imminent. For two weeks his cell phone was dead: as he later explained, the service (funded by the hospital) had been turned off for nonpayment. I wondered whether any of this was deliberate stalling on Grigorii Mikhailovich's part. Had I failed to set our relationship in the right direction by not bringing him a gift, or was he reluctant to bring my project to the director's attention for his own reasons?

Upon returning to St. Petersburg from a brief trip home to New York, I received word from Tikhomirov's office that my proposal had been forwarded to the city's Department of Public Health and that I was to write up a "research contract" (*dogovor o sotrudnichestve*) stipulating my own responsibilities, as well as those of the hospital, during the course of research. Having dutifully drafted the contract and shepherded it through the offices of several municipal administrators, I returned to the addiction hospital to receive Tikhomirov's signature. He was a small, bearded man with a squint who seemed to spend most of his time deskbound. After signing the document, he pointed to a clause stating that I would "present myself to patients as a graduate student in social anthropology." "Let me give you a piece of advice," he said. "When you speak to the patients, it's better to tell them you're a psychologist. They're used to speaking to people like that."

The suggestion concerned me, for several reasons. At the time, my expectations about how people would identify me—as well as the methodological issues that this identification would entail—were based both on my previous experiences as an adult in St. Petersburg (a brief fieldwork trip as an undergraduate and several monthlong stints of language study) and on my readings in the ethnographic literature. As I had been born in the city, then called Leningrad, and emigrated to the United States with my parents at age four, I was perceived by people who knew about my background as an émigré—a well-established and long-standing social category in Russia. Like all ambiguous and hybrid categorizations, this one could be interpreted in different ways by interlocutors and presented in different ways by me, sometimes emphasizing affinity between us (I was "returning home") and at other times accenting distance (I was "an American"). Language inflected my personal story as another ambiguous marker for identification. Despite my often shaky grammar, my Russian has little enough accent for me to pass unnoticed as a foreigner in many everyday conversations. This ability could, however, lead to moments of abrupt discord in conversations, particularly when my interlocutor's assumption of speaking to a fluent native suddenly ran aground on my lack of local knowledge.

Yet this project was different from those I had worked on in my previous visits; I had never worked in a clinical setting in Russia, and I knew that my field sites, my chosen topic of alcoholism, and my interest in speaking with both physicians and patients would present a new set of challenges. Given my lack of medical training or experience with research in this environment, I expected to be unambiguously viewed as an outsider by physicians. However, I also wanted some entrance into the lives of patients: at the very least, I hoped to learn of their clinical experiences, and I knew that my first introductions to both patients and physicians (and the ways I would be identified by them) could either facilitate or foreclose possibilities for ethnographically rich encounters.

For the hospital director, identifying myself as a psychologist was just a pragmatic methodological shortcut; he explained that introducing myself this way would expedite my interviews by giving the patients a frame of reference with which they were familiar. Some of the assumptions implicit in his proposal struck me as reasonable. For instance, it was clear that introducing myself as an anthropologist might not strike the right note, given some of the ideas circulating locally about anthropology. (One of the hospital administrators told me that upon learning of my disciplinary background, he had wondered whether I planned to measure the circumference of patients' heads—presumably drawing on popular associations of anthropology with early twentieth-century physical anthropology.) However, "psychologist" hardly seemed an improvement. Though I certainly hoped that patients would somehow benefit from my listening to their stories, I was worried that they might misconstrue our conversations as formal therapy and thus assume I was a staff member. At the time, I thought there were several reasons for such a concern about misrecognition: a range of conversational genres were construed by local addiction doctors as psychotherapy and people who carried out group therapy or social work were sometimes categorized as sociologists. The risk of perceived connection to clinic staff has been especially important for ethnographers working in postsocialist settings, as in any place where medical professionals are closely associated with state authority (Rivkin-Fish 2005; Skultans 2005).

As I began to visit the hospital regularly, it became clear that while my concerns about patients' misrecognition of our encounters were misplaced, the best I could do to avoid being associated with clinical authority was to mitigate physicians' representations of me. In most cases Grigorii Mikhailovich acted as an intermediary, putting me in touch with the physicians in charge of particular wards. Most were uneasy with the idea of my spending time informally on the ward; instead, they allowed me to speak to patients individually in consultation rooms. Some went even further and insisted on selecting patients for me to speak with. One had the habit of approaching patients in the ward's hallway and asking loudly, "Sasha! Do you want to help advance international science? Just answer a few questions from our American colleague!"[5]

Of course, even within these relatively constrained circumstances, there was room for much difference in the framing of our interactions. Some patients were withdrawn, answered questions tersely, and resisted my attempts to open up a broader conversation about their lives. It is important to remember that we were often discussing subjects—their diagnosis as alcohol-dependent or the circumstances leading to their stay at the hospital—that were, for many, difficult to speak about. My interlocutors were primarily men, and while male drunkenness is (still) often conceived in heroic terms in contemporary Russia, a diagnosis of alcoholism continues to carry a heavy stigma.

Not surprisingly, then, it was often (though not always) most difficult to have extensive and engaging conversations with the rare middle-class patients whose lives remained relatively undisrupted by their drinking or drug use. On the other hand, many of the hospital's patients had spent significant portions of their lives in prison and assumed toward me a posture that was at once formally deferential and firmly unforthcoming. Other patients—particularly those who had been taught to narrate their life stories as "drunk-a-logs" in the local 12-step rehabilitation program described below—were eager to relate the details of their lives. A few explicitly presented their stories to me as object lessons in moral failure or the dangers of the bottle.

Perhaps not surprisingly it was physicians who were much more likely to explicitly describe our encounters as beneficial to them. For instance, after several hours of conversation about the burdens of paperwork and stifling bureaucracy, the lack of sufficient material resources, the frustration caused by recalcitrant patients, and her general sense of futility caused by her inability to significantly affect the course of most addictions, a physician in the acute ward of the hospital exclaimed, "It's nice to be able to speak to someone about this. No one listens to *our* complaints." At other moments I was treated less as a listening ear and more as a colleague, a fellow "expert" (albeit in a very different discipline). Such identifications were, of course, never particularly stable—the narcologists remained keenly aware that I would represent them and their specialty—but they were sufficient to enroll me into a kind of complicity with their professional secrets.

Much of my fieldwork was carried out in the narcological hospital as well as in local dispensaries of the municipal narcological service. I also spent a month at one commercial addiction clinic and interviewed narcologists and psychiatrists in private practice, sat in on a series of training lectures on narcology for physicians, and attended open sessions of Alcoholics Anonymous and séances conducted by a self-proclaimed "Orthodox psychotherapist." However, the other significant field site was the House of Hope on the Hill (HOH) (Dom Nadezhdy na Gore), a center in the St. Petersburg area providing free-of-charge rehabilitation for alcoholism.

I had heard about the House of Hope during an early visit to St. Petersburg, but it was in the United States that a colleague put me in touch with Eugene Zubkov, a Russian American psychiatrist who has played a key role in the House's foundation and operation. Prior to his emigration to the United States, Zubkov had worked for nearly a decade at the Bekhterev Psychoneurological Research Institute, one of the most respected centers for psychiatric research in the Soviet Union. In the early 1990s, he had been hired to manage the Russia-focused philanthropic efforts of a former tobacco executive and supporter of Alcoholics Anonymous. Early efforts had focused on bringing physicians and psychiatrists, clergymen, and members of the cultural intelligentsia to the United States to tour rehabilitation centers (and in many cases to undergo treatment), with the aim of bolstering the stature and legitimacy of 12-step methods in Russia. By the mid-1990s, Eugene Zubkov and his American employer had developed a new strategy. Drawing on the Minnesota Model, a widely used 12-step-based protocol for inpatient substance abuse rehabilitation, they founded the House of Hope (J. Spicer 1993).

When I expressed interest in conducting research at the House of Hope and made it clear that I was willing to make myself useful, Zubkov's response was enthusiastic. Since the money funding both the House and its clinical technologies flowed from the United States, there was a great deal of translation to be done in the management of the center, and I was soon working on English and Russian texts for reports, letters, brochures, and Web postings. At the same time I began regularly taking part in daily activities at the House. By contrast with the situation in the addiction hospital, here there were no bureaucratic hurdles, no forms to fill out, no research contracts, no review of my project. In exchange for my work translating texts, the doors of the House of Hope were open: I was allowed to interview patients, join them for their lectures and conversations, and sit in on meetings with the counseling staff. The only restriction was that I was not allowed to sit in on group therapy or closed 12-step group meetings.[6] In fact, here the limits to productive encounters were shaped not so much by bureaucratic exigencies as by my self-identification. Whereas at the addiction hospital I had no choice but to temper my obvious association with the staff, at the House of Hope I found that I was always a potential fellow in recovery or an addict in denial. As I discuss in chapter 5, for some members of the House of Hope community, it seemed clear that my choice to research alcoholism treatment was motivated by my own (presumably unacknowledged) addiction.

What became clear to me, particularly as I shuttled between these two field sites, was that my possibilities for self-identification were opened up or foreclosed by ascriptions of identity made by my interlocutors, and that such opening up or foreclosure in turn shaped our mutual potential for identification *with* one another. Moreover, different ideas about illness and addiction were implicit in the ways I and my motivations were identified by my interlocutors and in the ways these identifications circumscribed the possibilities for encounters in the field. To put it in overly simplified terms, at the addiction hospital the identification of alcoholism was an act of diagnosis carried out by physicians. At the House of Hope it was an act of self-identification carried out by participants. For physicians at the hospital, alcoholism was a disease epistemologically accessible through particular symptoms—some self-reported, some visible to the physician. One narcologist at the hospital explained to me that she could typically see the ravages of long-term alcohol use on the body of a patient. "You, for instance," she added. "It is clear that you are not an alcoholic." This reliance on visual cues and physical markers of illness has a basis in a neurophysiological style of reasoning long dominant in Russian psychiatry. It was also a simple reading of my middle-class American habitus: it was clear that I wasn't an alcoholic because I didn't look like one. At the House, the experience of fellow suffering was valued over professional expertise; anyone could and might be an addict.

Learning something about these starkly contrasting conceptions of alcoholism was not only a matter of interpreting texts and statements made by my interlocutors, although these certainly were necessary sources. Equally important were what Jeanne Favret-Saada has called "situations of involuntary and unintentional communication," which "although they are commonplace and recurrent [during fieldwork], are never taken into consideration for what they are: the 'information' they have brought to the ethnographer appears in the text, but without any reference to the affective intensity which went with it in reality" (1990, 195). That such situations are just as commonplace and recurrent in the clinics, laboratories, and offices where fieldwork is increasingly carried out as they are elsewhere is a point that would be too self-evident to belabor were it not for the perception that these spaces, so redolent of modernity and ostensibly so homogeneous, threaten the productive ambiguity and uncertainty central to the production of ethnographic knowledge. Part of the methodological challenge of working in such settings is not only maintaining our sense of unfamiliarity but also remaining open to learning something from the (sometimes profound) failures of identification.

Plan of the Book

The core of this book's narrative is ethnographically driven, developed primarily from my observations, interactions, and conversations in St. Petersburg's Municipal Narcological system, the House of Hope on the Hill, and a number of private clinics and practices. Chapter 1 is structured around an investigation of the "Russian demographic crisis," examining the multiple kinds of knowledge that have both helped to produce the demographic crisis as an event and in turn been enabled by it. I set these epidemiological discussions alongside the narratives of patients in the addiction hospital. The aims are to provide some key background for understanding the significance of post-Soviet Russian addiction medicine in subsequent chapters and to place the singular stories of patients in a productive tension with the larger narratives of Russian demographic crisis and history.

The following two chapters trace the emergence and transformation of narcological institutions. Chapter 2 examines the emergence of Soviet narcology as a medical subspecialty and as a set of institutions, treating it as a an aggregation of infrastructures, concepts, styles of reasoning, and therapies, many of which were instantiations of distinct ideas about alcoholism and drunkenness and were linked to the history of particular forms of expertise and knowledge. Moreover, I interpret several narcologists' seemingly nostalgic accounts as reconstructed memories of the Soviet narcological system as intention. The following chapter is framed by an ethnographic account illustrating how narcology has been shaped by the commodification of services, the pervasiveness of violent methods in business, and a patronage-based bureaucratic culture: namely, a commercial war between two clinics. Through this story and others, I examine how these transformations in a "therapeutic economy" (Nguyen 2005) were experienced by physicians and their patients, and particularly how they transformed the grounds for the clinical relationship.

In the final two chapters of the book, I turn to therapeutic interventions—first focusing on techniques that have emerged from narcology, then on the domestication of Alcoholics Anonymous in Russia. Chapter 4 examines a set of popular aversion and suggestion-based techniques that account for most of the long-term methods of treatment for alcoholism offered in Russia. I argue that narcologists work to amplify patients' responses through attention to the performative aspects of the clinical encounter as well as through management of the methods' broader reputation as effective therapies, a phenomenon I call "therapeutic legitimacy." In chapter 5 I trace the development of Alcoholics Anonymous groups in Russia, focusing on the particular configuration of people and institutions from Russia and the United States that gave rise to the House of Hope. I examine AA as an "illness sodality"—a network of associations held together through the work of technologies and identifications.

In the conclusion I bring together and build upon the arguments developed earlier in the book. In particular, I compare the logics of suggestion-based modes of treatment for alcoholism with those of the 12 steps, with a focus on how these divergent clinical technologies treat the self. Finally, I draw out some of the implications of my argument for the anthropology of medicine and psychiatry.

1

States of Crisis

At the height of post-Soviet social ferment in the early and mid-1990s, the Russian population began declining by several hundred thousand people a year, and talk of a dire "demographic crisis" became increasing widespread. This trend, which continued well into the twenty-first century, resulted in an overall decline of the population by 4.6 million between 1993 and 2004 and has led some scholars to argue that Russia may shrink from its current population of 143.3 million to 100 or even 50 million by the middle of the century (Shlapentokh 2005). Soviet researchers had noted declines in fertility and increases in mortality since the 1960s and had debated how best to understand and potentially intervene on them, but during the immediate post-Soviet period these trends—particularly the rise in mortality rates— accelerated abruptly (Rivkin-Fish 2003). Moreover, although this increase occurred across the population, it was especially drastic among middle-aged men. Male life expectancy in Russia fell precipitously from 63.8 years in 1990 to 57.7 years in 1994, a decline that one group of health statisticians called "beyond the peacetime experience of industrialized countries"

(Notzon et al. 1998, 793). While groups of demographers, epidemiologists, and public health researchers disagreed fundamentally on how to interpret the relationship between decreasing life expectancy and rising mortality among Russian men and broader processes of post-Soviet transformation, there was significant agreement that alcohol consumption and alcohol-related harm had played a central role (Demin and Demina 1998; Notzon et al. 1998; Cockerham 1999, 2000; Field and Twigg 2000; Pridemore 2002; Dmitrieva et al. 2002). As the most common epidemiological narrative had it, Russian men "responded to [the] stress [of social and economic upheaval] by drinking themselves to death" (Parsons 2014, 7–8).

The debates about the ultimate or proximal causes, about the political or existential meanings of this phenomenon assemble under the trope of crisis—demographic crisis, mortality crisis. Indeed contemporary uses of the term "crisis"—in Russian *krizis*—echo the medical meaning of its ancient Greek root, *krino*, a term that often referred to a clinical judgment regarding the course of an illness (Koselleck 2006, 360). "Since then," Reinhart Koselleck explains, "the concept of crisis assumed a double meaning that has been preserved in social and political language. On the one hand, the objective condition, about the origins of which there may be scientific disagreements, depends on the judgmental criteria used to diagnose that condition. On the other hand, the concept of illness itself presupposes a state of health—however conceived—that is either to be restored again or which will, at a specified time, result in death" (361). Transposed to the domains of the social, political, or historical, the term retains something of this clinical kernel, signifying "a diagnostic of the present," as Janet Roitman reminds us: "[Crisis] implies a certain telos—that is, it is inevitably though most often implicitly directed toward a norm . . . crisis compared to what?" (2011, 2014). In other words, as with clinical diagnosis, talk of social or political crisis evokes an etiology, a course of treatment and some set of implicit ideas about the social that constitute a "presuppose[d] state of health" (Koselleck 2006, 361). For Roitman the key question is not whether we in fact have a crisis on our hands at any moment when the idea is invoked but rather what kinds of political, institutional, or ethical work the declaration of crisis enables. As she aptly puts it, "Crisis is a blind spot that enables the production of knowledge" (2014, 39). Sometimes this makes crisis the site of fierce debate; it may draw in multiple epistemic cultures and act as a site where distinct assumptions about knowledge run up against one another. But perhaps just as often (maybe even simultaneously) crisis renders "certain things visible and others invisible," naturalizing particular assumptions about the social, facilitating particular interventions and foreclosing the possibility of others (ibid.).

In Russia, krizis has been a pervasive trope in everyday talk, mass media, and political discourse since the late Soviet perestroika period, when public debates among members of the intelligentsia focused on the "crisis of socialism" (Shevchenko 2009, 20–21) and conversations increasingly turned to the "complete disintegration" (*polnaia razrukha*) of Soviet society (Ries 1997, 46). After the dissolution of the Soviet Union in 1991, the crisis framework came to be used in all these domains as a means of communicating, attempting to understand, and capitalizing on the numerous processes that introduced so much uncertainty into the lives of Russians throughout the 1990s: monetary reforms that wiped out most people's life savings, the liberalization of prices in the "shock therapy" of 1992, the tense political standoff between Yeltsin and the parliament in 1993, the disastrous and bloody Chechen wars, and the 1998 devaluation of the ruble. If crisis typically suggests a certain urgency—an acuteness, if not a state of emergency—during the 1990s in Russia it came to designate a chronic condition: a seemingly unending series of crises or one long continuing crisis (Shevchenko 2009). Indeed, as Olga Shevchenko has argued, *krizis* was not only "a term of choice for describing one's immediate experiences, but it structured the very logic of assessing separate events—from something as minor as a street quarrel to major disasters such as plane crashes or outbreaks of disease (and everything in between)—as indicative of one all-encompassing societal disorder" (2009, 62). In the absence of other widely accepted framing tropes or narratives, this idiom of total crisis became a means of understanding, communicating, and ultimately living through the uncertainties, disappointments, and deprivations of the 1990s (73). Moreover, this sense of total disorder and breakdown furnished an important set of justifications for Vladimir Putin's policies of consolidating power and "modernization" during the years that followed. Indeed, talk of crisis subsided during the first decade of the 2000s, as revenue from oil and gas exports buoyed the Russian economy, and only returned to public and political domains with the global economic crisis of 2008 (Feklyunina and White 2011).

Concerns about the demographic crisis not only have persisted throughout this period but have been closely entangled with understandings of other crises—crises of the Russian state, its sovereignty and security; crises of the economy and its "modernization"; crises of the Russian nation and its spirituality; and crises of Russian men and their masculinity. A general consensus about the crisis as a demographic fact has served as a platform for diagnoses that diverge not only in their assessment of the illness but even in their understanding of who the patient might be.

For example, while the declining population and health crisis was described by foreign observers for two decades as evidence that Russia was, in the words of one US demographer and pundit, "too sick [and too depopulated] to matter" geopolitically (Eberstadt 1999), parallel arguments made by scholars, politicians, and journalists in Russia refer not only to *population* decline but often to an imminent spiritual and biogenetic "degradation" and death of the Russian *nation* (naturalized by some into an ethnic or "social organism"). Some observers—such as the author of a newspaper article titled "Collective Suicide" (Gafutulin 2005)—have understood this national death to be self-inflicted, while another group has described the demographic crisis as a plot facilitated by ethnonational others both within and outside Russia. Reference to the "genocide of the Russian people" or a "Russian Holocaust" is not unheard of in this context (Elizar'eva 2002, cited in Oushakine 2007, 176). Many of these debates have clustered around the peculiar image of the "Russian cross" (*russkii krest*)—the intersection that appears when graphs of rising mortality rates and declining birthrates over the past decades in Russia are transposed onto one another. As Serguei Oushakine has argued, this hybrid image both identifies the population of the Russian Federation with the Russian people or nation and shifts technical discussions of "social policies, health and child care or the epidemics of alcoholism toward the predictable fascination with the nation's suffering" (2010, 159). In other words, there is a slippage between population figures—often those of the entire Russian state—and Russian ethnonationality, evoked as the entity under threat.[1]

This chapter examines the multiple kinds of knowledge that have both helped to produce the demographic crisis as an event and in turn been enabled by it. Starting from the vantage point of the narcological clinic, I trace the numerous etiologies and diagnoses that the narratives linking the demographic crisis to alcohol have fostered. Many of these narratives draw upon long-standing debates, such as more than a century of Russian and Soviet arguments about the proper role of the state in the governance of

alcohol and drinking, and the tensions between the biopolitics of population health and the fiscal politics of revenue extraction. In part to provide
background for the discussions in subsequent chapters, I interweave the
narratives of several patients at St. Petersburg's Munipical Narcological
Hospital with these broader discussions of the biopolitics of alcohol, heavy
drinking, and demographic changes throughout the past hundred years
in Russia, as well as the forms of knowledge these shifts have given rise
to. Although the lives and words of the men in the hospital bore traces of
broader processes and shifts, the relationship was in no way direct or deter-
minative. I recount some of their stories not simply to suggest that they
are illustrative or representative of something bigger than themselves but
also to place these singular stories in a productive tension with the larger
narratives of Russian demographic crisis and history. Implicit in the dif-
fering explanations for the demographic crisis are distinct conceptualizations of health and of the social. As "diagnostics of the present," narratives
of demographic crisis index different understandings of the social and its
attendant norms, logics, and forms of exclusion.

Social Bodies

On a warm summer morning, I followed the narcologists Alexander Sergeevich and Petr Dmitrievich as they conducted their daily rounds in the
patients' spare living quarters in Ward Two of St. Petersburg's Municipal Addiction Hospital. Each room had four or five simple beds to a side.
The walls, painted to eye level with a muddy pink or green and then a
dirty white to the ceiling, were barren, with the exception of an occasional
ratty calendar depicting women posing in bathing suits. The air smelled
intensely of acrid sweat, and despite the relatively large windows (thick
iron bars behind them), it seemed barely to circulate through the building.
Several patients lay on their cots, faces covered with a jacket or blanket,
overcome either by the pain of withdrawal or, as Alexander Sergeevich
explained, by the cocktail of medications meant to blunt both this pain
and their intense craving for alcohol or heroin—the two substances that
patients at the hospital were most commonly dependent on. Narcologists
often prescribed what they called neuroleptics—a class of drugs more commonly referred to in North America as antipsychotics—as a part of these

cocktails, for patients in withdrawal from both opiates and alcohol. These were first-generation or typical antipsychotics that caused telltale side effects, sometimes called extrapyramidal symptoms. As we moved through the ward, many patients approached us with awkward movements, some shuffling, some trembling, others speaking with difficulty—their voices garbled and wavering beyond their control. I later learned that this use of antipsychotics was highly contested, not only by addiction specialists throughout the world but by many Russian narcologists.[2]

Like other narcologists at the hospital, Alexander Sergeevich and Petr Dmitrievich had complained to me about the amount of time they spent filling out paperwork. With no administrative support or computers, they estimated that the various forms and detailed files they were required to keep took up at least two-thirds of their time, leaving little for direct interaction with patients. So the doctors walked quickly through the rooms where patients slept and lived, asking each briefly how he was feeling (*Kak samochustvie?*). Patients who were past the initial process of detoxification surrounded the doctors and peppered them with questions about medications and discharge dates. Two young men with bruised faces asked about their drug regimens. Several others handed the doctors handwritten notes, some notices that they were leaving the hospital. The face of one young man—no older than twenty—had a grayish tinge; his roommates reported that he had been throwing up earlier in the day. Some patients stood at attention, military style, and most addressed the narcologists using the formal voice, calling them "doctor." "Doctor, can I be put on antidepressants?" As the figures of greater authority in these exchanges, the physicians were the ones expected to shift between formal and familiar registers, and they did so, depending on the patient and the level of intimacy they hoped to achieve in their brief interaction.[3]

The patients in Ward Two were all male (other wards at the hospital were mixed, and one was primarily female), and while there was certainly variation in their social and professional status (several patients were professionals or workers who had been brought to the hospital by their families), most were either marginally employed or had long been without jobs. Others had spent significant portions of their lives traveling the "institutional circuit" of hospitals and prisons (Hopper et al. 1997); by the narcologists' estimate, as many as half of the patients were ex-convicts. Some were living in the hospital as they had nowhere else to go; indeed,

each ward seemed to have at least one or two patients whom the physicians allowed to stay semipermanently; these men usually helped out
with minor tasks, sometimes effectively working as janitors or orderlies.[4]
The physicians in Ward Two, as well as other wards, called this broader
category of patients, who occupied about two-thirds of the hospital's six
hundred beds, "socially destroyed" or "degraded." Such terms communicated in a condensed way the scope of these patients' losses: jobs; social
roles; relationships; mental, moral, and physical capacities; belongings.
For the physicians, these terms also had specific clinical meanings and
consequences. "Socially destroyed" patients were unlikely to have family
to return to, which was important for how a longer course of treatment
or sobriety might be planned. Even more significantly, as I discuss in a
subsequent chapter, such patients were understood to have so little left to
lose, so little at stake, that physicians found it particularly difficult finding
a "hook" with which to exhort them to change their behavior. In referring
to patients as "declassed" and "degraded," physicians also indexed certain
imaginaries of "the social." The idea of degradation, for instance, implied
a downward social trajectory and suggested an erosion that was simultaneously moral and bodily, in a way that was applied equally to particular
persons and to the entirety of post-Soviet Russia. For some, though not
all, of the clinicians, a socially destroyed patient was not only one whose
social roles, bonds, and capacities had been lost but also one who had been
destroyed *by* the social—or by the upheavals of political economic and
institutional change (cf. Friedman 2009).

In informally categorizing patients along a gradient of social degradation, physicians referred as often to their preferred drink as to the state
of their bodies and social lives. Regularly consuming "alcohol surrogates"
(window cleaner, cologne, food flavoring, and other substances containing
ethanol but not intended for consumption) placed one at the far end of
this gradient. In Venedikt Erofeev's late 1960s countercultural cult novel
Moskva-Petushki (a stream-of-consciousness account of an inveterate alcoholic's attempt to reach a town near Moscow on a suburban train), the nar-
rator, Venechka, offers readers a recipe for a cocktail he calls "The Tears
of a Komsomol Girl." Its ingredients include lavender, verbena, "Forest
Water" eau de cologne, nail polish, toothpaste, and lemonade (Erofeev
(1970) 2000, 81–82). Like much else in Erofeev's novel, this recipe and
others are tragicomic emblems of the sublime in the utter abjection of

Venechka's life. Among patients at the addiction hospital, the consumption of surrogates was rarely, if ever, so epicurean—but it was common. According to Alexander Sergeiivich and Petr Dmitrievich, the majority of patients they treated for alcoholism were drinking an inexpensive hawthorn-infused tonic (*nastoika boiarashnika*) sold in most drugstores and kiosks alongside medications. Patients drinking this substance seemed not to experience an alcoholic euphoria at all but simply to fall into a delirious stupor. Nor was this in any way restricted to the hospital or St. Petersburg. An epidemiological study carried out in Izhevsk, a Siberian city, between 2003 and 2005 found that as many as 8 percent of men aged twenty-five to fifty-four had consumed surrogates over the course of the past year (Tomkins et al. 2007). A patient named Nikolai told me about how he had been introduced to drinking cologne in the army and had switched to window cleaner during the mid-1980s anti-alcohol campaign, when vodka and other mainstays were being rationed. "I ended up in an emergency room, with cirrhosis of the liver, and didn't drink for six months." The physicians spoke about him as more or less a lost cause.

The Substance and Time of Patienthood

Nikolai belonged to the larger of two distinct groups of patients on Ward Two. These were the alcoholics—generally men ranging in age from their late thirties to their sixties—for whom the majority of the ward's beds were set aside (this was the case for most of the hospital's six hundred beds as well). The smaller group of patients was made up of young men in their early twenties being treated for heroin addiction, whom clinicians and laypeople alike called *narkomany* (drug addicts). The two groups had distinct clinical profiles. In the case of narkomany these were associated with the intertwined epidemics of intravenous opiate use, HIV/AIDS, hepatitis, and other infectious diseases in the former Soviet Union. Of the ten or so patients being treated for opiate addiction on the ward at any time, the physicians estimated that an average of eight were HIV-positive, a figure that seemed to hold roughly for the entire hospital. The HIV/AIDS epidemic has been closely linked to injection drug use in Russia and in other former Soviet states since it spread to the region in the mid-1990s, and some estimates suggest that over half of new cases are still linked to injection drug use (Federal AIDS Center 2012).[5] The vast majority of IV drug users at the hospital had also tested positive for hepatitis C.

As Alexander Sergeevich pointed out, alcoholics and drug addicts were not only epidemiological populations and clinical categories but also social clusters. "The alcoholics don't like those guys," he said, gesturing toward several young men in T-shirts and sweatpants who were making their way down the hall. As if in confirmation of Alexander Sergeevich's point, a few minutes later we heard shouting in the hallway leading to the ward's exit. Two of the young men had scuffled with Vasili, an older patient with a large walrus mustache. By the time we arrived, a nurse was already berating them, as they explained that they were only going out to smoke, while Vasili picked his thick glasses off of the floor and inspected them for damage. Later Alexander Sergeevich approached Vasili as he sat watching a game show on the ward's television and asked, "Are you going to be able to keep your cool and avoid any more incidents? We don't want to get the police [*militsiia*] involved."

Such moments manifested often-discussed tensions and perceived differences between alcoholics (*alkogoliki*) and narkomany. Underlying this typology, which was organizationally instantiated through the allocation of hospital beds according to diagnosis and colloquially reinforced in conversations about essential differences, was the idea that each substance affected bodies, psyches, and life trajectories with a distinct temporality. As a narcologist at the Bekhterev Psychoneurological Institute explained, "[Alcohol] destroys people over the course of years, while drugs do this over the course of months." This understanding of alcohol's sedimentary effects had long been inscribed in clinical categories such as "chronic alcoholism" (which was distinct from "everyday drinking" [*bytovoe pianstvo*]), the notion of "three stages of alcoholism," and the idea of the "extinguished vomiting reflex." These were clinical concepts that (as I discuss in greater detail in the following chapter) were no longer formally recognized or endorsed by the twenty-first century but remained part of the tacit repertoire for older clinicians. They suggested not only a chronicity with a particular tempo and rhythm but also a certain pattern to patients' entanglements with the therapeutic economy: years, sometimes decades, of regular habitual drinking or binging at increasingly closer intervals and eventually, repeated returns to the hospital for treatment. Drinking bouts or binges (*zapoi*), referred to in the medical literature as a drinking style or pattern, not only had their own temporality but were described by most patients at the hospital as distinct—perhaps liminal—times and spaces that one "entered" and "exited." In fact, most of the long-term therapeutics worked on a similar temporal logic: suggestion-based methods of facilitating concrete periods of sobriety or (to think of it another way) of forestalling a drinker's entry into the next binge.

Heroin was described as having a radically different temporality, linked not only to an accelerated process in which the patients became dependent but also to the way in which this process lined up with and shaped people's trajectories of bodily and moral development. Most heroin users in the hospital had begun using in their late teens or early twenties—and were understood to have had little in the way of a developed personality prior to their addiction. Without experience or a perspective on other forms of life, many clinicians understood them as more profoundly amoral than alcoholics—a view that was widely shared by substance abuse professionals working outside the hospital. A 12-step counselor and recovering alcoholic used an aphorism to suggest that alcoholics and drug addicts were at different states of moral decline or desperation: "The alcoholic will steal your wallet and a week later promise to return it. He'll feel guilty about it even if he doesn't return it. But the drug addict will steal your wallet and then return a week later and try to extort more money from you for returning it."

The temporal differences between alcohol and narcotics were not limited to an understanding of their effects but extended to the ways in which each substance was represented in relation to Russian history. Here the almost universally held assumption was that whereas alcohol (particularly vodka) was deeply familiar and intimately meaningful, linked to Russian national substance even in the pathologies it produced, drugs (particularly heroin) were profoundly alien and inherently corrupting. As one narcologist put it, "For some reason, in our mentality [*mentalitete*] drinking is a normal everyday vexing [*obidnoe*] phenomenon, while drug abuse [*narkomaniia*] is something foreign and alien [*inozemnaia, chuzhoe i chuzhdoe*]." Here discussions of alcohol and drinking practices in Russia touch upon long-performed myths and stereotypes of nationality, authenticity, and suffering. Accounts from the fifteenth and sixteenth centuries to the present day have depicted the issue through a primordial cultural logic, attributing to "the Russians" an insatiable appetite for alcohol and finding this "nation" to be (in the words of the seventeenth-century visitor Adam Olearius) "more addicted to drunkenness than any nation in the world" (quoted in S. White 1996, 6).[6] In these long-running debates vodka appears as a kind of *pharmakon*, a poison with particularly baneful effects in Russia or a spirit that holds "the people" (*narod*) together, but in either case as having some privileged relationship to Russianness.[7] As I discuss at length in the following chapter, these culturalist discourses are closely linked with a series of long-running debates about the relationship between patterns of consumption and the political economy of alcohol, primarily vodka, in Russia—and specifically, about the links between the social meanings (or use-values) of alcohol and the key role it has played in the tsarist and Soviet states' generation of fiscal revenues (Christian 1990; Herlihy 2002; Takala 2002; Makinen and Reitan 2006; Transchel 2006).

While vodka was in many ways intertwined with the Soviet political economy, for most of the late Soviet period, the use of psychoactive substances (other than alcohol, tobacco, and pharmaceuticals) involved cannabis grown inside the Soviet Union and opiates that were homemade or produced on a small scale and were relatively unprocessed (Conroy 1990).[8] Opiates began to flow across the border from Afghanistan in the 1980s during the war, and the relaxation of border and trade controls that came with the dissolution of the Soviet Union in 1991 made it even easier for various highly processed narcotics to flow into Russia. Despite this, the use of heroin did not become common and visible in urban centers until the mid- to late 1990s (Paoli 2002). This sudden visibility of heroin use prompted a moral panic in the mass media, reinforcing and feeding perceptions of narcotics in Russia as deeply foreign and polluting (Meylakhs 2009). Such assumptions further resonate with the framing of drug addiction by the Russian state as a problem of security, often linked to the problems of terrorism and illegal immigration. These became particularly dominant during the first decade of the 2000s as drug trafficking became increasingly understood (not only in Russia) as often intertwined with the financing of international terrorist networks and as more heroin began to flow into Russia through central Asia in the wake of the US-led war in Afghanistan (Renz 2011).

This distinction between vodka and heroin as substances that produced inherently distinct types of pathology and indeed, distinct kinds of persons, made so much sense to physicians and patients alike that it was referred to despite some evidence to the contrary. That is, while physicians and other professionals working with addiction throughout St. Petersburg spoke about their clinical experience with patients who used many kinds of drugs, and reported an increase in alcohol use among young people of an age and background who, several years previously, had almost exclusively been using heroin, the typology of alcoholics and drug addicts in the clinic remained firm.

The Political Economy of Heavy Drinking

Even for those wary of cruder culturalist accounts of primordial drinking cultures, it might be easy to think of alcohol simply as a means of escape from intolerable conditions of everyday life in Russia—during both the late and post-Soviet periods. But such a reading would overlook some of the key roles that alcohol—and particularly vodka—played in the Soviet political economy and continues to play in the post-Soviet world. These are the sites where practices of sociality, consumption, and exchange mingle, where enactments of intimacy and self-interest bleed into one another. Indeed these practices and sites were ubiquitous in the stories of the men at the Municipal Addiction Hospital.

Ivan—a sandy-haired and stocky businessman in his midthirties—showed me his trembling hands and explained that nearly all his business meetings had to be conducted over vodka. After completing his army service in a special-forces (*spetsnaz*) unit during the mid-1990s, Ivan and a business partner had begun buying and selling goods in the train station that serviced freight traveling between St. Petersburg and Moscow. It was, as he put it, "a gold mine." This was the period of early capitalism in Russia, during which the state's institutional capacity and reach receded and fragmented radically, and networks of what one scholar has called "violent entrepreneurs"—known as *kryshi* (roofs)—arose to provide security and enforce contracts (Volkov 2002).[9] Regardless of whether a business was legal or illegal or occupied a gray area between the two, in this institutional climate its relationships with other organizations were heavily personalized—grounded in relationships between individuals that were forged in face-to-face practices of deal making. As Ivan and his partner saw their business grow, they became involved in such interactions at increasingly higher levels, where, as he put it, "you couldn't get by without a glass." Ivan explained the process: "Two companies meet in a small office and one tells the other—I'll give you one wagon [of freight] and you'll give me two wagons. A person can't refuse [alcohol] in those contexts—people would look at him differently. The deal [*sdelka*] could fall apart. So I had to drink both in order to get things done [*protolknut'*] and to calm down when I got home." Here drinking is not simply a means of forging an economic relationship but a kind of test, whereby the manner in which one drinks is a potential sign of one's character and trustworthiness. Refusing to drink in such a setting can often be interpreted as a lack of respect for one's host—a topic of much discussion and humor in Russian popular culture (cf. Pesman 2000, 184)—but equally important is how one conducts oneself while drinking. One of my acquaintances (who was not in treatment) told me about how drinking with his superiors at his job as an engineer during the late Soviet period made it clear to both him and them that he would never be fully accepted into their circle—which had severe consequences for his career advancement. Not only was he unable to drink as much as the higher administrators, but he felt his relative lack of fluency with the bountiful lexicon of Russian profanity (*mat*) and his overall comportment marked his non-working-class origins, his self-ascribed identity as intelligentsia, and perhaps his Jewishness. Informed by the widely held assumption that alcohol always disinhibits people and encourages them to reveal their true selves, in such drinking settings various nonverbal, embodied, and enacted aspects of one's comportment could definitively mark one as *ne svoi*—"not one of ours." For Ivan, this meant that heavy drinking was an occupational hazard and that any attempt to address the condition that he called alcoholism—characterized by his shaking hands—meant changing professions. "Two weeks ago my wife and I decided to forget about this thing—and went to the narcologist," he continued, adding, "I won't go back there. . . . I won't go back there. I'll start over—I'll even work as a shipyard laborer."

As Ivan implied, such drinking practices are particularly significant because the forms of sociality they sustained and the relationships that were produced and maintained through them have been so important to how things get done" in certain domains of postsocialist Russia. And indeed, such informal practices of exchange and sociability were equally central to the political economy of state socialism. As many scholars have argued, since the Soviet state and Communist Party held a monopoly on all legitimate channels of distribution—for goods, services, and information as well as access to jobs or positions of authority—any practices by which social actors circumvented or poached from these channels were by definition informal or unofficial. They were in a kind of symbiotic relationship with the administered economy—entirely dependent upon it for resources, just as they undermined its stated goals. These practices, which ranged from the blat system—exchanges of favors—and the so-called second economy to patronage relationships within the state bureaucracy to the barter relations established between socialist firms, were also deeply personalistic (Berliner 1957; Grossman 1977; Kornai 1992; Verdery 1996; Ledeneva 1998). What has been remarked upon much less often is how central alcohol was to these forms of sociability, as a staple of the drinking practices through which the relationships were produced and maintained (Hivon 1994; Ledeneva 1998; Pesmen 2000). While the post-Soviet period saw many of the specific institutions that undergirded this system collapse, the informal practices of exchange and sociability have flourished—and in many ways sustained and provided continuity for people throughout the 1990s and early 2000s. While such practices span a dizzying array of types of exchange and sociality, in many cases drinking did more than help create and cement relationships: it allowed for the blurring of any clear distinction between the economic and the intimate, or some might say, allowed for people to mutually misrecognize calculated exchange as kind-hearted help.[10]

This ambiguity was all the more acutely felt because alcohol was—and frequently continues to be—not only the means of ritually cementing key relationships but also the object of exchange. Evgenii, whose work involved transporting, among other things, kegs of beer and cases of vodka, explained the use of alcohol as a surrogate currency simply: "The plumber comes to fix something and I give him a bottle: that's the liquid dollar [*eto zhidkii dollar*]." Once again, practices involving the exchange of alcohol—which ranged from barter to tacit exchange for services or favors to gifting—were well established throughout the Soviet period, when vodka was often referred to as *zhidkaia valiuta*—literally, "liquid hard currency." Throughout the Soviet period firms would often receive shipments of industrial alcohol—which they used to barter for goods they actually needed. The practice of distributing alcohol in this way went far beyond those industries in which it had a direct use—and amounted to a tacit acknowledgment by central planners that alcohol could be used to barter in an economy of shortage. This was particularly the case in settings such as the far north: one of the patients at the hospital had worked as an aerial photographer in the tundra, where, he explained, "everything is paid with alcohol [*spirt*]." During the 1990s large areas in Russia experienced a currency shortage for prolonged periods of time, and as forms of barter were taken up to allow for exchange, alcohol—whether vodka, *samogon* (moonshine), or industrial alcohol—was again used as a currency (Rogers 2005). The underlying assumption of these exchanges was that, unlike the Soviet (and in some cases the post-Soviet Russian) ruble, vodka had a stable value, and indeed, vodka had many characteristics that contributed to its use as a surrogate currency: it was portable and nonperishable, and— perhaps most important—it had a singularly widespread use-value.

"A Massive Natural Experiment"

For epidemiologists, demographers, and researchers in public health— particularly those interested in social determinants—the collapse of the Soviet Union has taken on the status of what UK epidemiologists Sir Michael Marmot and Martin McKee have called, respectively, a "ghastly natural experiment" (Marmot 2004, 43) and "a massive natural experiment" (McKee and Leon 2005, 1206)—that is, a vital source of new knowledge for population health. To understand how this came to be the case, how the demographic crisis became conceivable as a natural experiment, it is worth returning to the final Soviet anti-alcohol campaign.

In May 1985, two months after the ascension of Mikhail Gorbachev to the post of general secretary, the Central Committee of the Communist Party of the Soviet Union launched what would be the last Soviet anti-alcohol campaign—arguably the last attempt at a centralized campaign of social engineering directed by the party-state.[11] Public discussions of the early to mid-1980s acknowledged alcoholism and alcohol-related harm as a social problem to an extent unprecedented in Soviet history. In 1985, according to official statistics, there were 4.5 million registered alcoholics in the Soviet Union—and public health officials estimated that the actual number was up to three times as high (Nemtsov 2011). Many of these discussions were driven by a group of authors—a mix of editors, scientists, and physicians—who portrayed the problem of alcoholism in strongly nationalistic and even anti-Semitic terms and argued that the only solution was complete or near-total prohibition. (Though these arguments were veiled at first, they were made in an increasingly open manner throughout the 1980s). The shape of this argument was nothing new: rather, it evoked similar claims made during the nineteenth century: the Russian people were being destroyed by the poison of alcohol fed to them by something like a Jewish-Masonic conspiracy (White 1996; M. Levine 1999). Though these claims were made openly only by some of the more militant prohibitionists, they shaped much of the entire discourse about alcoholism in the late 1980s.

During the course of the anti-alcohol campaign it was this tough prohibitionist stance that came to dominate, and various well-known proponents of moderate drinking (referred to as "cultured drinking" in the debates) were marginalized and attacked (White 1996; M. Levine 1999). The campaign brought together radical cuts in alcohol production and sales, as well as price increases, with sloganeering by a newly founded nationwide temperance society. The rationing of vodka quickly led to queues that were extremely long, even by Soviet standards, in some cases leading to near riots. As discontent with the anti-alcohol measures grew, consumers increasingly turned to moonshine, reinvigorating long-standing practices of home distilling.

While the campaign had petered out by 1988, in part overshadowed by the broader political shifts of perestroika, its consequences were rather more far-reaching. Widely considered a failure in political, economic, and public health terms, for epidemiologists and demographers interested in the Russian demographic crisis, the anti-alcohol campaign has played an important role in helping to tease out the relationships between drinking, stress, mortality, and various types of morbidity. A network of collaborating researchers based in the United Kingdom, France, Eastern Europe, and Russia—centered on Marmot's research group at University College, London—has been particularly influential in making the argument of a strong link between decreases in life expectancy and alcohol-related harm in Russia. Drawing on estimated rates of alcohol consumption produced by the epidemiologist Alexander Nemtsov, these researchers have argued since the mid-1990s that fluctuations in mortality correlated with what was known about changes in alcohol consumption (Leon et al. 1997). Not only did life expectancy at birth increase by two years during the final Soviet anti-alcohol campaign and subsequently drop, but the greatest fluctuations in life expectancy took place in regions associated with higher levels of alcohol consumption—northern and western Russia as well as certain areas in Siberia (McKee and Leon 2005). Additionally, some of the largest proportional fluctuations took place in deaths classified as "alcohol-related"—accidents, suicide, and pneumonia (Leon et al. 1997). While the vast majority of "premature" deaths in Russia are attributed to cardiovascular disease, this group of authors has argued for a strong link to alcohol here as well. Although moderate quantities of alcohol are considered cardioprotective, they have argued that the particular *style* of drinking prevalent throughout Russia—that is, "heavy, episodic drinking," referred to in medical literature (and in Anglo-American colloquial usage) as bingeing and in Russian as zapoi—may be linked to sudden cardiac deaths among young men (Britton and McKee 2000).

However common such drinking might have been, making persuasive claims about the relationship between mortality, drinking practices, and broader social factors has been complex. Epidemiology deals in largely correlational claims, and in order to translate correlations between statistical trends or patterns into hypotheses about causal links between various factors, epidemiologists and public health researchers often base their claims on assumptions drawn from decades of stress research. For example, the authors of one epidemiological study on the drop in male life expectancy in Russia wrote, "The rapid rise in per capita alcohol consumption since the late 1980s may be partly a result of reduced social controls" (Notzon et al. 1998, 798), adding that "[stress, anxiety and depression] along with growing hopelessness in the face of increasing unemployment, negative economic growth, and social strife, may in turn underlie the rapid growth in per capita alcohol consumption" (ibid.). The Durkheimian kernel of such arguments is the idea that profound political and economic transformations disrupt the cohesiveness of social groups as well as the relationship between expectations and possibilities, creating not only stress but a sense of anomie (McKee and Leon 2005). A further notion, not necessarily following from the first, is that such dysphoric experiences are unequally distributed over socioeconomic hierarchies; the assumption is that people with higher class or status positions have greater social, economic, and psychological resources to draw upon and thus experience less stress (Cockerham 1999, 41).

While not all researchers studying the Russian demographic crisis subscribe to these ideas, they have been particularly central to the work of Marmot and his colleagues, who first developed what has come to be known as the "social gradient of health" theory on the basis of the Whitehall study of British civil servants. Indeed, it was Marmot and his colleagues who described the demographic crisis in the former Soviet Union, as well as other formerly state socialist Eastern European states, as a natural experiment—the results of which they interpreted as bolstering and furthering their theory as well as research on the social determinants of health more broadly. Both the original 1967 Whitehall study and its follow-up twenty years later argued that the risk of cardiovascular illness—and higher mortality—was inversely linked to social class or status (Marmot et al. 1991). Lower status has, in turn, been interpreted as more highly associated with psychosocial dynamics that lead to a stress response, namely a "lack of control over [one's] life," and a "lack of opportunity to participate socially in a meaningful way" (Kriesler and Marmot 2002). The studies based in Russia and Eastern Europe were thus understood as demonstrating a similar dynamic at work on the level of entire states. Between 1989 and 1999 this region experienced four million "excess deaths"—an epidemiological term referring to mortality above historically expected rates. As Marmot has pointed out, an important reason for interpreting these deaths through the lens of the social gradient theory was that these countries had not been— during the 1970s and '80s—suffering from anything like absolute poverty according to measures such as infant mortality or child malnourishment. In short, in seeking to link these deaths with the profound transformations taking place in postsocialist states during this period, Marmot, McKee, and their colleagues have developed a complex narrative in which alcohol plays a key role and that hinges on such psychosocial concepts as "control" and "participation"—which are, in turn, supported by basic assumptions drawn from the stress research literature.

And while these social epidemiologists are careful to call the aftermath of the Soviet Union's dissolution a natural experiment, its natural quality is called into question by some of the more contentious and provocative claims made by their own group. In 2009, McKee and two of his colleagues published a paper in the *Lancet* on the results of a study examining the association between the increases in adult mortality in postsocialist Eastern European states and the mass privatizations that took place in these countries during the 1990s. The researchers found that "mass privatisation programmes were associated with a short-term increase in mortality rates in working-aged men" throughout postsocialist Europe and Eurasia and that higher unemployment rates were linked to mortality in the former Soviet Union (Stuckler, King, and McKee 2009, 404). Though these claims have been, unsurprisingly, disputed by many, they point to an "experimentality" (Nguyen 2009; Petryna 2007) that, far from being "natural," was the product of "shock therapy" privatization schemes promoted by many neoliberal economists during the early 1990s.

Lost in a Forest: The Crisis of Masculinity

Anton Dmitrievich, the head doctor on the ward, had explained to me that Andrei had suffered a "psychotic episode." The doctor had trained as a psychiatrist, and prior to joining the addiction hospital he had worked at one of St. Petersburg's psychiatric hospitals. Andrei's case interested him for professional reasons, and he thought that it might similarly interest me. Yet what ultimately most struck me about Andrei was not the alcoholic psychosis that he had experienced but how he narrated his life as a series of failures to live up to the masculine norms of post-Soviet Russia. His story resonated with another crisis that has long been understood as intertwined with the demographic crisis in Russia—the so-called crisis of masculinity.

Gangly and thin, wearing thick glasses and a checkered shirt, Andrei looked younger than his thirty-eight years. He had grown up in Leningrad in a working-class family, his mother a chauffeur, his stepfather a dock-worker. The family experienced the privations of living space common to urban dwellers during the late Soviet period. "The four of us lived in one room in a communal apartment until we received an apartment. And then my youngest sister was born, so we were five." The stepfather drank occasionally. "Once he hit her, and then they divorced. She was left alone with three children: the youngest was one year old, my middle sister five, and I was twelve. I was the eldest, so I helped her out."

Andrei described his conscription into the army and his time there as the source of a trauma that had stayed with him throughout his life. "In the army they seriously disrupted my psyche [*podorvali psikhiku sil'no*]," he explained. The institutionalized practices of hazing (*dedovshchina*) in the Soviet and post-Soviet army have been widely described as contributing to numerous deaths and serious injuries annually (Elkner 2004). In many battalions, generational distinctions between the young conscripts and the *dedy*, or "old men," are reinforced or crosscut by ethnic-national ones, leading to similar practices of hazing (*gruppovshchina*). Using a common derogatory term for people from the northern Caucasus, Andrei explained,

> I ended up in a "black" battalion. I was in one of the battalions attached to the railroad. We had to chop down trees and make railroad ties. The officers are off hanging out [*guliaiut*], it's the *dedy* and that's it. And the forest. You have only yourself to rely on for help. We were young and they were chasing us around of course. . . . Out of my cohort of eight, four ended up in the nuthouse, three cut their veins and one just ran away—they caught him of course. I seemingly lived through it. I also wanted to do something to myself, to run away or something. But you understand I grew up in a women's collective [*zhenskii kollektiv*], and there it was all men, and all black: Chechens, Dagestanis, and so on. And I ended up in this kind of state, as though I exited [*vyshel*] and watched it all from the side, as though it wasn't me doing all this, but someone else. . . .
>
> . . . I went up to the commander and said, I'll fight with your guys, but just don't demote me. He says, "Well, if you survive, then OK." To approach him and say these words was very frightening. He could have cut me open. We're in the forest, you're there from spring to November, looking out for yourself alone. And there my psyche started to go, because of that.

Andrei described this milieu marked by fear, isolation, loneliness, and the threat of violence as the source of the problems with his "psyche" (*psikhika*). Andrei also hinted at his own interpretation for his vulnerability—a theme that he would return to throughout our conversations—"You understand I grew up in a women's collective." The underlying assumption here— that a man raised in a family of only women is unprepared for the expectations of adult masculinity—is one that first began to circulate in the context of late Soviet debates about changing gender norms and a crisis of masculinity. During the late 1960s members of the liberal intelligentsia began to point to high male mortality rates and declining life expectancies as signs that a generation of post–World War II Soviet men were unable to properly embody accepted norms of masculinity (Zdravomyslova and Temkina 2012). In explaining this failure, many observers turned to social and structural factors—such as the rise in female-headed households in the Soviet Union and the consequent lack of fathers to model appropriate masculine behavior.[12] Parallel discussions have continued into the post-Soviet period. Although the paradox here is that while the early post-Soviet period (1990s and early 2000s) saw an overall masculinization of certain domains of public life and a retrenchment of what some understand as traditional gender roles for men and women, there has also been a perception that men were somehow more susceptible or sensitive to the social ferment of the postsocialist period.

And indeed, it was during the early 1990s that Andrei had gotten married and found a job in a public bath. Andrei's description of the end of his marriage after only three years was painful, full of self-reproach and self-denigrating justification:

> I let her go myself. I felt that I was drinking—how to explain it. . . . We lived in a communal apartment [*kommunalka*]. We couldn't get an apartment and she had also grown up in a communal apartment with her parents. And we couldn't find better housing, so I decided to let her go, so that she could find someone better for herself. Of course this was hard for me as well. But it was my decision. She said, "Why?" And I said—I had to say something, so I said, I don't like you, I'm out of love with you, even though we had married for love. And then I started drinking—I would drink and cry.

Andrei had spent the next ten years working in various manual jobs, including one as a truck loader in a furniture factory. He explained why he had started drinking alone—as well as how he became caught up in a cycle of emotions that perpetuated his binges.

> I was living alone in a communal apartment and they started to rob me while I was drunk. You bring some people back to your place and in the morning you see they've stolen everything. So I decided not to bring anyone back, not to drink with anyone. Because they would secretly give me chlopheline [a tranquilizer] in my drink. You wake up, your leather jacket is gone, your boots are gone. . . . You know how it works: you're drinking on your own, and some others join in, and we all start drinking together. And then mine runs out and I say, let me try yours, and they give me the

loaded vodka. I wake up with nothing: just underwear and socks. . . . And then out of this situation comes another depression [*depresniak*] and on top of that you're feeling shitty [*tebe kolbasit*]. That's how my psyche broke. . . .

I don't have these moments when I just have to drink for no reason. It's when something goes wrong in my life. I lost my documents, I go into a binge. I lost track of myself, in other words I don't act responsibly. It is very hard for me to come out of these binges. When I'm there, I get anxious about how painful it will be to come out [withdrawal] and so I drink a little more, but then it only gets scarier. So you go into one for a week or two— and then you come out. And for those weeks you don't eat. Because I don't have that much money. So I just drink.

Often, it was only with his mother's help that he emerged from his binges. "I enter a binge and [my mother] helps bring me out of it. My sisters have turned their backs on me—'Why are you dealing with him?' [they ask] and she says, 'He's my son, as long as he's alive I'll deal with him [*budu vozit'sia s nim*].'"

Andrei wanted to move away from the communal apartment—"All around it was just swearing [*mat*] and drunkenness [*pianka*]"—so he followed his mother, who had recently remarried and moved away from St. Petersburg to a smaller town. There Andrei had become involved with a woman and fathered a daughter: "This city is small, and I was working with furniture—it was heavy work, and everyone drinks. Of course she was afraid, with the child, and would often leave for her mother's place. Again I would go away into loneliness. Again the binges, and again my mother would pull me out. So [the relationship] didn't work out." Andrei was proud of the fact that he had legally acknowledged his daughter (*udocheril*) and regularly sent her money. He returned to St. Petersburg, found a job working in a store, but was soon fired for drinking. "I was unemployed again and without money. I sold my TV; I needed to live on something, I can't ask my mother with her tiny pension. My sisters had turned their backs on me. And so I was left alone. I'd get hungry so I'd go and sell my jacket. I buy something to eat and of course something to drink as well. By this point it was nothing too decent . . . what do they call it—an alcohol-based baking additive."

During the past year Andrei had managed to get a job at a bread factory, unloading loaves from a conveyor and packing them into delivery trucks. "I worked clean for two months," he said. After his first paycheck his work crew had celebrated in a time-honored fashion: by collecting money to fund a party or drinking bout (Phillips 2000, 53). In the wake of this, he had lost his passport, bank card, and electronic key to the factory. He'd tried to buy himself time by purchasing a certificate of illness (*bol'niak*) from his polyclinic, but he had lost this as well.

> By then my money is running out already. And now again this got me down, this loss—and I went into another binge and this one lasted three weeks. I was taking out money and already couldn't go out—I'd just go to the kiosk and back—just to buy this baking additive. Also my daughter was supposed to come visit, and just when my mother left to pick her up, I lost my passport and went into this binge. They arrived and I wanted to go to the zoo with my daughter—I had a plan. And this was tearing my heart up so much—such shame. And I started to chastise myself [*korit' sebia*] that you've drunk yourself to this. And my mother was giving it to me too.

It was in the wake of this last setback that Andrei had experienced what his physician described as a psychotic break:

> A: And here the doubling of my personality [*razdvoenie lichnosti*] began. That is, this nonsense started, as though I'm not alone but with a friend: as though there are two of us. Just like I have two legs: there are two of us. I say—in my mind, "Let's drink up?" I talk to myself, and sit in my room and don't go into the communal apartment. The people there are normal, not heavy drinkers. . . . I just close myself in my room, no music, no TV, nothing. Just drink and smoke a little.
>
> E: Was this the first time you'd experienced this?
>
> A: No, well I told you, it happened once in the army. I could think that I'm a woman and tell myself, "Let's drink." [Andrei acts it out, stroking his own hand lovingly]. And so I drink as though he's drinking, and then for myself: this kind of situation. I was going nuts [*kryshu poekhala*]. Its true that I didn't hear voices, but when night comes closer, then it is frightening, you see faces, your head doesn't turn off. . . .
>
> . . . Now I no longer pity myself. I did this all to myself, after all. Sometimes you don't want to live, you want to fall asleep and not wake up—so as not to bother anyone.

Andrei had not previously received treatment from either a psychiatrist or a narcologist. He had been brought to the hospital by his mother, who had heard that there was a free service. When I asked Andrei about his hopes for the future, he explained, "I think I can exchange the room I have now for a smaller one. Then I'll have some money left over to buy a computer. And I can play computer games and be able to occupy myself."

Thrown-Away People

I met Sasha on one of the first days that I visited wards at the hospital. Gaunt and slight, his face and hands creased, Sasha had been born in Leningrad in 1958 into a working-class family that lived in a communal apartment; his father was a typographer, and his mother started out as a cook, eventually administering a number of cafeterias. Sasha attended a vocational school specializing in radio technology and later found work in a factory producing television sets. A brief stint in the army was followed by a series of different jobs. "I started to misuse alcohol, [*zloupotrebliat' spirtogo*] more and more often. Until I was twenty-three I drank, although I worked too. Of course, under the Soviet regime one didn't have a choice."

Sasha summed up the grim narrative of most of his life in a couple of sentences: "At twenty-three I was put in prison, and here begins a completely different life. Prison, prison, prison, prison, prison, colony, release, again prison, release, again prison, release, again prison, release, and here I am before you." Sasha had lived most of his life passing through the revolving doors of one prison to the next, following a trajectory that spanned the length of Russia's far-flung network of prison colonies, from Pskov to the Urals to Siberia and finally to St. Petersburg. Nearly all his prison sentences were related to acts committed while intoxicated—mostly burglary. Lately he had obtained a room in a communal apartment in the city, but he had stolen from his neighbors, who had retaliated by changing the locks to the apartment. Now Sasha preferred to live at the hospital while he tried to save up the money he owed his neighbors and hopefully arrange to swap his room for another. The physicians would occasionally discharge and readmit him to circumvent the monthlong limit on inpatient stays, and I often saw him sweeping, carrying food for patients, or running errands for Anton Dmitrievich, the head narcologist on his ward.

On one of these occasions, I passed Sasha in the hallway of the ward on the morning after a parliamentary election. We chatted briefly about the unsurprising results (another major victory for the party supporting Putin), and then Sasha motioned me into an empty examination room, where he gestured for me to turn on my audio recorder and launched into a tirade linking alcohol consumption to generational resentment:

> I think that people like me, or people close to me in spirit, we are not needed, not by the state, not by the police, not by anyone. We're thrown-away people [*my vyibroshennye liudi*]. So I think that all of these stores which are open twenty-four hours a day, are especially there for people of my generation— of the 1950s and '60s—which grew up on port wine—just to drown us in drink [*chtoby nas prosto spoit'*] so that we'll just die off. I think that way, and no one can convince me otherwise. Because all of my good friends have died—starting when they were thirty-eight years old, forty, forty-two—all of my friends. Some died from vodka, others died in the camps—in the camps they all died because of vodka. One died from a heart attack, but he also drank. As though it was all on purpose.

Sasha paused, seeming to mull over the idea he had just articulated. "The new generation, of the 1980s which grew up during perestroika," he continued, "everywhere you see they [employers] want thirty- to forty-year-olds—this is already a new generation. It doesn't recognize vodka, it doesn't recognize port wine; it recognizes narcotics." He pointed in the general direction of the room that housed the ward's several heroin addicts. "They are the dealers, brokers [*dilery, brokery*], all those other foreign terms," Sasha said emphatically. A nurse opened the door, frowned at us, and moved on. "Here, on every corner they sell vodka, alcohol, or hawthorn tonic at any hour. . . . You'll die. . . . We are not needed by anyone. The hospital doesn't need us. The people working in this hospital are just receiving money to treat us. That's it. . . . Here [*u nas*] the state's policies [*politika*] toward my generation are to drown us in drink so that we'll all die off." Sasha stood up. "I've looked for work," he said. "Everywhere I've looked, they want you to be forty-five years old maximum, and even this is rare, usually younger than forty. No bad habits and they want your biography to be [clean]. Who in Russia has a biography that isn't smudged [*zapiatnona*]? Ninety percent of people in Russia have served time [*sudimykh*]." With this he started toward the door.

In many ways Sasha's diatribe was not unusual—even adhering in part to the well-worn post-Soviet scripts of laments about "total crisis," complete social destruction, disarray, or "degradation" (Ries 1997; Shevchenko 2009). But the phrase that I could not stop thinking about for days afterward was "As though it was all on purpose." While far from the highly elaborated conspiracy theories I heard from others, Sasha's account had a similar logic—a logic that assigned a clear cause and responsibility for what I often took to be unintended consequences or the result of massively complex processes. Such arguments often arose in everyday discussions of the demographic crisis, sometimes voiced alongside those ideas about the supposedly deliberate extermination of the Russian people that frequently accompany a politics of xenophobia and ethnonational resentment. At times these explanations even echoed the many accounts of the occult that I encountered. Like the epidemics of witchcraft described by John and Jean Comaroff as "occult economies" (1999, 294) or the talk about mafia in postsocialist Europe described by Katherine Verdery, such explanations "attribut[ed] difficult social problems to malevolent and unseen forces" (Verdery 1996, 220) and evoked a social world manipulated by invisible agents.

And yet, such an interpretation—which would examine conspiratorial accounts as expressions of false consciousness or as inchoate articulations of discontent—falls short of explaining the other kinds of work that such talk accomplishes (cf. Boyer 2006; Pelkmans and Machold 2011). At the most straightforward level, Sasha echoed both contemporary talk about the demographic crisis and long-standing debates about moral meanings of the Russian and Soviet states' regulation of alcohol production and sales. Indeed, the idea that concerns about health and mortality of Russian citizens would be well served through closer attention to policies surrounding alcohol has been widely voiced and has been addressed by a range of state policies enacted in the past several years.

In his own diagnostic of the present, Sasha emphasized a crisis experienced by his generation and class of what he called thrown-away people. Such expressions of being "needed by nobody" (Höjdestrand 2009; Parsons 2014) are often heard in accounts of the marginalized in post-Soviet Russia. They communicate an acutely felt sense of purpose lost, of recognition averted, of meaning dissipated, which are only obliquely present in epidemiological and demographic debates and which remain largely absent from many arguments about public health and fiscal policy. For Sasha, it seemed that such affects might even remain invisible in the clinic. And yet, his mention of treatment in the hospital by people "just receiving money to treat us" suggests just a sliver of some other, prior, remembered or perhaps imagined kind of care.

Crises of masculinity, generation, national security, and economy were not the only ones understood as closely entwined with the demographic crisis. Throughout the past quarter century, a crisis in the healthcare system in Russia has also been repeatedly declared. According to many psychiatrists and narcologists, the crisis in the treatment of alcoholism and addiction has been particularly acute. It is those claims that the following chapters address.

2

ASSEMBLING NARCOLOGY

Elena Andreevna looked up from the pile of forms and other paperwork that covered her desk and sighed. It was only ten o'clock in the morning, but she already looked tired. She had spent the half hour before my arrival trying to convince a patient not to discharge himself from her ward. "This one insisted that he mainly drank beer, so I explained to him that beer contains estrogens and continuous consumption leads men to lose their libido," she said. In the end the patient had walked out, more or less telling Elena Andreevna that she could "treat herself!"

She had been working as a narcologist-psychiatrist since the mid-1990s, initially at the *oblast'* hospital, where she had first seen the consumption of surrogate alcohol in epic proportions and had witnessed the replacement of homemade opiates by processed heroin as the preferred drug of her younger patients. Like many narcologists, Elena Andreevna understood the changes she saw in the clinic as closely linked to the turbulence of Russia's early post-Soviet years, a consequence of what she sometimes called a "double morality." "What can we expect a man to do when he has no work and there is alcohol everywhere, and additionally when he expects that the state should give him everything?" she asked. "The state took everything away and didn't return anything. Yeltsin—I saw him as one of the bandits—and Chubais too. The people [*narod*] ended up entirely disoriented and abandoned in this situation." Irina Vassieleva, a narcologist whose desk sat on the opposite side of the office, took this moment to add that Yeltsin's own habitual drunkenness had not helped them in making the case for sobriety to their patients. "You never see Putin like this," she continued, making a distinction (endlessly repeated in print and conversation) that implicitly drew together the images of Yeltsin's dissolute personal behavior, his perceived weakness as a leader, and what she called contemporary society's "lack of discipline" (*razpushchennost'*) on the one hand and on the other hand, Putin's sobriety, his seeming resoluteness, his embodiment of an ideal of masculine strength, and the more general sense that everyday life was finally beginning to normalize.

Many of those conversations we would have later. That morning Elena Andreevna just raised an eyebrow at her colleague and continued speaking. Still frustrated by her encounter with the patient, she picked up the document that he had signed to discharge himself from the hospital, explaining,

Under Soviet power [*Sovetskoi vlasti*] this wouldn't have been possible; it was stricter then. After all, alcoholism and drug addiction [*narkomaniia*] need to be approached not only with voluntary treatment but also with some degree of compulsory [*prinuditelnogo*] treatment. In the past the collective [*kollektiv*], the party [*partkom*], could send him [away] and it was very uncomfortable to drink back then. And the register [*uchët*] at the dispensary was much more strict. Now unfortunately, this system, for various ideological [*ideinyi*] reasons like human rights [*prava cheloveka*]—the system is destroyed and everything is worse. And now many people looking at our old medical system are thinking—the Americans included—to build something like what the Soviet Union had. So not everything was bad. And the Alcoholics Anonymous movement was stronger then.

Many clinicians gave similarly sweeping accounts of the Soviet past during our first meetings, perhaps prompted as much by their awareness of my Americanness as by my questions, and by this point I was accustomed to them. I was also becoming increasingly familiar with expressions of what sounded like a longing for the social norms and institutional structures of the Soviet narcological system—in particular for its compulsory elements—made by narcologists, some of whom were far too young to have experienced these norms or institutions firsthand. Yet Elena Andreevna's account was still striking in its tone and affective intensity, a vision of Soviet narcology as strict and effective so totalizing that it incorporated any interventions toward which she was positively disposed, such as AA (which in fact had been introduced to the Soviet Union only in 1987 and had grown and become more visible in Russia only in the 1990s [Critchlow 2000a]).

Yet as I spent more time listening to Elena Andreevna and her colleagues over the following months, I began to see something more than nostalgia in their accounts of the Soviet narcological system.[1] While many of these narcologists described the Soviet system as characterized by a continuity of care that was largely dependent on its use of surveillance and social control, what struck me as even more significant was their fundamental emphasis on its orderedness. Ilya Sergeevich, a clinician who worked in one of the city's outpatient narcological dispensaries, said it best: "Everything was planned and written out," he told me once. "There was an algorithm." At the time I was also researching the history of narcology and the narcological system, and this emphasis on there having been an order to things seemed to have an affinity with the diagrams of the narcological system that appeared in Soviet textbooks on the subject: rectangles of different sizes, representing different kinds of institutions, are connected to one another by straight lines. The relationship between the institutions is not immediately clear in these diagrams, but it is clear that some hierarchy exists and that the parts of the system work together as a single entity.

Katherine Verdery has argued that if we take seriously Marx's observation about the centrality of commodity fetishism to market economies, then it is important to remember that "socialist systems too had a form of fetishism: plan fetishism, which produced the illusion of agency and obscured the anarchy and chaos that actually took place behind the scenes" (1996, 4). What Verdery describes here is not so much the concrete process of planning (for that see Collier 2011) as the plan as a kind of ideology or imaginary. I came to understand the retrospective accounts of Elena Andreevna, Ilya Sergeevich, and others in this way: not only as depictions of an imagined past that in part serves certain purposes in the present but also as an articulation of the Soviet narcological system as *intention* or *plan*. In other words, these clinicians were describing a small corner of a thoroughly planned system that could be remembered, at least by some participants, not in terms of concrete lived experience but precisely in the idealized abstraction of plans and blueprints. While seeing the past through rose-colored glasses, they were also seeing it "like a state" (Scott 1998).

In this chapter, I draw on Ilya Sergeevich's account of the algorithm, as well as those of others, and also on documentary and secondary sources, both to describe the history and shape of Soviet narcology as a domain of knowledge, expertise, and intervention and to reflect on the many traces of that system in the present, particularly its uses by contemporary actors. My own view of narcology and the narcological system lies closer to the metaphor with which I opened this book—that of the hospital building itself as an aggregation of reused and retrofitted materials and spaces. As this chapter and the following one will make clear, narcology was similarly an aggregation of infrastructures, concepts, styles of reasoning, and therapies. The narcological system that took form during the mid- to late 1970s was also made up of distinct kinds of institutions, some of which—like the inpatient hospital, the outpatient clinic, and the labor colony—were instantiations of distinct ideas about alcoholism and drunkenness, which in turn were often linked to the history of particular forms of expertise and knowledge. What held these various institutions together conceptually was the plan itself—their arrangement into a coordinated and interlocking system.

Legal provisions for compulsory treatment (*prinuditelnoe lechenie*), as well as the penal institutions into which chronic alcoholics were funneled, had been shaped by a Soviet conception (partly shared by biomedical practitioners and criminologists) of drunkenness as a habit that led to and underlay a physiological addiction to alcohol (Zenevich 1967; Connor 1972). As institutions exclusively devoted to the treatment of addicts began to be formed in the 1960s, and as an independent narcological service took shape during the following decade (in the wake of an anti-alcohol campaign), such ideas about drunkenness and alcoholism (which were rarely distinguished in nonspecialist writings) fostered a strong preference for techniques employing stigma, shaming, and other forms of social control as preventive means. For those addicts deemed chronic cases or who presented particular affronts to the "social order [*obshchestvennyi poriadok*] or the rules of socialist communal life [*obshchezhitiia*]," isolation in special institutions and compulsory treatment were mandated (Connor 1972; Tkachevskii 1974, 38; Beliaev and Lezhepetsova 1977).

This newly independent medical network required its own contingent of specialists; thus an additional series of government decrees legally created the medical specialty of "psychiatrist-narcologist" and mandated the creation of university departments, curricula, and texts for the training of physicians in this new specialty (Beliaev and Lezhepetsova 1977; Babayan and Gonopolsky 1985). Narcology had previously existed as a subspecialty of psychiatry, and even its newly independent form was conceived of as a sort of adjunct specialization, as the hyphenated name suggested (Galkin 2004). Thus the disciplinary assumptions of this nascent field were largely those of its parent: primarily, a dominance of a neurophysiological paradigm.[2] I examine how Russian addiction medicine has been shaped by a clinical style of reasoning specific to a Soviet and post-Soviet professional psychiatry, itself the product of contested Soviet intellectual and institutional politics over the knowledge of the mind and brain.[3] I argue that whereas psychosocial explanations and interventions played a central role in governing addiction in Western Europe and North America for much of the twentieth century, late Soviet addiction medicine was based on a very particular biomedical model, which claimed its origins in Pavlov's physiology of reflexes; it helped to shape the prominence of therapeutic methods for alcoholism based on mechanisms of aversion and suggestion.

Thus Soviet narcology was a hybrid discipline, shaped both by internal scientific and clinical discourses (which employed a neurophysiological paradigm to explain the mechanisms though not the etiology of alcoholism) and by the juridical notions that underlay its institutional organization (which conceptualized addiction in relation to problems of social order). And if the clinic was a particularly key site for the exercise of authority for narcologists, this authority was dependent upon a set of relationships and institutions that stretched far beyond the clinic—indeed, that were situated at the cusp of the relationship between the family and the clinic, the public and the private.

Problematizing Alcohol

Yet before addressing these questions, it is important to step back even further, to ask how alcohol has been problematized in Russia over the past two hundred years.[4] Understanding how alcohol has been variously constituted as a problem in Russia requires tracing briefly the ways in which the habits of individuals and customs of collectivities have crossed with the regulatory gaze of the state and the missionary aspirations of social groups around this substance.

Particularly important here is the strain in the literature on drinking and alcoholism in Russia that has focused on the relationship between patterns of consumption and the political economy of alcohol, primarily vodka. This literature (which itself varies vastly in its tone and aims) fore-grounds the links between the social meanings (or use-values) of alcohol and the key role it has played in the tsarist (and Soviet) state's generation of fiscal revenues (Christian 1990; Herlihy 2002; Takala 2002; Makinen and Reitan 2006; Transchel 2006). As such histories explain, the nineteenth-century tsarist state used a variety of institutional arrangements to pro-vide for up to one-third of its total revenues from the taxation of alcohol production and sales.[5] By the turn of the century, an otherwise politically disparate range of critics of the tsarist autocracy agreed on the charge that the state was profiting financially from the suffering of its subjects through the vodka monopoly (Phillips 2000; Herlihy 2002). While bureaucrats attempted to advocate moderate drinking through an official temperance organization, physicians, members of the clergy, and temperance advo-cates used alcoholism as a legitimate means to assert themselves politically (Herlihy 2002, 136).

For officials of the Bolshevik state, who in 1917 inherited a dry law insti-tuted at the outbreak of World War I, the conflict between fiscal and pub-lic health prerogatives was even greater. In debates among socialists about the proper conduct and everyday culture of proletarians in the nascent workers' state, heavy drinking figured as both a symptom and a buttress of capitalist class relations. Along with brawling, gambling, swearing, and "hooliganism," it was destined to be given up for more *kul'turnyi* (cultured) pursuits by new Soviet men, a development the Bolsheviks attempted to facilitate through a temperance campaign waged by its Society for the Struggle with Alcoholism [Obschchestvo po bor'be s alkogolizmom] (Phil-lips 2000; Transchel 2006). During the mid-1920s, however, fiscal concerns won out over those of health and culture: the prohibition was lifted in 1924, and a new state monopoly on alcohol sales was instituted. At a press conference the following year, Stalin explained the decision: "What is bet-ter, the yoke of foreign capital or the sale of vodka? This is the question facing us. Naturally we will opt for vodka because we believe that if we have to get a bit dirty for the sake of the victory of the proletariat and the peasantry, we will take this extreme measure in the interest of our cause" (quoted in Transchel 2006, 149). By 1931 Soviet temperance organizations were either disbanded or reoriented around the goal of supporting the first five-year plan (Transchel 2006). While drunkenness certainly continued to be discouraged by the party during the 1930s—indeed, prior to the mass purges of 1937, habitual drunkenness was the most common reason given for dismissal from the party—workers were now encouraged to reward themselves for their hard work with a drink (Gronow 2003; Hoffmann 2003).[6]

During World War II and afterwards the state continued to rely heavily on alcohol sales as a source of revenue. Between 1940 and 1945 vodka rose from 12 to 38 percent of the state's total ruble intake from trade (providing one-sixth of the state's income); by the end of the war it had again become the state's largest single revenue source (Hessler 2001). While reliable statistics were concealed in the following decades (from 1963 until 1988 the annual statistical handbook on the economy in the Russian Soviet Republic subsumed alcohol into a category called "other foodstuffs" along with other beverages, ice cream, coffee, and mushrooms), researchers have estimated that the production and sale of alcohol products doubled between 1960 and 1980 (Treml 1982; Takala 2002). Public health researchers have argued that this resulted in a steady increase in rates of alcohol consumption, particularly among working-class men, and a complementary steady decline in average life expectancy rates (Segal 1990; Leon et al. 1997; Cockerham 2000). And while published health-related statistics were also manipulated to conceal these trends, beginning in the 1960s there were repeated calls, particularly from medical professionals and academics, for measures to lower levels of consumption (S. White 1996). As we shall see, this was the setting in which the narcological system began to take shape.

Disease States

When narcologists and psychiatrists during the late Soviet period wrote about chronic alcoholism as a disease, they typically elided etiological arguments and focused on physiological mechanisms; chronic alcoholism referred more to the pathological consequences of regular, long-term heavy drinking than it did to a phenomenon linked to a bodily or psychological predisposition (Strel'chuk 1954; Galina 1968).[7] However, expert conceptualizations of alcoholism in the Soviet Union had not always been so narrow, nor had they always been monopolized by psychiatry.

From the Bolshevik Revolution through the 1920s the Soviet Commissariat of Public Health promoted investigations and interventions that examined the social etiology of illness under the rubrics of social- and psychohygiene (Sirotkina 2002). For Soviet social hygienists alcoholism was a "social disease" in that the social component of its development and "transmission" was held to be the primary one (S. Solomon 1989, 257). Specifically, social hygienists focused on the role played by such factors as stress, family background, wage level, and the drinker's "level of culture [*kul'turnnost'*]." The negative political implications of widening these "environmental factors" to a point at which they might have constituted a critique of Soviet society may have led many hygienists to focus on the "micro-social environment" of the family or immediate community (Solomon 1989).

Although social hygienists' and psychiatrists' views of disease were not inherently mutually exclusive, their drastically divergent object of study led them to recommend very different forms of intervention, fostering a professional rivalry over so-called lifestyle alcoholics (Joravsky 1989; S. Solomon 1989). Thus social hygienists argued that lifestyle alcoholics were to be resocialized and their habits transformed through a series of measures focused on public education (S. Solomon 1989). Additionally, social hygienists and sympathizing psychiatrists advocated the treatment of alcoholics through outpatient dispensaries, an approach which clashed with that of most psychiatrists who viewed alcoholics as a subset of their broader contingent of mental patients, whom they preferred to treat in hospitals or isolated psychiatric colonies (S. Solomon 1989, 266). Ultimately, social hygienists' claim to produce authoritative knowledge and treatment for lifestyle alcoholics was short-lived. In April 1927, the Soviet government issued a decree allowing drinkers categorized as "socially dangerous" to receive treatment without consent, effectively creating a legal equivalence between mental illness and alcoholism, and by 1930 the party-state had stopped funding social research on alcoholism (S. Solomon 1989, 1990).[8]

The eclipse of social hygiene by psychiatry in the management of alcoholism came at the same time that the latter was becoming increasingly dominated by a Pavlovian neurophysiology. Pavlovian theory had come to dominate the Soviet sciences of the mind and brain following a brief period in the early 1920s when a variety of schools and research traditions coexisted—including psychoanalysis. By this time many leading Bolsheviks already saw Pavlov's theories as politically valuable. The relationship between physiology and psychology was deeply contentious and ideologically significant, because it was in this sphere of knowledge that Marxists hoped to link their understanding of human beings as historical actors with an objective science of humans as material beings (Joravsky 1989; R. Smith 1992, 191). This project could not be achieved by a simple *reduction* of psychology to physiology; instead, it was attempted through the concepts and language of dialectical materialism. Ivan Pavlov's reflex theory was taken up in this context, not simply as an example of a concrete behavioral mechanism (as it was largely interpreted outside the USSR) but as a way of framing the relationship between human biology and the environment as "dialectical" (Graham 1987, 163; Joravsky 1989). Thus, although Pavlov's own politics were viewed as "reactionary" (until his rapprochement with the Soviet regime during the mid-1930s), his doctrine was embraced by the Bolsheviks and praised in 1924 by Nikolai Bukharin (at the time a leading party ideologist) as a "weapon from the iron arsenal of materialism" (quoted in Joravsky 1989, 212).[9]

When mass industrialization and the collectivization of agriculture were instituted late in the decade, Stalin and other party leaders shifted away from their previously conciliatory policy toward professionals and initiated the project of creating a cadre of specialists whose primary allegiance would be to the party-state rather than to their professional group (Fitzpatrick 1992). This shift in policy set the stage for the creation of a Soviet psychiatry that would, in its broad contours, persist at least until the late 1980s (Calloway 1992; Skultans 1997, 2003). Psychoanalysis, as well as various Russian psychological schools, was increasingly condemned as "idealist," while Pavlov's theory of conditioned reflexes was promoted in increasingly forceful terms (Todes 1995; Etkind 1997a; Miller 1998). Soon after the official endorsement of Trofim Lysenko's anti-Mendelian theories of heredity, a series of conferences on physiology, psychiatry, and psychology was held (between 1950 and 1952) at which Pavlov's doctrine was declared the objective foundation for the Soviet sciences of the mind and brain, and scientists who had previously dissented publicly "confessed" their errors (Joravsky 1989, 413; Windholz 1997; Zajicek 2009).

Although the research of Soviet psychiatrists and physiologists during the post-Stalin period became increasingly removed from orthodox reflex theory, representatives of the Pavlovian school retained powerful institutional positions in psychiatry (Segal 1975). Moreover, the psychiatry that emerged from this context was still broadly neuro-neurophysiological in its outlook. While an alternative Leningrad school, made up of many of Bekhterev's students, advanced a framework that emphasized environmental factors, the dominant Moscow school foregrounded biology in its understanding of mental illness. The official school of Soviet psychiatry also emphasized longitudinal and dimensional approaches to mental illness states (Wortis 1950; Babayan and Shashina 1985; Calloway 1992).[10] Psychiatrists and physiologists representing such approaches, such as Andrei V. Snezhnevskii (the clinician who presided over Soviet psychiatry from the early 1950s to the mid-1980s), held the primary administrative positions in clinical and research organizations dealing with mental illness.[11] This arrangement strongly shaped the forms of treatment that patients received. For instance, even though psychology reemerged as a discipline during the post-Stalin period, until the late 1980s only psychiatrists were legally entitled to practice psychotherapy (Etkind 1997b).

The dominance of neurophysiology in psychiatry—and the politicization of genetics—facilitated a focus on the functional mechanisms of addiction and away from its etiology, whether social or hereditary. This avoidance of etiological arguments was also shaped by the political sensitivity of alcoholism itself. Whether they were criminologists or psychiatrists, Soviet writers on alcoholism found themselves constrained in similar ways. On the one hand, they drew on Marxist arguments to bolster their contention that various forms of deviance were a fundamentally social phenomenon; on the other hand, the risk of articulating an overt critique constrained the sphere of the social to which this etiology could be ascribed. At least until the 1970s, popular and specialist texts alike continued to describe alcoholism as a "vestige of capitalism" (Galina 1968).[12]

Without recourse to etiological arguments, Soviet psychiatry focused more closely on the mechanisms underlying alcoholism—and particularly on alcoholic psychoses—than on the motivations or explanations of the behaviors leading to alcohol consumption. At the peak of Pavlovian orthodoxy in the sciences of the mind and brain it was sometimes argued that chronic alcoholism was simply a conditioned set of reflexes. In other words, if heavy drinking or alcoholism was a learned behavior, the theory of conditional reflexes was used to explain *how* that behavior was learned but not *why* it took place in the first place (Janousek and Sirotkina 2003, 438). Even well into the 1960s chronic alcoholism was often referred to in somewhat tautological terms, as in this popularizing medical text entitled *Harmful Habit or Disease?* (*Vrednaia Privychka ili Bolezn?*): "At the root of chronic alcoholism lies lifestyle drunkenness, conditioned by various factors, fed by traditions and customs. The systematic consumption of alcoholic drinks that emerges on this basis leads to a singular passion for alcohol, accompanied by numerous disturbances to one's health, that is, to chronic alcoholism" (Zenevich 1967, 20).

The legacy of Pavlovian thinking in narcology extended to diagnostics as well. In fact, it was in this sphere that I first encountered it during my conversations with narcologists. For instance, when I asked him about the symptoms or signs that distinguish alcohol dependence, the medical director of the municipal addiction hospital, explained,

> The dependence syndrome: there are several criteria according to which you can clearly tell that a person can't live without alcohol or some psychotropic substance, that he needs systematic use. . . . One of the signs is when the so-called defensive reflex has been lost. If you drink too much you have a hangover, and if you try to drink a little more you feel nauseated. If you are nauseated, that means your defensive vomiting reflex is working. That means you're not an alcoholic. If the reflex is lost, then this is already alcoholism. A person in this state just needs to drink and he's fine. A person who's not an alcoholic—even if people put pressure on him and say—comrade, just drink a little beer—just from the sound of it he gets nauseated. This is one of the signs, the symptom—the vomiting reflex, through which you can categorize all people into alcoholics and nonalcoholics.

Like other practicing narcologists I spoke to, this physician identified the vomiting reflex as the primary criterion for a diagnosis of alcohol dependence. In part because of its congruence with Pavlov's theory of reflexes, this marker was mentioned in late Soviet textbooks as coinciding with the beginning of the first stage of alcoholism (Babayan and Gonopolsky 1985, 100).

Textbooks on narcology written throughout the Soviet period generally referred to a progressive "three-stage" schema of alcoholism, distinguishing between an initial "mild, neurasthenic" stage, during which the patient experienced no physical cravings for alcohol; a second stage, characterized by a psychological obsession and physical craving, a plateauing of tolerance; and a third "terminal, severe, encephalopathic" stage (100–109). In his *Lectures on Narcology*, Nikolai Ivanets, the country's head narcologist during the 1990s and early 2000s, argues that this schema, which employed diagnostic criteria such as the loss of a vomiting reflex, defined alcoholism significantly more broadly than does contemporary Russian narcology, by including under its aegis the phenomenon of "alcohol abuse" (*zloupotreblenie*), or "problem drinking" (here Ivanets borrows and literally translates the Anglo-American terminology). In other words, more recent diagnostic criteria—namely, those of the World Health Organization's International Classification of Diseases (ICD)—draw a bright line between biological "dependence" and "abuse," the latter a category that to some degree maps onto the popular notion of drunkenness (*pianstvo*) (Ivanets 2001, 48).

Moreover, Ivanets emphasizes that under the new set of diagnostic criteria, the loss of the vomiting reflex, as well as the entire first stage of alcoholism, belongs to the "pre-clinical stage of the illness" (2001, 47). Along with an increased tolerance for alcohol, the loss of the vomiting reflex is simply a sign that the patient has ingested high levels of alcohol over a long period of time. Neither indicates physical dependence, the cardinal sign of which is "alcohol abstinence syndrome," described in Anglo-American literature as "withdrawal syndrome" (48).[13] While Ivanets writes that the abstinence syndrome was not widely accepted as the primary diagnostic marker of dependence in the Soviet Union until the 1950s or '60s (48–49), even in 2004 some narcologists referred to the earlier diagnostic criteria.

Yet by the mid-1990s, researchers in Russian narcology were arguing for a new conceptualization of alcoholism—or more specifically, "alcohol dependence" [*alkogol'naia zavisimost'*]. This new paradigm, which was first developed by Vladimir Altschuler—a researcher at the Narcology Research Institute in Moscow—in a 1994 monograph, describes "pathological desire" [*patologicheskoe vlechenie*] as the most important of several syndromes that make up substance dependence [*zavisimost' ot psykhoaktivnykh veshchestv*]. While many Soviet psychiatrists wrote about compulsive forms of craving, Altschuler's definition is distinct. Specifically, he argues that this craving or desire is psychopathological and that it manifests in what is sometimes called an overvalued idea that the consumption of a particular psychoactive substance is necessary (Altschuler 1994). As some critics of this conception have argued, this "doctrine" of "pathological desire" effectively categorizes addiction as a quasi-psychosis, a categorization with significant consequences for therapy and institutional care (Mendelevich 2013).

This is not simply one scientific conceptualization of addiction among many; rather it is one that has received significant institutional support in Russia. Altschuler's definition of addiction appears in officially sanctioned textbooks for the training of narcologists, and has been used as the basis for developing a strategy for treating opiate addiction legally enshrined in standards of care. This involves the heavy use of antipsychotic and antidepressant medications during detoxification and after. Second, it has often been argued that if craving is like a psychosis, addiction should be treated legally in the same way as are serious "psychiatric" disorders such as schizophrenia. Finally, critics argue that this conception of addiction helps to support a long-standing Russian state policy that unequivocally rejects opiate-substitution therapy and other harm reduction approaches (Mendelevich 2013).

Assembling Narcology

By the time the Soviet narcological system was established in 1975, many of its constituent institutions and bodies of knowledge were already in place and had been for several decades. Many of the institutions had been founded during one of the periodic campaigns that the Soviet party-state mounted in 1958, 1967, and again in 1972 against alcoholism, drunkenness, and the range of crimes against "public order" grouped under the diffuse rubric of "hooliganism" (Kirichenko 1967; Connor 1972; Tkachevskii 1974).[14] These campaigns in turn had particular social and institutional roots, related to (often conflicting) assumptions about drinking, addiction, and crime made in several expert discourses but equally to the way in which party-state power was exercised during the late Soviet period.

A number of historians have argued that expert discourses became increasingly important to the new forms of state power in the Soviet Union after Stalin's death in 1953. With the relative (and this is key) decrease in the use of overtly repressive techniques of domination (such as the widespread use of prison-labor colonies and summary executions), new modes of productive and disciplinary power became increasingly important as the party-state sought to create self-regulating subjects who had internalized a sense of communist morality (Kharkhordin 1999). Of course, many of the arguments made in the moralizing discourses of the 1960s were nothing new. From the mid-1930s onward, the Stalinist project of kul'turnost' (itself a revamped and Sovietized version of prerevolutionary norms regarding propriety, culture, and self-advancement) presented a diffuse set of behavioral ideals for upwardly striving Soviets, which included norms of "cultured drinking" (Fitzpatrick 1992, 1999; Volkov 2000; Hoffman 2003). However, beginning with the de-Stalinization campaign and the return to "Leninist norms" championed by Khrushchev in the late 1950s, these discourses were increasingly bolstered and produced by specialist disciplines such as psychology and criminology, which had been, respectively, disallowed or unable to significantly influence policy for more than thirty years (Connor 1972; P. Solomon 1978; Graham 1987). Thus the 1960s and '70s saw not only an expansion of Soviet specialist discourses on drunkenness, hooliganism, and other forms of social deviance but their increased influence in shaping policy decisions (P. Solomon 1978; M. Levine 1999).

However, while legal specialists and security officials disagreed over "the right combination of educational and repressive measures" necessary to combat the related ills of alcoholism and crime, in multiple debates that took place during these decades, compulsory treatment for noncriminal alcoholics emerged as a measure that everyone seemed to agree upon (P. Solomon 1978, 83). As one leading jurist wrote, "This compulsory influence [*vozdeistvie*] is one means of socially protecting . . . the interests of society [*obshchestva*]" (Tkachevskii 1974, 38).

The specific institutional germs of the narcological system were sown in the wake of a late 1950s campaign against drunkenness. During this time of de-Stalinization, laws dating from the 1930s, which mandated a minimum of one-year sentences for hooliganism, were liberalized, and restrictions were enacted on the sale and production of alcoholic beverages (Solomon 1978, 81). The campaign spurred calls for the development of special institutions for the isolation of chronic alcoholics (from both jurists and physicians), and the first of these therapeutic-labor prophylactories (*lechebno-trudovoe profilaktoriia*] (hereafter LTP) was opened six years later in the Kazakh SSR (Connor 1972, 67; Babayan and Gonopolsky 1985, Budartseva 2002; Pozdniaev 2005). Since compulsory treatment for alcoholism could be ordered only in criminal cases involving an intoxicated defendant, the question emerged of effectively extending this law to non-criminal alcoholics.[15] A recommendation to establish compulsory treatment made by the supreme court to the presidium of the Supreme Soviet led to the establishment of a working commission charged with drafting policy recommendations for the "struggle against drunkenness and alcoholism." Though the commission, which was chaired by a prominent criminologist and included sociologists, lawyers, and psychiatrists, suggested a series of measures to reduce the production of hard liquor and to campaign in schools against alcoholism, only its recommendation regarding compulsory treatment was carried out (P. Solomon 1978, 83–88).[16]

Thus a 1967 Supreme Soviet decree both simplified the procedures for commitment and broadened the category of persons to whom they were applicable (Connor 1972, 66). According to this decree (reinstated and strengthened in 1974), the system of LTPs was meant for those who "resist treatment or continue in their drunkenness following treatment, those who disrupt labor discipline, social order [*obshchestvennyii poriadok*], or the rules of socialist communal life [*obshchezhitiia*]" (Tkachevskii 1974, 38).[17] A parallel 1974 order extended provisions for compulsory treatment to drug addicts who refused treatment (Gilinskii and Zobnev 1998). Over the following years LTPs began to be constructed around Moscow.

These institutions were to be only one part of a broader system of narcological institutions: a decision passed in 1975 ordered the establishment of a narcological system independent of the existing system for psychiatric treatment (Babayan and Gonopolsky 1985). While it had the effect of acknowledging the importance of alcoholism as a public health issue, the creation of the narcological service was also driven by pragmatic concerns: for the past years psychiatrists had been complaining that increasing numbers of alcoholics were filling up beds in mental hospitals, leaving little room for patients suffering from other illnesses (Galkin 2004). Although this decision originated in the Ministry of Health, the new system was meant to cut across the jurisdictions of particular ministries: the new network of addiction-treatment clinics and hospitals would be part of the Ministry of Health; the LTPs and the sobering-up stations (*vytrezviteli*) would remain under the aegis of the Ministry of Internal Affairs

(MVD) (Beliaev and Lezhepetsova 1977; Babayan and Gonopolsky 1985; Pozdniaev 2005).

In addition to mandating the creation of this network, the Ministry of Health passed an additional set of provisions to produce medical workers to run it, in effect creating the "new" medical specialty of narcology. Although the term "narcology" was not new (courses and textbooks on the topic had existed for decades), prior to 1975 the specialty of "psychiatrist-narcologist" had not existed as a legally recognized and certifiable position in the Soviet medical system. Of course the legal designation of such a hybridized profession indexed the way that narcology continued to be viewed institutionally as an adjunct discipline to psychiatry (Galkin 2004). And yet during the late 1970s, and then again in the mid-1980s during the final Soviet anti-alcohol campaign, departments of narcology (institutionally distinct from psychiatry) were established at medical schools throughout the country (Babayan and Gonopolsky 1985). In the mid-1980s an independent institute for narcological research was established in Moscow (S. White 1996). To attract physicians to what was recognized as an undesirable specialty, incentives were created for physicians choosing to enter narcology, mainly in the form of reduced hours and material benefits beyond those already approved for psychiatrists (Babayan and Gonopolsky 1985). During this early period, specialist retraining for those who already had medical degrees took place over the course of months and did not require additional coursework or clinical practice in psychiatry (Galkin 2004). Narcologists and psychiatrists I spoke to who remembered this period recalled the enormous influx of physicians from various specialties into narcology: some debated the relative value of dividing narcology from psychiatry, even to a limited degree, while others questioned the professionalism and knowledge of those who had been attracted to narcology at the time.

Isolation, Surveillance, and Compulsory Treatment

The narcological system that emerged during the late 1970s as a result of these decisions was a complex of different institutions, themselves instantiations of distinct disciplinary and professional ideologies about the nature, etiology, and appropriate treatments of alcoholism. The narcological system's organization included different institutions meant to address a typology of heavy drinkers, alcoholics, and addicts that roughly mapped onto narcologists' three-stage theory of alcoholism. The first of these was the network of narcological dispensaries on the district (*raion*) level, which employed the social hygienists' ideal of treating lifestyle drunkards on an outpatient basis. More serious cases of prolonged intoxication, or those presenting greater problems to their families or in the workplace, could be taken for treatment for one month in the municipal addiction hospital—the organizational shape, predispositions, and priorities of which owed much to the psychiatric hospital or asylum. (Patients suffering from delirium tremens [*belaia goriachka*] or alcoholic psychoses continued to be treated in the parallel system of psychiatric hospitals). "Recidivists" could be committed to a narcological clinic attached to a manufacturing enterprise (*narkologicheskii statsionar pri promyshlennoi predpriiatei*), known colloquially as a *spetskombinatura*. Such institutions had proliferated during the early to mid-1970s: in 1975 and '76 alone twenty-seven had opened in Leningrad under the aegis of the city's addiction hospital (Beliaev and Lezhepetsova 1977). According to some accounts, they accounted for the majority of narcological clinics in the Soviet Union when the system was at its largest (Entin et al. 1997). Finally, so-called chronic alcoholics or addicts could be sent to LTPs, which were clearly modeled on labor colonies and prison camps (Babayan and Gonopolsky 1985; Tkachevskii 1990). While this list leaves out several institutions, it should illustrate a key point: though they emerged from separate discourses, medical diagnostic criteria for alcoholism and juridical criteria regarding socially dangerous drinkers mapped closely onto one another.

Moreover, as many narcologists saw it, the Soviet system was effective precisely because it created practices of surveillance over addicts that ran well beyond the narcologist and policeman into the domestic sphere (Elovich 2008). As Ilya Sergeevich argued, coworkers and family members played a positive role as disciplining agents of the public health system:

> The doctor played a secondary role [in sending a patient for compulsory treatment], the decision was made either by the family or, let's say, relations of production. If people saw that he was coming home or to work in who knows what condition, on Monday, once, twice, then he would get a warning. Then they would send him to a specialist, and say, until you bring proof that you've entered [the register] and that you're being treated and

that there is a guaranteed remission, you aren't allowed [back to work]. The person lost his qualification. The person felt himself pressured in other way, for instance in the queue for an apartment. In other words he would literally cut himself and his family out of society. And this worked very distinctly. And the first ones to be on guard were of course the wife, the mother, the father, the children. All you needed was a declaration, whether he wanted it or didn't want it, that didn't matter. If the family thought that papa dear or grandpa was acting inadequately, that was it.

Specifically, Ilya Sergeevich referred to the legal provisions that allowed not only family members but also coworkers or neighbors to initiate the proceedings that would result in a person's commitment to an LTP. Additionally, given the typical gendering of such things, it was usually wives or mothers who played this role of surveillance. Combined with the feminization of the medical labor force, as well as that part of the administrative bureaucracy that dealt with social issues (*obshchestvennost'*), this dynamic served to further a common view (one that has gained particular momentum in postsocialist debates throughout Eurasia and Eastern Europe), which associated the interests of women with those of the socialist state (Gal and Kligman 2000, 8).

A similar function of surveillance and social control was played by the sobering-up centers (*meditsinskii vytrezviteli*), where people found intoxicated in public were brought by the *militsiia* for an overnight stay. Though these centers were nominally medical, they were administered and staffed primarily by police (as they continued to be in the post-Soviet period) (Tkachevskii 1974; Gerasimova and Zubov 1991). Officially a night in the *vytrezvitel'* was meant to result in a notice to one's place of work: an arrangement that clearly facilitated police extraction of fines beyond those officially mandated (Tkachevskii 1990, 63). During the Soviet period the sobering-up centers, like medical facilities, were sometimes subject to pressures to fill quotas, which were dubious indexes of success, such as the demand by central planners of the Turkmen SSR that 3,300 people be serviced over the course of 1962 in the capital city of Ashkhabad (Connor 1972, 60). Though people brought in to the vytrezvitel' were meant to have their blood-alcohol level tested, this procedure was routinely flouted. One narcologist who had once worked as a medical assistant in a vytrezvitel' told me about how, instead of conducting multiple individual blood tests, he and his colleagues would often "get lazy . . . take blood from ten people," mix it together, and "check all their blood all at once." While one might interpret this simply as an anomaly, arguably it stands more as an index of a system that was less interested in accuracy than it was in exerting a general kind of social control. In other words, in practice the vytrezvitel' system was meant to function as part of the wider network of institutions exerting a kind of social pressure on potential drinkers—the threat being that of getting pulled into the vytrezvitel' regardless of whether or not one was in fact drunk.[18]

Dispenserization and the Register

A night in the sobering-up center during the Soviet period was meant to be followed by a trip to a psychoneurological or, after 1976 in Leningrad, narcological dispensary or outpatient clinic (Beliaev and Lezhepetsova 1977). Here the authority of narcologists was buttressed by the institution of dispenserization and the narcological register (*narkologicheskii uchët*). The register was essentially a list of patients diagnosed with a particular addiction kept by each district-level dispensary and was a key element linking the narcological service both to a residentially based system of urban governance and to the state's systems for medical surveillance and control (Babayan and Gonopolsky 1985).[19] Similar registers existed for other illnesses such as tuberculosis and, more recently, HIV/AIDS.

Like other medical services, treatments for addiction were provided by local dispensaries based on an individual's *propiska*, a document that combined the functions of a residence permit with those of an internal passport. The propiska system (originally a tsarist technology of internal passports that was revived in 1933) was, and continues to be, a means by which the state attempted to control urban in-migration.[20] (Of course this system gave rise to a brisk market in permits, as well as fictitious marriages arranged to obtain them, well before the post-Soviet period). The link between the register and this residency system, by means of dispensarization, provided a grid through which state actors attempted to manage the health of populations.

For narcologists, dispensarization and the register functioned as means of tracking patients under their care. Field has characterized this as "an important service . . . of a preventative nature" in that it allowed "the systematic observation and periodic examination both of patients with an identified condition and of healthy groups" (1967, 139–40). For public health administrators, the register operated as a means of "quality control," in the words of one narcologist, a source of statistics and a quantifiable measure of the output of narcologists' labor. While it is true that these statistics were rarely publicized, they were not always obscured from interested professionals, as has often been suggested of Soviet statistics. For instance, a 1977 publication of the Bekhterev Psychoneurological Research Institute gave the following breakdown of patients on the city's narcological register: 24 percent are being treated "systematically," 27.6 percent "drink following treatment and refuse follow-up treatment (but show no signs of pronounced social degradation)," 18.7 percent "require compulsory treatment," and 4.9 percent suffer from "pronounced alcoholic encephalopathy and psychoses . . . and require periodic treatment in psychiatric hospitals" (Beliaev and Lezhepetsova 1977, 14). (Of course these figures are somewhat compromised by the authors' failure to report the total number of patients.) As important as the numbers are the categories being employed, for they suggest that public health officials' cardinal concerns in regard to the register were precisely the sorting of patients along a gradient of increasing debilitation and social exclusion and, presumably, their subsequent placement into appropriate institutions. In short, the narcological register functioned as one quantified criterion according to which a dispensary could be measured as fulfilling or failing to live up to the expectations of centrally produced plans; it also served as a means of surveilling and sorting patients into clinically significant categories.

For patients themselves, the register had a distinct set of consequences. Patients on the register were unable to receive a permit for a gun or a driver's license and were prohibited from working in a number of occupations and from traveling abroad. Once on the register, one's name remained there for three years (Tkachevskii 1974, 1990; Gilinskii and Zobnev 1998). In short, the register was meant to keep addicts away from potentially dangerous situations, and the threat of appearing on it was to act as a deterrent to potential alcoholics as well. Physicians also had the authority to require patients on the register to return for inpatient treatment and could call upon the police to bring in recalcitrant patients. As we shall see, the narcological register, in a transformed capacity, has come to play an important role in the commercialization of post-Soviet Russian narcology.

Institutional Memory

I met Ilya Sergeevich at the district dispensary, where he worked as a narcologist for children and adolescents. He had been trained as a child psychiatrist in Leningrad but subsequently had worked for much of the 1980s in an LTP. As he explained, "I worked mainly in the far north, but it was a special contingent [of patients] [*spetskontingent*]. . . . It was a penal colony [*zona*][21] and a special institution [*spetsucherezhdenie*] where we treated alcoholics and drug addicts. At the time, during the years of Soviet power [*vlast'*], we had compulsory treatment, as we called it." When the LTPs had been closed down in the early 1990s, he and a colleague had returned to St. Petersburg and found positions in the city's narcological service.

Like many other narcologists, Ilya Sergeevich was quick to voice his discontent with the current state of affairs in his specialty. As he saw it, compulsory treatment had been the linchpin of a Soviet narcological system that had both successfully provided medical care for patients and shaped their conduct, largely through various modes of social control and surveillance. The key problem with the contemporary situation in narcology, he argued, was the lack of "any possibility to confine or limit [*ogranichit'*] the patient in a situation where he doesn't allow—not just his family—but himself to live." Whereas under the Soviet system, compulsory treatment allowed physicians to "isolate this person, at least until he comes to himself and then [allow him to] decide will he or not [accept treatment]," under conditions of voluntary treatment, which had been instituted around the same time the LTPs were shuttered, patients were unlikely to come for treatment until they were in an advanced state of decline:

> Now there's voluntary treatment. And so what happens? Until things haven't gotten very bad for this person, until the illness hasn't taken him to who knows what places, [we don't see him]. . . . And we tell him that this is a mental illness, chronic and progressive. Do we wait until tomorrow when he accepts this fact and comes to us? This never happens. Over the past ten years we've had more patients in serious decline, more difficult patients.

How does it all turn out? The person has gone to as many places as possible, used the services of private or government doctors. . . . Only when nothing is left in his soul, no health, no psyche to acknowledge his situation, then the only choice left is to return to us . . . and to do what? If not to receive charity then social [help]. The state takes this debris [*oskoly*] on itself when taking in this patient, because there has already been a diametric progression. . . . It takes too much material and moral expense on the part of clinicians to bring these people back to life.

For Ilya Sergeevich, compulsory treatment had been a necessary tool with which the state could fulfill what he understood as a central set of social obligations.

The crux of this system was the legal category of compulsory treatment, which was used primarily to commit patients to LTPs. In the language employed by narcologists, these conditions mapped roughly onto the group of patients belonging to the third stage of so-called chronic alcoholism (Babayan and Gonopolsky 1985). If the figures given above are to be trusted, narcologists believed that a sizable proportion of patients (at least one-fifth of those on the register) belonged to this stage or could be categorized in this way. The percentage that actually ended up in LTPs was much lower: in the 1980s this was about 3 percent of the three million who were on narcological registers at the time. Yet in absolute numbers this amounted to a significant figure: at least 112,000 inmates in 272 institutions in 1988 (S. White 1996; Entin et al. 1997).[22]

Ilya Sergeevich emphasized how a commitment to an LTP required the collaboration of family members, physicians, police, and occasionally fellow workers:

And if, God forbid, during this period [of observation] there was a relapse, who would come and tell us? Of course the family. That he went to go drink with his friends and the wife says, that's it tomorrow. . . . And if the person refused, then what authority could be drawn on? The doctor didn't hospitalize him, nor did his wife. A call would go out to the station house for accompaniment by a policeman [*militsianer*] and. . . . if we saw that the person was not agreeing to any conditions, doesn't need work, doesn't need family, says I'll just drink, then we would gather a council. First he went through the hospital, and then if there was a relapse, only then to the LTP. Where a year, half a year, two years was the maximum period: this was already dependent on his behavior, his desire to be treated.

Indeed, though a commitment to an LTP required the decision of a court, as well as the recommendation of a medical committee, proceedings could be initiated by family members or neighbors, and there was no requirement for a lawyer to represent the potential patient/inmate. Thus it not surprising that when the Soviet media began to publish criticisms of various institutions during the late 1980s, reports abounded of family members "abusing" the committal procedure (S. White 1996, 155). Moreover, no procedure existed for inmates to challenge their commitment or to receive compensation. In some cases, investigations yielded evidence of committals taking place in order to fulfill plans—that is, a promised quota of patient/inmates (156).

LTPs, which were administered by the same ministry (Internal Affairs) that oversaw the extensive Soviet network of labor and prison colonies, were modeled on these penal institutions in that they too combined confinement with compulsory labor. All employees, including physicians, wore uniforms with epaulets, and the camps were surrounded by barbed wire. While the security regime was less stringent than that of prison camps (guards at LTPs apparently did not carry firearms), attempts to escape an LTP were treated as a criminal offense (Connor 1972, 66–67; S. White 1996, 156).

During the late 1980s the effectiveness of LTPs began to come under scrutiny. The anti-alcohol campaign of 1986–88 had opened additional funding for the system, and the push to crack down on drunkenness led to high levels of incarceration—but because these efforts took place during a time when the policy of glasnost was making public calls for official accountability more prevalent, the LTPs also faced greater pressure to live up to high expectations for rehabilitating inmates. Many public health and party officials were seemingly disappointed with the official results. In one relatively successful center, 20 percent of the inmates were sober after the first year and 13 percent after the second, while the comparable figures for the entire country were closer to 2 or 3 percent (S. White 1996, 158). Moreover, there was evidence that the institutions acted as spaces where patients became exposed to criminal networks and practices (157). By the late 1980s there were reports of inmates at various centers striking, in some cases violently breaking out of the LTP, in others peacefully demanding that treatment for alcoholism be carried out by the Ministry of Health rather than Internal Affairs (156). In response to these pressures, regulations at LTPs were somewhat liberalized in 1988—efforts were made to facilitate a less formal and restrictive atmosphere, patients were allowed freer movement, and changes were made in the committal procedures, allowing patients representation by a lawyer (158). However, these measures seemed only to exacerbate the problems at the centers: for instance, in one of the LTPs in Moscow only 137 of 1,200 registered patients showed up after the reform (159).

As they were increasingly seen as ineffective and repressive institutions—out of sync with the contemporary valorization of human rights (*prava cheloveka*)—in 1991 the Russian Supreme Soviet began the process of dismantling the system, ordering the release of alcoholics committed only because they had refused compulsory treatment (S. White 1996, 159). In 1993 the federal law "On psychiatric help and guarantees of civil rights in carrying it out" removed the legal basis for involuntary hospitalization of noncriminal addicts. The following year the LTPs were formally disbanded (Entin et al. 1997; S. White 1996). At least some of the facilities were transformed into remand prisons or "investigatory isolators" (SIZO), where suspects are held while awaiting trial, and others into different kinds of prison colonies.[23]

During the 1990s and early 2000s, the LTPs and the legal provisions for compulsory treatment, along with certain types of treatment (described in chapter 4), came to represent the core of the Soviet narcological system. As they have been remembered and represented again and again, their meanings have shifted within the changing images of a now-demonized, now-valorized Soviet past. Grigorii Mikhailovich attributed the reluctance of many patients to use the state narcological services to the legacy of the LTPs: "After these LTPs, the fear that someone might be sent there pushed people to feel, when the commercial structures emerged, that you shouldn't go to a doctor in the state service." Like other emblems of the Soviet period, LTPs have also become, in contemporary discourse, a shorthand for the imagined effectiveness of strong state authority, with calls for their revival arising in discussions of alcoholism, drug abuse, AIDS, crime, and public order (Pozdniaev 2005). Among the narcologists I spoke to, the notion of reviving some type of compulsory treatment was strikingly prevalent. Such sentiments of nostalgia are often interpreted as signs of persistent Soviet or authoritarian relations of authority or as remnants or imprints of the Soviet "political culture."

Yet as I have suggested throughout this chapter, placing these arguments into the context of narcology's institutional origins in the 1970s and its rapid transformation during the late 1980s and 1990s may suggest a different interpretation of such accounts. First of all, narcologists who express support for compulsory treatment for their patients may be referring to a variety of different and divergent programs and institutions. Additionally, such arguments might be interpreted as voicings of frustration over a fundamental disciplinary crisis, expressed in the readily available register of nostalgia. Narcologists' clinical authority was heavily bolstered by Soviet legal provisions for compulsory treatment, as well as the broader intermeshing of medical and juridical organizations in the Soviet narcological service. As the following chapter explains, these elements were dismantled at roughly the same time as the discipline lost its monopoly on the production of knowledge about and treatment of addiction and as the state-funded medical sector took significant blows to its funding and medical services became increasingly commodified.

3

Selling Sobriety

On a bitterly cold and windy February morning, I walked through an industrial district in northern St. Petersburg with Mikhail Venediktovich to visit the addiction clinic that he directed. More than others involved in addiction management, Mikhail Venediktovich had actively fostered contacts among local social scientists; when I met him at a sociological institute, he had invited me to visit and possibly conduct fieldwork at his clinic. With his spectacles, goatee, tweeds, and modest mannerisms, Mikhail Venediktovich cut the figure of an academic more than a clinician or public health worker. He had in fact received his education not in medicine but in engineering and systems analysis, and he had worked during the final years of the Soviet Union in the energy sector. After going a year without pay at a research institute during the mid-1990s, Mikhail Venediktovich had founded a medical services firm along with a few acquaintances. At first the firm offered only ambulatory detoxification; additional services and inpatient facilities were added gradually. The clinic was officially called the Bekhterev Therapeutic-Prophylactic Medical Center, but everyone referred to it simply as the Bekhterev Center. This institution had no formal affiliation with the city's leading center for psychiatric research, the Bekhterev Psychoneurological Research Institute. It simply partook of the positive associations that potential clients might have with the early twentieth-century Petersburg psychiatrist Vladimir Bekhterev (or the institute), although this branding would eventually become a great source of trouble for Mikhail Venediktovich.

Mikhail Venediktovich did not portray his motives in opening the center in lofty terms of social good. He spoke openly of the clinic as a commercial venture: "I got into this absolutely by chance; there was the possibility of making some money and it was something new and interesting for me." At the same time, Mikhail Venediktovich was able to carry over something of his training in analysis of systems and infrastructure. Having adopted the issue of addiction as his own, he approached it not simply as a commercial opportunity but as a general sphere for social intervention. For instance, along with several others, he drafted a proposal for a municipal methadone program during the late 1990s. While the Bekhterev Center primarily offered alcohol and drug detoxification on a commercial basis (along with a variety of other medical services), during the late 1990s Mikhail Venediktovich founded Healthy Future, a noncommercial foundation that ran a rehabilitation program for drug addicts and carried out some prevention-oriented programs. The two organizations were legally distinct but were housed in the same building, and profits from the commercial clinic were sometimes used to help fund Healthy Future.

Detoxification at the center followed by a full course of rehabilitation cost about fifty thousand rubles (more than $1,700 at the time), an amount which ensured that the vast majority of patients came from the new professional or business classes. Workers at the center heavily encouraged their patients to complete their educations (the vast majority of heroin addicts in St. Petersburg are under twenty-five). While many counselors employed 12-step methods, Mikhail Venediktovich and members of his staff took issue with certain ideas central to Narcotics Anonymous—such as "once an addict, always an addict," a notion they felt only discouraged their patients, given the high stigmatization of drug addiction in Russia.

As we walked toward the center under the shadow of idle smokestacks and past rows of stacked shipping containers, Mikhail Venediktovich complained about his wasted morning. He had spent several hours at a meeting devoted to public health issues with a group of representatives from the municipal government, all of whom, he argued, were solely concerned with amassing money and power for themselves. "The municipal government gets worse with every election," he said bitterly. "There are fewer and fewer decent [*prilichnyii*] people in it. Everyone is bought [*kuplennyi*]." The nongovernmental organization (NGO) sector, on the other hand, was, in Mikhail Venediktovich's opinion, filled with well-intentioned but largely unprofessional and ineffectual people. Mikhail Venediktovich deeply valued professionalism and thus was wary not only of local antiaddiction organizations made up of mothers of drug addicts, but even of the former or recovering addicts whom his center hired as counselors.

No sooner had we entered the center than Mikhail Venediktovich was approached by a medical worker. "Did they tell you?" she asked. "There are about fifteen people upstairs." A crisis was unfolding at the center. On the main floor of the clinic a crowd of people was jammed into the office of the medical director while several clusters of large men in leather jackets stood idly in the hallway nearby. Thinking that a large group of patients had shown up and needed to be registered, I sat down on a couch in the hallway. Several minutes later, Mikhail Venediktovich emerged from the office and called me in. "Please pay very close attention to everything that goes on here," he requested. Suddenly conscripted into the role of witness, I needed a while to sort through three or four simultaneously shouted conversations to understand what was happening. A stocky woman, who turned out to be the director of the rehabilitation program, was standing behind a desk vigorously telling a uniformed officer that she would not sign the document he was waving at her. Another officer, wearing a badge around his neck, was demanding to see other documents from a doctor who kept repeating, "We're doctors. Are we hurting anyone here? Are we causing anyone harm?"

Throughout that day, most of which I spent in the director's office watching the crisis unfold, and over the following weeks I learned that this was only one battle in an ongoing commercial war being waged between Mikhail Venediktovich's center and another addiction clinic. That morning the center's administrators had been visited by two separate, and ostensibly unrelated, groups of people. One was a visit by two agents of the Federal Service for the Control of the Drugs Trade (Federal'naia sluzhba po kontroliu po oborotom narkotikov) (FSKN), the recently formed federal "supra-agency" charged with carrying out all aspects of a war on drugs, who claimed to be conducting a surprise inspection of the center's license. The other was a clerk of an arbitration court delivering a decision allowing the seizure of certain items of medical equipment pending a lawsuit. He was accompanied by the representatives of a private security company and a group of "movers," who were supposedly meant to participate in this seizure but in fact—argued the physicians—were there to intimidate them and their patients.

Though this lawsuit emerged from a series of events and changes in the center's legal status, which I describe below, Mikhail Venediktovich and his colleagues were sure that both visits had been orchestrated by one of their principal competitors. As I later learned, this competitor had previously been a business partner of Mikhail Venediktovich's involved in the Bekhterev Center. After the two had split, both continued to claim the brand name "Bekhterev Center" and the associated logo. The scene I witnessed, the physicians explained, was one in a series of attempts by this other Bekhterev clinic to shut down their operation.

When I began my research, I assumed—very naively as it turned out—that treatment and intervention into substance abuse would vary across what I thought would be relatively clear-cut distinctions between certain sectors—namely, the state, market, and civil society. In other words, I thought that state-run or state-funded clinical settings would differ in fundamental ways from commercial ones, which in turn would be distinct from not-for-profit or charitable institutions. And though such distinctions were not insignificant, it became quickly clear to me that they were blurred and crosscut to such a degree that they seemed to conceal more than they revealed about the operation of addiction treatment services in St. Petersburg. State-funded clinics contained units that functioned effectively as commercial entities; for-profit clinics like Mikhail Venediktovich's were often partnered with NGO entities; and the managers of charitable centers worked to improve the recognition of their brand. People participated in multiple spheres as well: narcologists in the state system moonlighted in private practice, and patients regularly cycled between treatments in various types of institutions (at least as long as they could afford it). Moreover, many physicians, administrators, and other participants in various clinical institutions that were legally understood as municipal, commercial, or charitable conceptualized themselves as all operating in a market in which their institutions competed for patients with other institutions regardless of their formal sector.

In this chapter I interpret the movements of practitioners, patients, and money across these varied institutions as part of what Vinh-Kim Nguyen has called a therapeutic economy, which he defines as "the totality of therapeutic options in a given location, as well as the rationale underlying these patterns of resort by which these therapies are accessed" (2005, 126). In what follows I use this concept to highlight the relations of exchange and regimes of value underpinning the domain of treatment for alcoholism in St. Petersburg, tracing its transformation from a state socialist political economy of favors and access to an irregularly regulated market. In the next chapter I continue to build on the idea in my discussion of therapeutic legitimacy, showing how talk about therapeutic methods and enactments of belief, affect, and volition are seen by narcologists as shaping their clinical efficacy.

A Market of Favors

Eugene Zubkov, a narcologist who had become a major proponent of Alcoholics Anonymous during the 1990s, ascribed many of the problems of contemporary Russian narcology to the way in which the Soviet political economy shaped the doctor-patient relationship:

> [During the Soviet period] Russia was a market of favors. Money on its own, without contacts, had no value. You had to have the opportunity to spend that money. So all of narcology was shaped as a market of favors, and doctors were heavily interested in having control over the patient [*zainteresovan s kontrol'iam nad bol'nym*]: a situation which hasn't changed. The doctor was paid very little, and so he wanted his own contact in the store where clothes were sold, and so on.

Zubkov's characterization evoked several aspects of the political economy of Soviet medicine as well as the particular form that the professional authority of physicians took under these conditions.

Michele Rivkin-Fish (2005) has argued that the systemic analysis of state socialist political economy developed by Katherine Verdery helps to explain the healthcare field as well. In Verdery's terms, this means that the state monopolized the means of health production (all the infrastructure of the medical system, as well as the system of medical education) and controlled the distribution of medical services. Simultaneously the state sought to legitimate this appropriation through its ideology of "socialist paternalism," claiming to provide for its citizens' needs by redistributing goods and services (1996, 26). In the case of health care, the party-state claimed to guarantee its citizens the universal provision of medical care without direct charge. While this claim, often exhibited as evidence for the achievements of socialism, arguably had a profound effect on the development of redistributive "welfare state" institutions in Western Europe and North America (particularly in the climate of the Cold War), its effect on the legitimacy of the Soviet state among its own citizens was rather double-edged (Rivkin-Fish 2005, 23–24). Though patients were by no means conceptualized as consumers, Verdery's (1996) argument that "the [socialist] system's organization exacerbated consumer desire by further frustrating it and thereby making it the focus of effort, resistance and discontent" is key here as well. For in the same way that promises of material plenty often served to underscore the shortages experienced by many citizens, the state's promises of universal health care also served to heighten the frustrations caused by shortages of medical supplies and services and long queues for many procedures, as well as clinical encounters often perceived as impersonal and brusque (Davis 1989; Verdery 1996). Additionally, the claim of "free of charge" medical services was not strictly true, even in official terms, as patients paid for prescription drugs (albeit at heavily subsidized prices); as I discuss below, an entire sphere of payments for health services circulated outside official acknowledgment (Ryan 1978, 28).

The roots of patients' frustrations also lay in the institutional structure of the medical system. Like other state sectors, the healthcare system that emerged during the mid-1930s in the Soviet Union was characterized by a highly bureaucratized and hierarchical set of institutional relationships that ran from the Ministry of Health (itself answering to the executive committee of the Communist Party) to republic-level ministries to regional and city ministries, all the way down to the microdistrict (*uchastok*)—the level on which medical care was provided to residents (Field 1967; Ryan 1978; Rivkin-Fish 2005). The provision of material and human resources to these units, as well as their expected outputs, was laid out in plans developed by an agency of the Ministry of Health, as well as by a department of Gosplan, the central planning agency (Davis 1989, 239). While the party-state's five-year plans set health-related goals based on demographic measurements (such as the lowering of mortality and morbidity rates during the 1970s and '80s), the metrics used to measure success within the Health Ministry's plans were often disconnected from such outcomes: they concerned the quantities of medical personnel or hospital beds or focused on the number of procedures conducted rather than their quality or effectiveness (Field 1967; Davis 1989; McKeehan 2005).[1]

Simultaneously, the very same structural aspects of the Soviet health care system made it more difficult for centrally produced plans to be fulfilled. First of all, the system of official healthcare provision was far from simple. Rather than a single network, there were several: two separate "closed" networks (*zakrytyi set'*) of clinics existed for members of the party elite and employees in prioritized industries, and even the "open" networks (*obshchii set'*) designated for everyone else differed depending on whether they were situated in a large city, a small city, or a rural setting (Davis 1989, 242). Of course, an entirely separate network of healthcare facilities existed to serve the military. The sheer scale and complexity of this system was often more than the limited resources of the central planning offices could handle; even according to their own criteria of success, some things simply fell by the wayside (Davis 1989, 239).[2] These tendencies were further exacerbated by the fact that health care was funded according to what some analysts have called the "residual principle," receiving whatever funds were left over in the central budget after appropriations were made for high-priority sectors like the military and heavy industry (Sheiman 1994).[3]

In part because of these conditions, various informal or unofficial economies flourished in the Soviet medical sector, as they did in much of the rest of the system (Grossman 1977; Sampson 1987; Verdery 1996; Ledeneva 1998). Like the ubiquity of shortages and queues, various "shadow economies" and informal institutions of exchange were further symptoms of a system in which political and social capital, rather than economic capital, was the most valued resource (Bourdieu 1986). In the absence of officially recognized private property and given the state's monopoly on legitimate production and distribution, rights of use or access were worth more than those of ownership. As Zubkov put it, "Money on its own, without contacts, had no value. You had to have the opportunity to spend the money." Physicians therefore sought to create long-standing relationships, often based as much on mutual obligation or friendship as on the exercise of their professional authority. Patients for their part often drew upon extensive acquaintance networks, taking part in a practice colloquially known as *blat*, not only to obtain certain scarce medications but often to receive a type of care that they viewed as motivated by personal interest and attention (rather than bureaucratic obligation) on the part of physicians (Ledeneva 1998). This kind of phenomenon has continued to characterize much of contemporary Russian health exchanges since the dismantling of the planned economy (Salmi 2003; Rivkin-Fish 2005).[4]

Fiscal Crises

During the final years of the Soviet Union and just after its collapse, legislators and health administrators discussed how the Russian nationalized system of health care was to be reformed. These discussions, which continued throughout the 1990s, focused in part on the optimal form of governance for health care: specifically the right balance between markets and state regulation. In general, the market principle was never questioned as an appropriate mechanism for the healthcare: opponents of radical marketization based their arguments on questions of fairness rather than arguing against the principle of commodifying health services (Rivkin-Fish 2005). During the initial drafting of healthcare legislation in the early 1990s, the concept of a state-administered economy was seen as so discredited that officials did not consider drawing upon systems such as the British National Health Service as a model, opting instead for an amalgam of the US and Canadian systems (McKeehan 1995). The Health Insurance Act, which was signed into law in April 1993, provided for parallel systems of insurance: mandatory (which would provide a basic level of care) and voluntary (paid for by individuals and employers, this was to be the institutional basis for a nascent medical insurance industry). The act, which was heavily promoted by the World Bank, mandated the creation of mandatory health insurance funds (*fondy*), a set of independent, nonprofit agencies that would act as mediators between the state, employers, commercial insurance companies, and healthcare providers.[5]

Not surprisingly, the result of the rapid switch to this system was not the creation of a healthcare system operating on the ideal principles of market competition but the development of parallel systems of highly commercialized medicine and institutions that still function somewhat as they did during the Soviet period.[6] With inflation spiraling upward throughout the 1990s, and particularly in the wake of the 1998 monetary crisis, fiscal resources were unable to keep up with the costs of providing the minimum levels of care that the mandatory insurance system promised as a right to Russian citizens. Thus in Leningrad Oblast the cost of providing mandated obligatory care in 1994 was 86 billion rubles, at the same time that the district government's entire budget was 95 billion (Twigg 1998, 596). On a national level, public health spending had dropped to 2.9 percent of the GDP by 1998, a level that covered only 75 percent of the estimated costs of mandated care (Balabanova, Falkingham, and McKee 2003, 2124). In addition to inadequate—or misplaced—funding, aspects of the institutional and spatial structure of the system worked against the ideals of the new system. In many (perhaps most) parts of Russia, Soviet-era hospitals and polyclinics retained their territorial monopoly on healthcare provision, entirely undercutting the possibility for competition. Legislation that prohibited privately owned clinics from participating in the obligatory insurance system also hampered the ideal market that reformers had envisioned (Twigg 1998).

The situation was somewhat different in specialties such as narcology and psychiatry, which treated what were categorized as "socially significant illnesses" (*sotsial'no znachimye bolezni*) and thus were funded not from insurance but directly from the budget (Galkin 1996, 73). While a parallel system of "social funds" was proposed to fund mental health and addiction treatment, the system was even slower in taking shape than the mandatory medical insurance program. (Significant federal attention to the narcological system was not paid until 2010, when an effort toward "modernization" was initiated [Narcology Research Institute 2012].) All of this accounts for the overall contraction of the state narcological system during the 1990s. It is worth remembering that the relative impact of these budgetary contractions was perhaps greater in the narcological system, which had received a major fiscal boost just a few years prior during the anti-alcohol campaign.

In addition to the demise of the LTPs during the early 1990s, the entire system of clinics attached to manufacturing enterprises in St. Petersburg was closed as the managers of newly privatized factories sought to shed unprofitable units. For narcologists, this was significant in that this system of "industrial narcology" had arguably accounted for the largest portion of inpatient beds (Egorov 1997). While outpatient clinics remained in each of St. Petersburg's twenty-one administrative districts, as well as in the central addiction hospital to which they funneled patients, many district governments (such as Amur, Volgograd, and Kirov oblasts and the Tuvan Autonomous Republic) shut down their narcological systems entirely (11). These closings were reflected in the overall statistics for Russia, in which the total number of state narcological dispensaries dropped from around 325 in 1988 to 217 in 1997; the number of inpatient beds and narcologists fell to 33,707 and 3,827–41 and 74 percent of their respective 1988 levels (Egorov 1997, 9–10).[7] While many regions have also been opening or reorganizing their narcological services (with a visible movement toward institutionally separate networks for adults and adolescents), these units remaining in the state system experienced an intense shortage of funding during the 1990s and early 2000s. To be sure, there have been new funds in recent years—particularly those aimed specifically toward the treatment of drug addiction. This does not in itself suggest a solution, however, as arguably it has precisely been the coexistence of deeply underfunded institutions alongside unusual opportunities for personal enrichment that has fostered much of the disciplinary confusion and self-recrimination in narcology.

Self-Financing Units

Shortages of funding in the narcological system were exacerbated by the fact that, starting from the late 1980s with the emergence of medical cooperatives and increasingly in the 1990s, the state system was effectively competing with multiple commercial clinics, which sprang up to provide various addiction-related services. As they became partly or largely self-financing (*khozraschetnyi*), physicians and administrators in the state narcological service sought to keep their institutions going in much the same way as did actors in other sectors. Retaining the institutional structure of a state organization, hospitals and clinics, as well as individual wards and networks of physicians, began to function as commercial enterprises, charging patients directly for their services. While this was to some degree a continuation of Soviet practices, in which the medical system was shot through both with cash payments and with informal exchanges of favors and access, both the degree and tenor of these exchanges altered during the post-Soviet period. They encompassed both officially sanctioned practices and those that were formally illegal. As we shall see, they also carried a newfound urgency in post-Soviet narcology: on the one hand, institutions and their employees faced the real possibility of fiscal crisis with consequences such as the nonpayment of salaries; on the other hand, the possibilities for personal enrichment were far greater than they had ever been. Narcology became a sphere of medicine in which both of these motivations were to play a role, one in which the extremes of fiscal shortage and lavish wealth appeared in disconcertingly close proximity to one another.

Thus while the municipal hospital's role in the city's system of addiction treatment provision was to provide services free of charge, in fact it also offered a number of services for a price. As Lyudmila Petrovna, a narcologist in the hospital's acute care ward, explained,

> Of course we have a portion of the services that are for pay. Without these the hospital simply wouldn't be able to survive. Also, I want to say, psychotherapy does not have the right to be free, the person values only that which he pays for. Seriously. We have the "budgetary" [*budzhetnyi*] patients: those who have lost everything and whom we still have to help somehow. And we of course have the self-financing beds: the spaces are better, the medications are more expensive; not better but more expensive. And for these people we can prescribe certain antidepressants that are a bit more expensive.

While the majority of patients at the hospital fell into the budgetary category, some paid three thousand rubles (equivalent to $100 at the time) to stay in a separate room rather than stay with the rest of the patients in spaces with eight or more cots. The hospital also offered a short course of detoxification (three days), similar to services provided by many of the city's commercial clinics. Yet most of the hospital's narcologists insisted that the main difference between the for-fee and free services, as well as between the hospital in general and its commercial competitors, lay in cosmetic conditions (*vneshnoe uslovie*).

Alexander Sergeeivich argued that it was primarily for this reason that the hospital failed to attract more middle-income patients or professionals:

> Mainly this hospital is set up for people without a very high social status or low financial state. . . . Rather, it was designed for everyone but somehow the powers that be [*vlasti*] aren't trying to make it amenable to people who are used to . . . to comfort, to more or less adequate conditions. Although these people end up here too, but rarely. Because the treatment here and in the commercial clinics is not significantly different. The main difference is in the appearance of the conditions.

Reiterating the point, his colleague gestured toward the crumbling plaster wall above his desk: "You see the state of it." Such a concern with material conditions had led administrators at the alcoholism ward of the Bekhterev Psychoneurological Research Institute to initiate construction of a separate set of "elite rooms." While the institute was primarily devoted to clinical research and was administratively separate from the municipal addiction service, as a state-financed institution it faced a similar set of budgetary constraints. Although all the patients there paid a relatively small fee (sixty rubles per day) for inpatient treatment, the administrators recognized that some could and would pay significantly more for elite treatment, a strategy that drew upon the widespread commercial practice of offering tiered services by price, most often consisting of a special VIP level above the normal range of services.[8]

Privacy Commodified

While material conditions were certainly a part of what distinguished khozraschetnyi services from budgetary ones, another important difference lay in the fact that patients were able to pay for "anonymity." The existence of this service can be traced to the institution of the narcological register, described in the previous chapter. During the 1990s, state and municipal clinics treating addiction began to offer patients the possibility of treatment without registration, for a price (Galkin 1996). This became the legally sanctioned practice of every clinic in the municipal network in St. Petersburg. Part of its justification was that similar anonymous services were already available in commercial clinics. Since the laws barring those on the register from owning guns or receiving driver's licenses remained unchanged, the result was the creation of a two-tiered system, with very different degrees of state surveillance. Treatment was nominally free of charge for those who would accept having their names on the register, while others, who paid, could escape the penalties and restrictions. From the point of view of some physicians and public health reformers, this system served to further penalize the socially marginalized and poor. Others pointed out that the practices of anonymity made it more difficult to hold physicians legally accountable for their actions.

Even those physicians who defended the practice did so in a guilty tone, insisting that anonymous treatment simply capitalized on a (now unjustified) suspicion that some patients had of the state service. For instance, the administrator Grigorii Mikhailovich assured me that the confidentiality of patients' records and doctor-patient privilege was guaranteed by the sixty-first article of the 1993 General Law on Health Care of the Russian Federation (Tsyboulsky 2001, 259; see also Tichtchenko and Yudin 2000, 230). Nevertheless, he explained, "The fear that someone will tell someone or get the information—this still lives." Thus the addiction hospital provided the service of anonymous treatment, which was "easier for [the patients], and easier for us, because we get extra money," he added, laughing. Yet in the same breath Grigorii Mikhailovich recounted recent attempts by police to access the register, undercutting his argument that confidentiality is secured by a new post-Soviet legal regime: "Just before the three hundredth anniversary [of St. Petersburg], I was sending away policemen. . . . One of them wrote to me saying, 'Give us the lists of the people who have been treated here.' And I replied . . . 'You won't get any lists.'"

Deliberately or not, Grigorii Mikhailovich's account laid bare the institutional incentives for narcologists to stoke fears of such unscrupulous policemen, thereby bolstering the "need" for anonymous treatment. Grigorii Mikhailovich acknowledged that the current demand for anonymous treatment grew partly out of the punitive character of the Soviet system; in his view, "This is what the anonymous treatment is connected to: the fact that there was this punitive system." Yet it was in the interest of physicians like Grigorii Mikhailovich to perpetuate the notion that the confidentiality of patients' records was still not secure. In other words, in order for narcologists to create a demand for anonymous service, patients had to be continually reminded that their information might fall into the wrong hands and led to fear that legal protections of confidentiality and doctor-patient privilege were weak.[9] Given the lack of institutional protections for privacy during the Soviet period and the continued vulnerability of personal information to theft or sale during post-Soviet years, it was not difficult to convince patients of the need for anonymous service.[10]

Murder in the Clinic

As I have argued, narcology was created as a specialty by the Soviet state under conditions that encouraged physicians with an economic motivation to enter it. Given the low (official) pay of physicians relative to other workers in the Soviet period, any financial incentives were able to attract professionals from various medical specialties to narcology. The rapid commercialization of narcology during the 1990s encouraged this tendency, particularly since it coincided with a period of intense economic depression. For physicians or medical researchers whose small salaries were often delinquent or delayed for years, the promise of a specialty with a higher pay scale was clearly attractive. Though most of the narcologists I spoke to said they had entered medicine for a variety of reasons (many came from families of physicians), almost all explained that they had chosen narcology in particular for financial reasons. "At the moment, in Russia, it's rather profitable to work specifically as a narcologist," Anton Dmitrievich explained. Since narcologists in the state service continued to receive salary bonuses above those given to psychiatrists (which in turn made psychiatry higher-paying than general practice), he was willing to leave behind the higher prestige of psychiatry to work with addictions. "If not, I would have stayed in big psychiatry." The self-financing services described above also increased the salaries of narcologists.

Despite their higher pay relative to that of other physicians in the state service, narcologists were quick to point out that they made far less than their colleagues in commercial clinics or private practice. Indeed, commercial narcology was often used as a temporary professional destination for physicians seeking to earn quick money. On the other hand, narcologists starting out in the state system were paid an official salary of about four thousand rubles a month (approximately $150). As one physician put it, "That's about how the state values the labor of a narcologist."

And yet, at least for some of those at the top of the hierarchy in the state service, this salary was only the tip of the iceberg, only a small portion of the money they made through various services. While most narcologists saw the potential for personal enrichment in what was formally a commercial sector, the degree to which the commercial and state sectors were entangled with each other became clear with a prominent story involving the head doctor of the addiction hospital, Sergei Tikhomirov.

On August 26, 2004, the deputy director of the hospital, Larisa Artyukhovskaia, was killed by a bomb that had been left at the doorway to her apartment. A similar remote-controlled device was found near Tikhomirov's apartment, leading the procurator's office to initiate a broad investigation into the conflicts over control of the narcology business in the city. Early in October, none other than Tikhomirov himself was arrested and charged with the incitement of the murder of his deputy. Arrested along with him were Marat Dreizin, the director of a commercial narcological center, and Pavel Beliaev, an employee of the city's pathological-anatomical bureau (which oversees the morgues), known in the St. Petersburg underworld as "Pasha-Kvadrat." Beliaev was known as the head of a criminal group, the members of which were employed as orderlies in the city's morgues, earning them the name the "gang of orderlies" (*grupirovka sanitarov*).[11]

According to journalistic reports of the police investigation, Tikhomirov had developed a particularly lucrative business on the basis of his position as the northwest district's head narcologist. One of his duties in this position was the licensing of commercial narcology clinics (for the treatment of alcoholism), a service for which he apparently charged approximately $2,000. Additional funds reportedly came from the anonymous treatment of wealthy drug addicts. Reports differed on whether Artyukhovskaia, who was in charge of the hospital's finances, had refused to participate in Tikhomirov's business or whether she had simply refused to share the profits she herself stole from the hospital. In either case, investigators charged that Tikhomirov had arranged for the orderlies to carry out Artyukhovskaia's murder and, in order to clear himself of potential guilt, to make a seeming attempt on his own life. Also under question were the circumstances under which Tikhomirov had assumed his post in the first place: his predecessor had resigned after being severely beaten and threatened with bombs (Andreev 2004; Bezrukova 2006; Tumakova 2004).[12] Yet given how commonplace practices such as Tikhomirov's selling of licenses have been in recent years, it seems possible that he and Artyukhovskaia had clashed over some other, perhaps more profitable schemes. As media articles on the affair suggested, this spate of violent attacks associated with St. Petersburg narcology probably would not have occurred before increasing levels of (both state and private) funding began to appear for drug addiction treatment.

Two Clinics and the Power of the State

Mikhail Venediktovich's troubles had begun several years prior to the incident that I happened to witness. As he told it, he had noticed recurring discrepancies in the accounting books for the Bekhterev Center and suspected that his partner was embezzling funds. After several confrontations failed to correct the situation, Mikhail Venediktovich and his partner decided to divide the business between them. The idea, at least as he portrayed it in hindsight, was that each of the new clinics would be given a new name. Their advertisements, ubiquitous in the medical pages of free newspapers that were stuffed on a weekly basis into the mailboxes of Petersburgers, were also adorned by logos that were barely distinguishable. Both portrayed an open hand with either a single figure or a family group silhouetted in the palm. While Teplitstkii's Bekhterev Center offered a range of medical services, including gynecology and cardiology, both clinics specialized in addiction: specifically detoxification and treatment of withdrawal symptoms, as well as longer-term rehabilitation.

They were far from the only clinics offering such services: detoxification continues to be one of the most crowded and profitable parts of the commercial medical sector in the city. Between the mid-1990s and early 2000s, hundreds of organizations were licensed to carry out narcological services of one kind or another in Moscow and St. Petersburg (Egorov 1997, 9). The free newspapers, as well as other venues for relatively inexpensive advertising, were filled with advertisements for "rapid ending of binges" and "removing of [drug] withdrawals," many claiming to complete such procedures over the course of "six to eight hours." Such clinics also typically advertised longer-term aversive therapies such as disulfiram implantations and coding (described in the following chapter), and many offered ambulatory house calls. Some also offered treatment for other phenomena framed as addictions, such as smoking and compulsive gambling.

Many narcologists admitted that these services often acted as revolving doors for patients. For drinkers this meant "breaking a binge," allowing them to resume their consumption; for heroin users, such services were seen as a means to simply lower the dose they needed to take to obtain a high. At least for drinkers, detoxification services seemed keyed to particular local practices of consumption, albeit ones that were conceptualized as pathological.

Patients in various institutions rarely spoke in terms of consuming or drinking alcohol. Most referred to entering and exiting drinking binges, in a way that suggested a separate time and space. Both patients and physicians spoke about binges in terms of their length—three days, two weeks, two months—but patients in particular depicted them as definitely demarcated states or spaces: one clearly knew when one entered a binge as well as when one emerged from it. While the phenomenon of drinking binges is prominent in international medical literature on alcoholism, this local vernacular understanding of a binge—and the practices it described—was clearly distinct from the medical one. Clinics offering detoxification services then were less interested in propagating a medicalized terminology or understanding of sustained drinking bouts than in capitalizing on the meanings of such practices among lay populations.

Addiction clinics also benefited from the popular perception of a heroin epidemic overtaking Russia's youth, which became widespread during the mid- to late 1990s. While the increase in intravenous drug use among young people, and the concomitant spread of HIV infection, was very real indeed, the mass media representation of this phenomenon was often keyed in a hysterical and moralistic tone that some sociologists have referred to as a "moral panic" (Thompson 1998; Meylakhs 2009). Thus although alcohol-related deaths far outnumbered those associated with drug use in Russia, policymakers and public health administrators began to increasingly emphasize narcotics as a primary site for state intervention (Mendelevich 2004). If alcoholism was often portrayed as a timeless national tragedy, as old as Russia itself, drug use (rarely distinguished from drug *addiction*) was depicted as a new and frightening foreign scourge. Just as it had been during the 1920s, another period of radical social upheaval in Russia, drug use was discursively linked to images of "deviance" to a far greater degree than alcoholism, justifying a greater role for legal and penal state agencies in the matter.

At the same time as little effort was being made to regulate services targeted toward drinkers, efforts were being made to place the treatment of drug users under the aegis of state supervision. One of the results of these efforts was the 2002 creation of the FSKN. Whereas previous narcotics agencies had existed in the Russian Federation during the 1990s, the FSKN was distinguished by its size (it reportedly began with some forty thousand staff members), its institutional autonomy from federal ministries, and the scope of its mission, which ranged from policing narco trafficking and carrying out anti-drug-use propaganda to regulating the provision of treatment for drug addiction (Butler 2003).

The institutional imperative of the FSKN to monopolize authority in its given sphere, as well as its role in Vladimir Putin's much-vaunted goal of rebuilding the "vertical" of state power, was well articulated by a representative of the agency who spoke at a workshop for substance-abuse NGOs I attended in December 2003. To the concern of other workshop participants, the agent argued that "if an organization is effective, you need to pull it closer to power [*nado pritiagivat' ego k vlast'iu*] and give it particular goals to fulfill."[13]

Many narcologists viewed the creation of this agency as an attempt by those in the spheres of criminal justice and security to assert a conception of drug addiction as primarily a problem of public order over a medical one. In pointing out the essentially punitive character of the organization, some cited reports that the majority of FSKN agents had previously worked in the recently dismantled federal agency for tax collection. Some also noted that the agency's first director, Victor Cherkessov, had made his career in the KGB "chasing dissidents." At the same time, both recognized that they would eventually have no choice but to deal with the organization and that its existence meant that certain laws, already on the books, would now be enforced.

For instance, a federal law on narcotic substances passed in 1998 specifies that "the treatment of patients suffering from drug addiction is to be conducted only in institutions of the state and municipal health system."[14] While several physicians I spoke to mentioned this law, it was interpreted for me by Grigorii Mikhailovich, the medical administrator at the municipal addiction hospital. He argued that this law primarily represented the views of people in the state's security organs [*pravokhranitel'nye organi*]. Not only did it make him uneasy by defining drug addiction in legal rather than medical terms, but the clause in question stemmed from a misplaced anxiety about physicians selling narcotics. "These guys from the FSKN seem to have nothing better to do than to chase after doctors—they need to be dealing with drug trafficking! A couple of weeks ago, one of my doctors got a visit from two large young men asking her to sell them drugs—clearly an undercover operation carried out by these guys." Of course such anxieties were not *entirely* misplaced: when I arrived in his office that day, Grigorii Mikhailovich had been on the phone dealing with an incident involving a narcologist who had been selling prescriptions.

However, rather than spurning the entire notion of the state's remonopolizing treatment for drug addiction, Grigorii Mikhailovich emphasized the imprecisions of a law "written by people who are not medical specialists":

> The problem is in the definition of treatment [*lechenie*]: it isn't clear what "treatment" is. It seems that the people who wrote this law had in mind a situation where I give you a tablet. They don't, for instance, include psychotherapy in their understanding of treatment. And only some forms of "treatment," even when it is strictly defined in such medical terms, are included here. For instance, vitamin therapy, or therapy to treat all kinds of other illnesses which might accompany addiction, is not included.

Grigorii Mikhailovich implied that this vagueness of definition could make it easy for commercial clinics to get around the formal objectives of the law at the same time as it facilitated the unfair penalization of other clinics for practicing forms of treatment not included in the law's intent. More generally, it was not so much the wording as the broader institutional context that facilitated the use of this law, as well as the actors it mobilized, as an extension of commercial competition by other means.

Anything Is Possible: Commercial War

After the creation of the FSKN, Mikhail Venediktovich and his associates decided it was in their best interests to follow the requirements of the 1998 law. This meant reconstituting their business as a municipal institution, which they did in the autumn of 2003 with the support of a government committee. In this new legal incarnation (its third) the Bekhterev Center was meant to receive funding from the municipal budget to help reduce the cost of addiction treatment, thereby making it accessible to a broader group of potential patients. When these funds were not forthcoming, the center began to treat patients for drug addiction under the auspices of the municipal institution.

Within a month things began to get ugly. Unbeknownst to Mikhail Venediktovich and his colleagues, their "municipal institution" was declared null at a meeting of the local government committee that had originally authorized it. A "liquidating committee" was formed and supposedly charged with recovering certain pieces of medical equipment. In December 2003, clinical workers were taken by surprise when a group of men, some of them dressed in camouflage, representing the liquidating committee arrived at the center, shut down its operations, and escorted both physicians and patients—many of whom were heavily drugged by their ongoing detoxification—out of the building. Since this initial raid had no legal basis, the center's work was only briefly interrupted.

However, when the liquidating committee returned in February 2004, on the day I happened to be visiting, its visit was framed in legal terms. A lawsuit had been filed in an arbitration court by representatives of the municipal committee that had entered into a contract with the Bekhterev Center. The committee laid claim to various pieces of medical equipment and medicines, which it claimed had been purchased through the municipal budget. As the center's lawyer explained to me, the Russian arbitration codex includes a special provision for cases involving property disputes that allows for property held by the defendant to be seized and held, pending a trial, presumably to prevent him from selling or hiding it. All of this can take place before the defendant is even notified that a suit has been filed against him. In this case, the plaintiffs had asked the court to deny the defendants access to their building, to seize the property in question, and to have it held with the plaintiffs. While the court had apparently refused the first of these requests, it had granted the second and third.

To Mikhail Venediktovich, his coworkers, and their lawyer, this was another sure sign that the court had been "bought." The lawyer in particular felt that such a decision was unprecedented, and, along with the doctors, he discussed how much money their competitor must have spent to buy this decision. Their conviction about the roots of the lawsuit was bolstered by the appearance of agents from the FSKN, who had scheduled a surprise inspection of the center that very day. I spent much of that day in the office of the center's stocky medical director, Yuri Nikolaevich, as he, along with the nervy bald toxicologist Alexander Germanovich, the lawyer, Mikhail Venediktovich, and others chain-smoked out of communal cigarette packs and developed strategies for dealing with the dual onslaught.

Whatever its provenance, the effects of this day's events were based on much more than the formal legal basis of a lawsuit and a regulatory agency's inspection. Both visits had the strong performative effect of intimidating the center's administrators—or at least were perceived as attempts to intimidate by threat of force and to display the power and influence of the person behind the scenes who was pulling strings to make it all happen. This was particularly true in the case of the leather-jacketed movers, whom Mikhail Venediktovich and others essentially interpreted as representatives of a security agency—synonymous with a bandit or mafia group.

The phenomenon of such raids was a common feature of the Russian business world throughout the 1990s and early 2000s. As I learned from other acquaintances, it was colloquially known as *"maski* show"—originally the name of a mime troupe—but applied in this case because of the ski masks typically worn by raiding security personnel. This form of attack, with an added element of threat added by the visible wielding of guns, was used equally in conflicts between businessmen and by the state in crackdowns on the conglomerates of several so-called oligarchs during Putin's administration. The trope of hidden identities is central to the performative effects of this form of power, in that people experiencing such raids initially do not know whether the security people bursting in the door are agents of the state, of their own firm, or of a competing firm or are simply a bandit group. Rather than relying on the authority conferred by the legitimizing face of the law, the very power of this tactic lies in masking and blurring the institutional identification of those wielding force.

As Vadim Volkov (2002) argues, this blurring has a structural and social basis in that throughout the 1990s, so-called mafia groups performed many of the functions typically carried out by the (in this case, absent) state. The groups, which Volkov calls violent entrepreneurs (they convert violence or force, or the threat of it, into capital), function in basically the same way whether they are illegal mafia groups, legal private protection agencies (themselves made up of former state protection agencies), or current state employees—providing protection and ensuring that contracts are honored.[15] In other words, a similar relationship of protection and patronage, known as a *krysha* (roof), can be provided by a security group (either formally legal or not), a particular state agency, or a network of actors connected by personal ties and debts that often crosscut these institutional boundaries.

The organizers of the raid on the Bekhterev Center certainly drew upon such tactics even as they attempted to frame it as a legitimate legal action. Though none of the movers wore a mask, they categorically refused to give their names or show identification when asked by Mikhail Venediktovich. At the same time, even the attempt at a seemingly legal process in this case raises the question of whether a certain legitimacy of the state has been successfully reconstructed in recent years. If this is the case, then—as we shall see—it is perhaps less legitimacy in the classic sense, connoting practices of good governance and rule of law, than a conviction that the state (more specifically, certain of its agencies) is once again becoming the most powerful of kryshas, the most potent and reliable source of protection.

Of the two attacks suffered by the center that day, the surprise inspection was more easily dealt with. The main FSKN agent, wearing a federal badge around his neck, couched his demands entirely in a formal and bureaucratic logic. When one of the clinicians initially protested the inspection, claiming, "We're not harming anyone," he responded, "Actually we come across plenty of doctors who claim that they keep illegal drugs on hand simply to help patients through withdrawal." When the physicians produced a photocopy of the center's license, the agent was not pleased: "I need to see the original license. This photocopy doesn't mean anything to me unless it's notarized." When Mikhail Venediktovich pointedly asked him why his inspection was occurring on the same day as the attempted seizure of equipment, the agent assumed the rhetoric of a powerless bureaucrat: "I'm just a clerk, I'm just carrying out my boss's orders," although he later acknowledged, "This is some war you guys have going on here."

At this point Yuri Nikolaevich decided to take a more conciliatory approach and to engage the agent. He offered him tea and chatted with him for nearly an hour. The two exchanged stories about the troubles the Scientologists were causing to Russian narcology. Yuri Nikolaevich asked the agent for advice regarding the finer points of the new agency's regulatory regime. The agent, for his part, was very interested in making sure that the center was not carrying out subdermal implantations of naltrexone, an opiate antagonist (similar therapies are described in the next chapter), a technique that was, at the time, not approved by the Ministry of Health. Seemingly appeased, the agent sat at a desk and wrote his report out in longhand. After everything, his only formal complaint was the lack of the original copy of the center's license—which the physicians promised to bring to him the following day—and a missing tag on the safe that held controlled medications.

As he prepared to leave, the agent recounted several stories about seizing illegal drugs in ambulances. He argued that a number of drugs currently classified as uncontrolled should be reclassified as narcotics and complained about the flow of such substances from Ukraine and Belarus, where he claimed regulation was lighter. After he had left, Yuri Nikolaevich said to Alexander Germanovich, "Don't you think I handled that well? He came in here all excited, but when I talked to him, he calmed down." Alexander Germanovich was having none of this and launched into a short tirade about the effects of such a punitive understanding of addiction on public health. "It's because of people like him that young people addicted to drugs are contracting HIV and dying of overdoses."

Having dealt with the agent, the center's administrators still had the other half of the crisis on their hands. As they saw it, the problem was potentially deeper than the document from the arbitration court suggested. For one, they insisted that the equipment claimed by the municipal committee had not been purchased by the city's funds: in fact, the list of property exceeded anything that the center actually had on hand. The real problem did not lie with the potential seizure of medical equipment. The various defibrillators, electrocardiographs, blood-pressure monitors, and cots could easily be replaced. However, the doctors feared that the seizure of this equipment was only the first step in a broader strategy by their competitor to shut them down entirely.

Medical licenses in Russia are granted according to the particular clinical specialty or type of care being practiced. Whether it applies to narcology, cardiology, or gynecology, a medical license stipulates certain standards, including particular pieces of equipment and medicines, which a clinic must have on site. The Bekhterev Center's physicians and administrators worried that immediately after a seizure of their equipment they might receive a surprise visit from the licensing bureau, which, finding certain required items to be missing, would revoke their license.

For this reason, the physicians' main goal was to make sure they ended the day with the infrastructure required to practice. Simply replacing equipment was not enough: since the court's decision listed more items than the clinic owned, any new equipment could simply be seized on the following day. In other words, it was also necessary to provide documentation proving that each piece of new equipment did not belong to the municipal organization. "We don't have the receipts for these electrocardiographs," Yuri Nikolaevich exclaimed. "We bought them years ago. If you come to my house and claim my refrigerator, how am I going to prove that it's mine?" The administrators discussed whether the best course of action was to write up backdated letters documenting the receipt of medical equipment as "gifts" from one of the doctors or simply to lock all the materials in the gynecology ward, an area that, everyone agreed, even the movers would refrain from entering. The only moment of levity that day occurred while the doctors decided which pieces of equipment they were prepared to forfeit. Taking out a "broken" blood-pressure monitor, Alexander Germanovich disconnected the display dial, explaining, "This is the most expensive part." In its place he connected a pump, creating an absurd device that consisted of tubing connecting two rubber pumps: "We'll give them this," he laughed.

Yet such moments did not hide the intense anxiety Alexander Germanovich expressed throughout the day. A professor of narcology and toxicology at the university, he had, like many other academics, begun practicing in a commercial clinic in order to supplement his small and irregularly paid salary. Yet as the official director of Bekhterev's municipal institution during its brief existence, he had already had criminal proceedings initiated against him for illegally treating drug addicts. During a half hour of relative calm that day, he told Yuri Nikolaevich and me that he was considering leaving narcology altogether. "Too many unlikable [*nepriiatnye*] people." Moreover, he emphasized that the "disorder [*bespredel*] we were witnessing not only characterized this medical specialty but Russia as a whole. "You see what kind of legal system we have?" His tirades, themselves typical of Russian speech genres that link tropes of "total collapse" to an ethic of virtuous suffering, grew only more intense once he learned that I was visiting from the United States (Ries 1997).

Although the lawyer came up with his own strategies, which included filing suit against the security company for lost revenues, in the end the Bekhterev Center emerged from this episode in its commercial war through the intervention of its own patrons. At one point during the day, there was talk of Mikhail Venediktovich's calling up his own "unlikable people." Soon a jovial man in his fifties, wearing a black jacket and carrying a string of worry beads, arrived in the office and vigorously shook everyone's hand. Introduced by Mikhail Venediktovich to the court officer as the center's technical director, the man spent much of that afternoon negotiating with the representatives of the liquidating committee as well as, apparently, the competing clinic. Toward the late afternoon he had worked out a compromise according to which the equipment would remain at the Bekhterev Center; the liquidators were allowed to leave one guard in the building to make sure nothing was removed.

Back in the office, he instructed the physicians to write up an account of that day's events and enclose it in a letter of complaint to a particular representative of United Russia, the pro-Putin coalition party that had swept the parliamentary elections two months earlier. In a moment that played out uncannily like a political ad, Alexander Germanovich intoned, "There is no future for Russia, no future." To this, the technical director, who at that moment was jotting down the contact information for the United Russia deputy, replied, "You're wrong. Russia has a future." The unspoken subtext, as I interpreted it, was not so much a matter of political party affiliation as of whether a system of institutional authority based on personal ties and patronage could still evoke the vision of a future worth putting one's hopes on.

Within the following days, assistance arrived through the personal intervention of St. Petersburg's head narcologist, Vladimir Nikolaenko. In an open letter addressed to the city's then governor, Valentina Matvienko, Nikolaenko argued that particularly in light of the "deficit of beds" in the municipal addiction clinic, "the actions of the head of the liquidating committee . . . undermine the existing system of narcological services" (Dyleva 2004a, 10). It was not clear to me whether Nikolaenko's ties to the center predated this event or whether it represented his assumption of a new role as patron. In either case, this relationship between the Bekhterev Center and the city's head narcologist was further cemented in the following months when the center agreed to conduct clinical tests of an experimental system Nikolaenko had devised for the treatment of addiction.

There were other long-term aftereffects of the raid. When I visited the Bekhterev Center a month later, Mikhail Venediktovich had just been released from the hospital after suffering a mild heart attack. As we discussed my research into the local differences of addiction medicine in St. Petersburg, he insisted that there were no "real differences," only "differences in conditions":

> Here there's always something. The last time they came from the FSKN, all the guy could find was that we didn't have the appropriate tags on the safe that we keep controlled substances in. And then he said, well you should have contacted me in advance so we could have worked something out. And this means that they are basically offering to act as a krysha. And you know how many agencies there are competing for that role? There's the sanitary epidemiological service, the licensing committee, the fire marshals. . . . In every other country the way that licensing works is that a professional organization of physicians or whoever establishes certain criteria and gives licenses to its members. Here we don't have anything of that sort—medical licensing is carried out by a state agency—and basically, it's another situation in which you have to pay a fairly large sum of money.

At the same time, he was ready to work with the new agency: after all, what choice did he have? "Sure, they'll be stealing an enormous amount of our money, but at least we'll be able to continue our work."

Like many other Petersburgers I spoke to, Mikhail Venediktovich spoke of a world in which a logic of fundamental economic interest and profit seeking could explain everyone's actions. In such a world, the commodified substances and objects of addiction—vodka, beer, heroin, gambling machines—were seen as following the same circuits, underpinned by the same market logic, as the clinical interventions that sought to manage addiction. Though there was nothing particularly unusual about this insight, it was made repeatedly by people working in the clinical sphere as a kind of commentary on the absurdities of the addiction treatment market (cf. Schüll 2012). For instance, Mikhail Venediktovich argued that the hyperinflated costs of drug tests made it "more profitable to sell drug tests than to sell drugs." An acquaintance active in the 12-step movement repeated an apocryphal story about drug dealers in the city who opened their own treatment centers so as to make money from the entire circuit of addiction and its treatment. At the same time, Mikhail Venediktovich and others relied on personalizing strategies to manage what they perceived as a rapacious market (Rivkin-Fish 2005).

An interesting postscript to the Bekhterev Center raid emerged several months later when I came across an article in a local newspaper describing the events. The article was written by a reporter who had not been present on that day but had subsequently interviewed Mikhail Venediktovich and other members of the staff. I recalled that during the course of that day, Mikhail Venediktovich had asked me about my impressions of the events I was witnessing. Unable to come up with much, I mumbled something about never having seen anything of the sort in the United States. The title of the article, "Treat Drug Addicts? No, 'Bloody' ['*mochit'*'] Narcologists," made ironic reference to President Putin's assertion that he would similarly "bloody," or destroy, Chechen separatists. (This unabashed use of an argot seemingly shared by the criminal world and its pursuers in the security sphere was often referred to by members of the intelligentsia as evidence both of the president's "lack of culture" and of his "KGB mentality.") The article opened with a brief description of the February raid, followed by this statement: "An accidental witness of these events, an American citizen, a graduate student at Yale [*sic*] University, Mr. Raikhel, thinks that such a situation is unthinkable, impossible, in any case in the setting of the USA. But here [*u nas*] anything is possible!" (Dyleva 2004a, 10).

4

PROSTHESES FOR THE WILL

Vyacheslav was one of the first patients I met at the addiction hospital. As we sat under the cracked and water-stained walls of a small examination room, the fifty-year-old factory worker described his stay at the hospital as part of a cycle. Every year Vyacheslav went on a drinking binge, which always ended with his being voluntarily hospitalized. During his month at the hospital, Vyacheslav's physicians detoxified his body with intravenously delivered vitamins as well as a heavy pharmacological regimen, including the liberal use of tranquilizers and antipsychotics, a treatment protocol that had changed little since the Soviet period (Fleming 1996; Ivanets 2001; Fleming, Bradbeer, and Green 2001; Elovich 2008).

Before discharging him from the hospital, Vyacheslav's physicians gave him an injection (colloquially known as a *torpedo*), which, they told him, contained a long-acting form of disulfiram—a drug that induces a heightened sensitivity to alcohol—that would remain in his bloodstream for a year. Vyacheslav did not pretend to understand how the medication worked—that was the job of the specialists. "There's also a special injection they can give you in your vein," he explained, adding, with deference to the authority of his clinicians, "It's all figured out by the professors so that it gradually dissolves." He knew that his body had been somehow modified, rendered incapable of processing alcohol, and he knew that drinking in this state posed a grave danger to his health, perhaps even to his life.

And so, as he explained, Vyacheslav always waited until the course of the torpedo was over before embarking upon another binge. Once he had tried another procedure: the physicians had implanted a capsule under his skin, which they said would slowly release disulfiram for five years. That time Vyacheslav had not been able to wait it out: "I didn't drink for two and a half years. Then I paid them and had the implant removed [*rasshilsia*]." Typically this cycle repeated itself every year, he told me, with no evident regret or concern. Vyacheslav explained that, along with his family, he was successfully managing his tendency to indulge in drink, although he added that abstaining from alcohol noticeably dampened his social life.

Vyacheslav described his torpedo as a physiologically based treatment, which was more or less the way that physicians depicted it in conversations with patients and advertisements. However, later that week Anton Denisovich, Vyacheslav's physician, gave me a radically different account of the treatment. When I asked him about the forms of longer-term treatment offered to patients at the hospital, he explained, "Mainly it is *khimzashchita* or placebo therapy, or we orient them toward rehabilitation programs." By this point in my fieldwork, I knew that *khimzashchita*, which literally translates as "chemical protection," was an umbrella term used to refer to different forms of disulfiram treatment, including Vyacheslav's injection and his subdermal implantation. I had also read in an English-language medical journal that Russian narcologists sometimes used "placebo therapy." However, none of the physicians I had spoken to had mentioned it, and I was surprised at Anton Denisovich's depiction of disulfiram therapy in this way. "Can you explain khimzashchita?" I asked. "How should I explain it to you? As if you were a patient?" asked Anton Denisovich and then began without waiting for an answer:

We inject the medication disulfiram. It comes in different forms: intravenous, capsule form, or subdermal implantation. All of these forms are long-acting. If the medication is taken intravenously or orally, it dissolves in the stomach and ends up in the bloodstream and then enters the body's tissues, combines with proteins in the liver . . . and for a certain period of time this medicine remains in the bloodstream. This medication cannot be taken with alcohol, as it blocks the enzymes that break down alcohol. If a patient on this medication drinks and alcohol enters his bloodstream, the possible side effects are dangerous to his health or life-threatening. It can be anything from a flushing or reddening of the face to serious or crippling consequences or even death. . . . This is told to the patient and he signs a paper explaining that he understands the procedure. And then the procedure takes place.

I was confused. "Then why is it placebo therapy?" Anton Denisovich hesitated awkwardly for a moment, perhaps realizing that he was about to reveal a minor professional secret. "Well," he resumed, "because it is. . . . Because, as you understand, all patients cannot take these substances, in part because some of them won't wait out the entire period, and this would just be dangerous for them. So it's better to give him a placebo and give him the gift of several months of sober life than to inject the real medication."

As I gradually learned through conversations with narcologists at the hospital and in commercial clinics over the subsequent months, it is common practice to inject or implant patients with neutral substances (often vitamins or saline) in place of disulfiram. Moreover, as narcologists see it, whether or not they use active disulfiram, the therapies they refer to as khimzashchita rely heavily on suggestion and have more in common with hypnosis than with neurochemically based interventions. When they did not describe it as placebo therapy, as Anton Denisovich had done, most narcologists characterized khimzashchita as a form of psychotherapy and emphasized its parallels with a technique known as emotional-stress psychotherapy, or *kodirovanie* (coding). Like khimzashchita, kodirovanie is a therapy meant to keep patients from drinking by seemingly convincing them that their bodies have been altered so as to make the consumption of alcohol harmful or fatal. Unlike khimzashchita, kodirovanie does not involve the ingestion, injection, or implantation of any substance at all. Instead, the therapist is said to alter the patient's brain through his actions, which sometimes involve vigorous physical manipulations and a strict ritual structure. Both narcologists and their patients often implicitly acknowledged the similarities between khimzashchita and kodirovanie by classifying them together. Proponents of the therapies have called them "mediating psychotherapy" (*oposredovannaia psikhoterapiia*) in print, and many patients refer to both types of treatment as kodirovanie (Entin 1991, 132).

It is difficult to overstate the ubiquity of such clinical technologies in post-Soviet Russia. The Kazan-based psychiatrist Vladimir Mendelevich (2004), an avid opponent of khimzashchita and kodirovanie, reports that such methods "constitute up to 80 percent of all treatment methods offered by official and unofficial Russian narcology" (see also Ivanets 2001; Sofronov 2003). In 2004, both methods were heavily advertised in the medical pages of free newspapers that were regularly stuffed into the mailboxes of Petersburgers. Russian-language online forums on alcoholism and addiction are filled with questions posted by patients anxious to understand how these methods work and to ascertain their efficacy. In both the state-run and commercial clinics where I conducted fieldwork, the vast majority of long-term treatments offered to patients relied on mechanisms of suggestion and conditioning. In addition to khimzashchita and kodirovanie, these included emotional-stress psychotherapy, subliminal suggestion, and several recently imported methods, such as neuro-linguistic programming (NLP) and Eriksonian hypnosis.

In addition to being widespread, these therapies are highly contested in Russia, condemned on a variety of clinical, ethical, and political grounds. They are criticized by proponents of Alcoholics Anonymous for ignoring the underlying emotional and spiritual roots of alcoholism and by advocates of harm reduction for being falsely represented as "cures" for a chronic disease (Mendelevich 2004). Even many clinicians who offer khimzashchita or kodirovanie point out that while these methods are often successful in facilitating short-term remissions, patients rarely see the need to supplement them with longer-term psychosocial interventions, leading to a cycle of decreasingly successful and increasingly short remissions (Valentik 2001, 244; Sofronov 2003). Not surprisingly, visiting Western European and North American physicians have criticized what they see as these treatments' disregard for a normative model of patient autonomy; instead of treating patients as autonomous, rational, and potentially self-knowing individuals, these methods are described as relying on people's ignorance and belief to frighten them into sobriety (Finn 2005; Parfitt 2006). Noting that the effectiveness of therapies such as khimzashchita or kodirovanie "depends on the therapeutic ability of those who dispense" them, "as well as the patient's and their relatives belief in miracle cures," a team of British and Russian physicians argued during the mid-1990s that this belief "has directed attention away from more progressive psychological approaches and has weakened patients' confidence in their ability to overcome dependency by becoming aware of the problem and mobilizing their own will and intelligence" (Fleming, Meyroyan, and Klimova 1994, 359). According to such accounts, the mechanism underlying khimzashchita and kodirovanie is very simple: it consists of the physician's convincingly telling his patient, "'If you drink—you die'" (Chepurnaya and Etkind 2006).

The theme of fear as a motivator in such clinical technologies was often linked to political or culturalist interpretations about which methods were more appropriate for Russian or post-Soviet people. Alexander Germanovich, a toxicologist working at a commercial clinic offering alcohol detoxification and rehabilitation, often employed khimzashchita in his own clinical practice. His explanation was representative, not simply because he drew a clear analogy between the clinical encounter and the relationship between citizens and their state but also because of the emphasis he placed on the centrality of fear to khimzashchita.

> [I]n addition to the purely chemical effect, there is a suggestive effect. A suggestive-stress [*suggestivnoe-stressevoe*] effect. Suggestion [*vnushenie*] to the person that all of this [drinking] is dangerous and not allowed. Of course this is all built on fear. In America this is probably used rarely—implantation, because there the personality [*lichnost*] of the patient and his potential possibilities [*vozmozhnestei*] are taken into account much more than in Russia. This is characteristic for us, that we treat people differently—both medicine and the state. People have much less freedom of choice among methods of treatment here. In America, they are mainly oriented toward "counseling" [spoken in English], you know this, toward self-help groups. Russia is gradually moving in that direction, it will also get there eventually. Khimzashchita is, of course, yesterday's method.

Like others, this doctor focused on the element of fear as a motivating factor in khimzashchita to draw an analogy with "Russian" relations of authority: a comparison that was sometimes drawn in political terms—as a legacy of totalitarianism—and sometimes through the lens of cultural arguments about "Russian culture and mentality." Underlying such arguments was a stereotyped figure of the Soviet subject: stripped of its individual self through the hypnotic power of the physician or state and dependent on that authoritative figure to solve its problems. Although many narcologists complained about the passivity of patients who wanted quick fixes and silver bullet treatments for their addiction (complaints often infused with an analogy of patients as wards of the welfare state), opponents of aversive methods argued that physicians fostered such passivity for their own monetary gain.

Such characterizations of khimzashchita and kodirovanie as techniques by which money-hungry and amoral physicians scare unwitting patients out of drinking, as throwbacks to Soviet relations of authority or as modes of biopolitical social control (Chepurnaya and Etkind 2006), fail to capture the complexity of clinical logics, institutional concatenations, and domestic modes of governance that have allowed these modes of treatment to become as ubiquitous as they are in contemporary Russia. Of course, rapacious physicians with pecuniary motives are certainly part of the story, and individual motivations aside, the therapies described in this chapter have depended on, and helped to reinforce, clinical encounters premised on a steeply hierarchical physician-patient relationship. Yet focusing exclusively on such interpretations obscures a number of issues that are central to understanding the continued prevalence of khimzashchita and kodirovanie and their roles in the lives of countless drinkers and their families.

Chief among these is the relationship of these therapeutic technologies to the subjectivity or the self of patients. North Americans are accustomed to the idea that treatments for alcoholism and drug addiction either demand that patients conceive of themselves as persons of a certain sort or teach them to do so. It is not simply that 12-step programs like Alcoholics Anonymous—which are certainly the most culturally visible forms of long-term treatment for alcoholism in North America—require people to publicly self-identify as "alcoholics" and "addicts" and to narrate their life stories appropriately (Cain 1991; Wilcox 1998). Rather, as Laurence Kirmayer has argued, various systems of psychotherapy depend "on implicit models of the self, which in turn, are based on cultural concepts of the person" (2007, 232). Such models of the self are implicit in certain capacities that most psychotherapies demand of patients. Sometimes grouped under the rubric of "psychological mindedness," these include a capacity to articulate one's life story according to particular narrative conventions; an awareness of oneself as possessing an unconscious—the linguistic corollary of which Summerson Carr has called an "ideology of inner reference" (2006); a capacity for self-reflection; an ability to recognize and identify one's emotional responses to experiences; and a desire "to accept and handle increased responsibility for the self" (Kirmayer 2007, 236). Even psychopharmaceuticals—which are often described as undercutting this psychological model of the self—are often conceived of by their North American consumers as technologies through which the "true self" is rendered accessible or transformed (Elliott 2004; Saris 2008, 266n4).[1]

As I learned in my conversations with Vyachslav and other patients at the addiction hospital, khimzashchita and kodirovanie are different in this regard, not because they ask patients to conceptualize a different sort of self but because they scarcely seem concerned at all with the self or its transformation. Vyacheslav did not identify himself as an alcoholic. And though his physician described him as suffering from a biologically based disorder, recognizable through somatic symptoms, neither did Vyacheslav speak of himself as suffering from a brain-based disorder. In large part, this is because the methods of behavioral modification that make up narcology's clinical armamentarium do not encourage patients to identify in this way. Rather than transforming patients' subjectivities, these methods work by harnessing their preexisting ideas, beliefs, and affects—with an end result that is experienced as a change in behavior or practice without a change or transformation of the self.

In order to understand how this may be, it is necessary to take another historical excursus. In describing the project that he calls—drawing on Michel Foucault (1983)—"historical ontology," Ian Hacking writes of being motivated by an "obscure conjecture that when it comes to philosophy, many of our perplexities arise from the ways in which a space of possible ideas has been formed" (2002, 26). The genealogical solution with which Hacking, along with many others (e.g., Young 1995), addresses these problems is useful not only to philosophy in the disciplinary sense but also to the perplexities of everyday forms of life posed by fieldwork. In this case, understanding khimzashchita and kodirovanie as they are practiced today requires that we trace their origins to Soviet psychiatry's clinical style of reasoning, discussed in chapter 2. Here I return briefly to that history to examine how the instantiation of Pavlovian theories in mid-twentieth-century Soviet scientific, medical, and penal institutions formed a space of possible ideas from which khimzashchita and kodirovanie emerged.

Pavlov's Progeny: Suggestion as Psychotherapy in Soviet Psychiatry

When asked to describe khimzashchita and kodirovanie in the simplest of terms, many narcologists in St. Petersburg explained that these were "psychotherapeutic" methods. At first I found this rather confusing because neither of these methods looked like what I understood psychotherapy to mean—that is, some long-term talk-based intervention during the course of which a patient gains insight into his or her condition. As many social critics and historians have pointed out, the prevalence of this general understanding of psychotherapy in North America attests to the deep influence that Freud's psychoanalytic ideas continue to exert (Campbell 2007, 20–28; Illouz 2008). While the dominance of explicitly psychoanalytic ideas in psychiatry and popular culture alike is said to have been toppled in the 1970s and '80s by biological psychiatry, many North American assumptions about psychological interventions and subjectivity continue to reflect a Freudian legacy.

It is in this regard—in having followed a Pavlovian, rather than a Freudian, path during the early to mid-twentieth century—that Soviet psychiatrists and narcologists diverged most noticeably from their North American (and to a somewhat lesser extent, their Western European) counterparts. Though the theory of psychoanalysis became anathema in the Soviet Union from the early 1930s onward, alternative theories of the unconscious as well as modes of psychotherapy continued to be developed, particularly during the post-Stalin period. Theoretical work on "the psyche" was revived with Alexander Luria's neuropsychology and S. L. Rubinstein's writings on consciousness (Graham 1987; Joravsky 1989; Miller 1998). This period also saw the appearance of increasingly sophisticated Soviet critiques of psychoanalysis (which, with the coming of the Cold War, became emblematic of American and Western European "bourgeois psychotherapy"), exposing discerning readers (those able to "read through" to the notions being critiqued) to the ideas of Freud, Jung, Adler, and even Erich Fromm and Jacques Lacan (Miller 1998). Other Soviet researchers and clinicians, such as Dmitri Uznadze (1886–1950) and Vladimir N. Miasishchev (1893–1973), a Leningrad psychiatrist and director of the Bekhterev Psychoneurological Research Institute, developed explicitly nonpsychoanalytic theories of the unconscious (ibid.).

In regard to clinical interventions, however, with a few notable exceptions—and a parallel tradition of "rational psychotherapy"[2]—the majority of techniques framed as psychotherapy during the Soviet period employed mechanisms of hypnosis and suggestion (Wortis 1950, 88; Kirman 1966; Segal 1975; Lauterbach 1984; Etkind 1997b). While hypnosis had been widely used in psychiatry during the nineteenth century, it increasingly lost favor in psychoanalytic circles, as well as in the transnational psychiatric community, during the twentieth. In tsarist Russia it was used with some frequency as a treatment for alcoholism (Herlihy 2002). Yet throughout the early Soviet period, researchers continued to use techniques of suggestion, emphasizing their basis in the physiological reflex theories developed by Pavlov and Vladimir Bekhterev.

Hypnosis and suggestion were central to the research of Bekhterev, an eclectic psychiatrist who studied with Jean-Marie Charcot and developed a theory of "associative reflexes" in many ways parallel to Pavlov's (Kozulin 1984; Valsiner 2001). Bekhterev ([1897] 1998) viewed suggestion as a fundamental way in which human beings communicated and influenced one another, and he drew on crowd theory and notions of "moral contagion" in developing a social theory with suggestion at its core. Often described in the Soviet literature as the "founder of Russian psychotherapy" (Platonov 1959, 11), Bekhterev grounded his interest in psychotherapy firmly in a physiological theory of reflexes. His influence on the development of Soviet psychotherapy is often described by reference to a group of therapies known as "the Bekhterev triad": explanation, hypnosis, and autosuggestion (Babayan 1985). Notably, Bekhterev was also deeply involved in contemporary social debates around alcohol and drunkenness and frequently used hypnosis to treat alcoholism.

Ironically, the ideas of Bekhterev, who was significantly more engaged in progressive politics than Pavlov and welcomed the Bolsheviks' assumption of power in 1917, fell out of official favor during the late 1920s (Joravsky 1989). And though his legacy was partly restored during the post-Stalin period, when it proved particularly important for the "Leningrad school" of Soviet psychiatry, it was the dominance of Pavlov's theories that accorded legitimacy to practices of hypnotic suggestion and, less directly, placebo therapy, by reframing them in entirely physiological terms (Chertok 1981, 11). In elaborating his theory of higher nervous activity, Pavlov relied on the notions of excitation, inhibition, and equilibrium to describe basic processes taking place in the nervous system, which he correlated with experimental evidence produced through conditioning. For Pavlov, inhibition encompassed all processes that weakened conditioned reflexes, and was dividable into the categories of "external inhibition," "internal inhibition," and the inhibition associated with sleep (Smith 1992, 200–201). Pavlov described hypnosis as a transitory state that resulted when the inhibitory process that led to sleep occurred to a less extensive degree (Platonov 1959; Pavlov 1994, 84). Further, he argued that "suggestion in hypnosis can be rightly interpreted as such a phase of inhibition when weak conditioned stimuli (words) produce a greater effect than the evidently stronger and real external stimuli" (Pavlov 1994, 85). In other words, Pavlov conceptualized hypnosis as a state of consciousness that facilitates suggestibility.

This account helped to render hypnosis scientifically legitimate by placing it firmly in the realm of the material, allowing it to be incorporated into mainstream psychiatry (Slobodianik 1963; Hoskovec 1967; Babayan and Shashina 1985, 99). A Soviet textbook on psychiatry claimed that "the strictly objective Pavlovian method of investigating higher nervous activity dispelled the fog of mystery and the subjective psychological conceptions that had for so long wrapped the problem of hypnosis in darkness" (Babayan 1985, 99). Pavlov's theories also led to the development of various clinical interventions that were generally categorized as psychotherapy.

Whether one interpreted such accounts as reductive or as dialectical, Pavlov's theories helped to render hypnosis scientifically legitimate, allowing it to be incorporated into mainstream psychiatry (Babayan and Gonopolsky 1985; Babayan and Shashina 1985; Rozhnov and Burno 1987). In helping to legitimate hypnosis, the Pavlovian dominance in psychiatry led to the development of multiple suggestion-based interventions categorized as psychotherapy. Indeed, throughout much of the Soviet period, psychotherapy was synonymous either with rational psychotherapy or with methods based on suggestion (Wortis 1950, 88; Lauterbach 1984; Etkind 1997b). These methods included various types of individual and group hypnosis; "direct suggestion," in which the patient remains in a waking state and is aware of the procedure; "indirect suggestion"; and techniques of autosuggestion and the "autogenous training" developed by German therapists (Lauterbach

1984, 81). As I describe below, such methods made up the majority of long-term interventions used to treat alcoholism in the Soviet Union.

Engineering Aversion: Conditional-Reflex Treatment as Therapy and Punishment

Eugene Zubkov, an émigré narcologist who has become active in the 12-step movement in Russia, spent one of our first meetings detailing the various ills of Russian narcology. His critique was based largely on first-hand experience: Zubkov had received his medical degree in the late 1970s, just as narcology was taking shape, and had spent much of the following decade working at the Bekhterev Psychoneurological Research Institute. Out of the various treatments that emerged from this discipline, he identified conditional-reflex therapy—sometimes referred to as "apomorphine treatment"—most closely with the Soviet period.

> It was invented by a professor of the Serbskii Institute, Ivan Vassiliivich Strel'chuk, for which he received the Stalin Prize. I remember this very well: I used it. Apomorphine is a substance that, when injected, makes you vomit. They'd ask what kind of alcoholism a person has: vodka, beer or whatever. Then the person would drink this substance, the doctor would give him apomorphine and in forty-five seconds he would throw up. During the next session, he drinks a glass of cognac and they give him apomorphine and he vomits into a tub. Thirty or forty people would gather in a room and they all puked.

In itself, the idea of inducing a physical aversion to alcohol in patients was far from new. An early version of aversive therapy against alcoholism was employed by the pioneering American physician Benjamin Rush during the 1780s (White 1998, 4), and during the twentieth century, apomorphine therapy was used against alcohol and drug addiction by British physician John Dent, whom William Burroughs credited with breaking his addiction to heroin (Dent 1949; Burroughs 1957).

Soviet medical researchers, however, grounded their efforts in Pavlov's theory of higher nervous activity. In Pavlovian terms the idea was to condition a reflex to the taste, smell, sight, or mention of alcohol based on the unconditional or instinctual reflex to an unpleasant stimulus. After initial attempts using electrical shock, researchers settled in 1933 on the use of emetics like apomorphine to condition subjects so that they experienced a nausea reflex upon tasting or smelling alcohol (Sluchevsky and Friken 1933; Zhislin and Lukomskii 1963). This was a direct translation to humans in the clinic of the work conducted twenty years earlier in Pavlov's laboratory, where researchers had used apomorphine to condition laboratory dogs to gag in response to a particular sound (Zhislin and Lukomskii 1963). The project of carrying over such clinical practices from animals to humans had been seen as a complex one by Pavlov and his collaborators, in part because it required one to assume a radically simplified model of human behavior (or at least some aspects of it). Reflex action of the sort demonstrated in Pavlov's laboratory worked on the level of a body outside (or beneath) the sphere of conscious thought, willed action, and morality (Todes 2002).

In the political climate of the 1930s, however, the airing of such doubts about the applicability of Pavlov's findings to human beings was difficult, and potentially dangerous. And whereas conditional-reflex therapy remained a fairly marginal phenomenon in most of Europe and North America,[3] in the Soviet Union it became one of the primary techniques for the clinical treatment of alcoholism, and it remained prevalent until the late 1980s. In late Soviet narcology textbooks conditional-reflex therapy was given pride of place as a first-line therapy for use after detoxification, and it was instated as a recommended means of treatment in narcological clinics through the country (Babayan and Gonopolsky 1985).

In its most widely used form, credited to the psychiatrist Ivan V. Strel'chuk, the treatment was meant to create an aversion not only to alcohol as a substance but also to the broader context of drinking practices. A popular textbook encouraged physicians to replicate a typical setting for alcoholic sociality in the clinic:

> A "drinking setting" is created, i.e., tables are laid with sandwiches, beverages are placed on the tables, and sometimes a bar with a counter is set up, its cupboards displaying bottles with alcoholic beverage labels. Sessions are held simultaneously with several patients. . . . A patient is given sandwiches to eat and two cups of warm tea to drink. An initially determined dose of apomorphine is injected subcutaneously while the patient is given a glass

with his "favorite beverage" to hold. The patient smells the drink, rinses his mouth, and about 5–20 minutes before the onset of vomiting drinks half of the beverage. After the injection the vomiting reaction usually lasts 2–30 minutes. Within this time the patient drinks up the remaining portion of the alcoholic beverage. (Babayan and Gonopolskii, 220)

Some opponents of the method argued that this led patients to develop an aversion that was much broader than initially intended. As Zubkov explained, "It worked, but what would happen: You go to a banquet and they pour cognac—what happens? You're walking down the street and you run into the doctor who treated you with apomorphine. Immediately you vomit all over the doctor." As a proponent of Alcoholics Anonymous, Zubkov of course had a particularly strong stake in undermining the legitimacy of conditional-reflex therapy. And yet his negative depiction of the technique notably hinges not on its lack of effectiveness but on its obviation of the patient's conscious agency. In Zubkov's somewhat sensationalized account, conditional-reflex therapy worked (perhaps too well) but failed in that it figured the patient as a bundle of reflexes.

Unsurprisingly, the treatment was extremely unpopular with patients. During his brief periods of freedom Sasha had experienced a variety of treatments for alcoholism, including conditional-reflex therapy:

In 1980, I was in a psychiatric hospital, and they started to treat me with so-called apomorphine. They gave me three injections in the shoulder, gave me some vodka to smell and gave a small bit to drink, which caused spasms of nausea. But after three or four courses, the doctors stopped this because my organism couldn't go through it. I was turning green, and I was feeling nauseous, not so much because of the vodka they had me smell or drink, but because the poison itself [apomorphine] had a horrible effect on me. So they said it was contraindicated for me.

Because the effectiveness of the therapy was thought to depend on the extreme unpleasantness of the experience, conditional-reflex therapy fit particularly well into the institutions of Soviet narcology that functioned under a logic of coercion. Thus while it was recommended in the general narcology service, the use of conditional-reflex therapy was mandated in punitive institutions such as the therapeutic-labor prophylactories. Tamara Metelkina, a narcologist who currently runs a small noncommercial addiction rehabilitation center outside St. Petersburg, worked during the mid-1980s in a *spetskombinatura*—a clinic attached to a factory to which recidivists were committed. At the time, the use of conditional-reflex therapy was also mandated in such institutions.

> Even by the textbooks of the time, it was clear to me that the patient must be motivated to be treated by this method—a situation you obviously didn't have in the spetskombinatura. . . . Often it was not alcoholism that these people had but "lifestyle drunkenness" [*bytovoe p'ianstvo*].[4] There were psychopaths and sociopaths, and it was very difficult to get into contact with these people. They saw me as a police figure. Nevertheless, I started to do some psychotherapy and some group therapy. . . . Then as soon as we started to do the conditional-reflex therapy all of the contacts were broken. People would rather go to prison than go through these procedures.[5]

Metelkina argued that the treatment was both deeply unethical—"I felt that it went against the Hippocratic oath of 'do no harm,'"—and, even by its own criteria, ineffective: "The patients never developed the reflex." Yet her chief concern was that while conditional-reflex therapy was assumed by its proponents to work on an amoral and precognitive animal body— as she put it, "This only made sense on the level of a dog or a rat"—in fact, any potential effectiveness depended on patients' motivation. This blindness of the therapy, and of the institution surrounding it, to the psyche of the patient was particularly demoralizing for Metelkina, who had originally trained as a physician with the intention of practicing psychotherapy, which she envisioned as requiring adequate intersubjective contact with patients. Conditional-reflex therapy shattered the fragile ties she had begun to cultivate with her psychopaths and sociopaths and eviscerated of any significant meaning the distinctions between therapy and punishment and between physician and police figure.

The appeal of conditional-reflex therapy for officials who *were* police figures, by formal position and by disposition, is not difficult to imagine. Less obvious are the sources of the technique's popularity with public health officials and many physicians. For one thing, during a period when political elites sought to portray the autonomy and difference of Soviet science from "bourgeois science," conditional-reflex therapy could be claimed as largely, if not wholly, a domestic development. Not only was the therapy based on Pavlov's theory of reflexes, but in an official culture highly focused on the applicability of science, it served as a clear demonstration that this theory could bear practical applications (Zhislin and Lukomskii 1963). Moreover, conditional-reflex therapy was consistent with the dominant medical conceptions of behavior. Since the theory of reflexes functioned as the officially condoned paradigm for understanding the mechanism through which behavior was learned, clinical techniques that sought to condition new reflexes appeared to be promising means for controlling unwanted habits. More specifically, conditional-reflex therapy seemed to restore and generalize the primary diagnostic sign of alcoholism: the loss of the vomiting reflex.

The technique was also easily adaptable to use with large groups of patients, presumably making it attractive both to ideologists and to planners interested in economies of scale. Not only did this method make the technology amenable to use in large hospitals and penal institutions by allowing several physicians to simultaneously treat dozens of patients, but the groups were thought to bolster the conditioning effect of the procedure. Grigorii Mikhailovich, the medical director of the addiction hospital, explained, "There were apomorphine sessions—there were these special rooms, give everyone a swab to smell, inject everyone, and everyone puked, all in a choir—a communist choir." This narcologist's depiction was only half joking: forms of group therapy were often described as congruent with Soviet values of collectivism (Babayan 1985, 98).

By the time of my fieldwork, conditional-reflex therapy was no longer in use in St. Petersburg. Along with labor colonies for alcoholics and laws allowing for compulsory treatment, it had been swept away during the brief period of the early 1990s when an enthusiasm for liberalism and human rights reigned in Russia. However, it persisted as an institutional memory, frequently evoked by narcologists in conversations about the relative failings and merits of their profession during the Soviet period. Often, drawing a distinction between the therapy and the conditions under which it had been practiced was a way of retrospectively distinguishing narcology from punishment and policing, an attempt to salvage an ethical stance for medicine. Thus while some narcologists claimed that conditional-reflex therapy was entirely ineffective or that it worked "too well," Grigorii Mikhailovich felt that it had simply been practiced under the wrong clinical conditions:

And this conditional-reflex therapy did not hold for long. At first the treatment worked very well. Very well. But then when people got some experience. . . . The alcoholics—many of them were forced into this method of treatment. In other words, without his agreement and conviction—but just in those times of the LTP. . . . You should have convinced people of this— that this method would help them. But when it was forced, he didn't have conviction and after that they would destroy this reflex. So a good method was discredited, because there wasn't a normal selection [of patients].

For Grigorii Mikhailovich, conditional-reflex therapy had become discredited because of improper patient selection: instead of being performed on motivated patients who had consented to the treatment, the method had been used on those committed to compulsory hospitalization and treatment. Moreover, his concern over the discrediting of conditional-reflex therapy reflects a broader set of issues that Russian narcologists grapple with. For him, and for many other narcologists, a therapy's effectiveness is wrapped up not only with medical criteria of pathology and wellness or even with issues of consent but with the clinical settings within which it circulates and the legal categories that facilitate their existence. Such concerns reveal not only the importance of the legitimacy of therapies to patients and physicians alike but the degree to which this legitimacy often depends on the institutional contexts and political meanings with which those therapies are associated.

Somatic Suggestions

As I have mentioned, when I brought up khimzashchita—the umbrella term for disulfiram-based interventions—in my conversations with narcologists, some initially represented it as a pharmacological treatment, while others depicted it as psychotherapy. Irina Valentinovna, a narcologist in the acute ward of the addiction hospital explained it this way:

Khimzashchita is a psychotherapeutic method. In principle, we give a regular [medication]—you can also give a placebo—this depends on the personality of the patient—and either we use a placebo or the chemical. . . . I give you this medication. I give you a prohibition [*zapret*] through personal psychotherapy [*lichnostnaia psikhoterapiia*]: for a certain period of time you don't have the right to consume alcohol [*spirtnoe*]. If he waits through the period, then we do another one. His self-image rises.

While it was clear that khimzashchita was meant to help facilitate what narcologists called periods of "remission" (sobriety) for patients, it seemed from Irina Valentinovna's description that the chemical content of the medication (disulfiram or placebo) mattered less than the meanings enacted by the narcologist and her clinical tools. I found myself both troubled by the deception seemingly entailed by this blithe equation of placebo with disulfiram and fascinated by the questions it raised. Was khimzashchita a somatic or a psychological treatment?

As depicted to patients and the public, khimzashchita relies on the effects of disulfiram, a chemical often referred to in Russia as *teturam* or Esperal', and elsewhere as Antabuse.[6] Disulfiram prevents the body from fully processing alcohol. By blocking the action of aldehyde dehydrogenase, a key enzyme in the metabolic pathway of ethanol, the drug causes a buildup of the toxic by-product acetaldehyde, with extremely unpleasant consequences for patients. Rather than the pleasurable effects of alcohol intoxication, people with active disulfiram in their bodies experience flushing, nausea, and high blood pressure soon after drinking—referred to in the medical literature as a disulfiram-ethanol reaction (DER) (Kenna, McGeary, and Swift 2004; Mann 2004).

The aversive physiological effects of disulfiram, which was originally used in the manufacture of synthetic rubber, had been common knowledge to those in the industry but were first noted by medical researchers in the mid-1930s (Williams 1937). A decade later two Danish researchers accidentally rediscovered these effects and subsequently developed the chemical as a treatment for alcoholism (Hald and Jacobsen 1948; Martensen-Larsen 1948; White 1998, 226–27). Over the subsequent seventy years disulfiram has played divergent roles in the public health and medical systems of various countries, reflecting differences in local psychiatric models of alcohol dependence and institutional and political economic conditions as well as notions about individual willpower and personal responsibility (Chick and Brewer 1999). For example, while it continues to serve as the cornerstone of alcoholism treatment in Denmark, the prevalence of its use in North America has long since waned (White 1998; Steffen 2005).[7]

Though disulfiram is often portrayed as the first pharmacological treatment for alcoholism, the mechanism underlying its effects has been described and classified in several significantly different ways, and these accounts are linked to specific clinical uses of the drug. Researchers framing disulfiram as a pharmacological rather than a behavioral treatment—particularly its early proponents—often described it as a "sensitizing" drug (e.g., Hald and Jacobsen 1948; Martensen-Larsen 1948; Ivanets 2001). Conversely, contemporary researchers argue that unlike more recently developed pharmacological treatments for alcoholism, such as naltrexone and acamprosate, the efficacy of which is based on a neurochemical dampening of patients' craving, the effects of disulfiram are psychologically mediated (Kenna, McGeary, and Swift 2004). Some researchers argue that disulfiram is meant to "create an aversion to alcohol, rather than modulate its neurochemical effects" (Mann 2004, 489), while others emphasize that it has immediate effects on behavior "by replacing delayed with immediate negative consequences" (Heather 1989, 471). In either case, we can conclude that it is a patient's anticipation or memory—whether conscious, unconscious, or bodily—of an unpleasant or frightening experience that is meant to change his behavior. As the authors of one English-language review argue, "When taken in an adequate dose, disulfiram usually deters the drinking of alcohol *by the threat or experience of an unpleasant reaction*" (Brewer, Meyers, and Johnsen 2000, 329, emphasis added).

As a pharmacological therapy that seems to work primarily by non-pharmacological means, disulfiram occupies an uneasy position in the biomedical literature and clinical practice. With a few exceptions, most researchers writing in the English-language literature refer to disulfiram as having "nonspecific or placebo effects" with some trepidation, or as evidence for its overall *ineffectiveness*. In part, this has to do with the deeply ambivalent attitude that most of biomedicine has taken toward treatment outcomes that are not attributable to a specific material cause, as well as to the subjective dimensions of human experience (Harrington 2006, 2008; Kirmayer 2006).[8]

As I have argued, however, the Russian/Soviet genealogy of ideas about suggestion and healing is radically different from its counterpart in the English-speaking world, and this had important consequences for the reception of disulfiram in the Soviet Union. The Danish developers of disulfiram therapy had initially employed it as a form of aversion therapy, and this style of treatment fell on particularly fertile ground in the Soviet Union (Hald and Jacobsen 1948; Martensen-Larsen 1948). When Soviet medical researchers first began to experiment with disulfiram during the late 1940s, their model for thinking about treatment for chronic alcoholism was conditional-reflex therapy. Indeed, many of the earliest publications about disulfiram in the Soviet medical literature were authored by the aforementioned Ivan Vasil'evich Strel'chuk (Strel'chuk 1951, 1952; Miroshnichenko, Pelipas, and Ivanets 2001, 139). Not only were patients told of the potential negative effects of drinking alcohol while on the drug, but these effects were demonstrated to them in physician-administered tests (Strel'chuk 1952; Babayan and Gonopolsky 1985). Writing at the height of the Pavlovian orthodoxy in Soviet psychiatry, Strel'chuk added that the drug induced in patients a "negative conditioned reflex to alcohol," and this reflex was observed even in "patients who had not taken Antabuse in nearly a year" (Strel'chuk 1952, 49). In other words, Pavlovian psychiatry's style of reasoning allowed researchers to conceive of patients as having the intended physiological reaction to disulfiram in the absence of the drug itself.

This awareness of physical effects without chemical intervention gave Soviet medical researchers and clinicians a means of managing one of disulfiram's major shortcomings as a therapy—namely, the problem of compliance. Although many studies have shown disulfiram therapy to be a potentially effective means of increasing the lengths of patients' remissions, adherence represents the major obstacle to efficacy (Fuller and Gordis 2004; Suh et al. 2006). Once ingested, the medication remains at chemically active levels for only several days, which means that patients must take the drug regularly in order for the threat of an adverse reaction to alcohol to remain (Eneanya et al. 1981; Brewer, Meyers, and Johnsen 2000, 331). While this may not represent a problem for highly motivated patients, for many others the challenge of adhering to this treatment is as great as that of abstaining from alcohol itself (Valverde 1998, 99; Steffen 2005, 180). In general, disulfiram therapy is most effective when a relative or clinician is able to monitor or supervise the patient's consumption of the medication (Brewer, Meyers, and Johnsen 2000; Fuller and Gordis 2004).[9]

However, in the absence of a need for the chemical itself, the issue of compliance became potentially more manageable. Strel'chuk's negative conditioned reflex to alcohol would persist regardless of one's daily motivation because it was conceptualized as operating on a bodily level. It is perhaps not altogether surprising that by the late 1960s, Soviet researchers were reporting clinical experiments with the use of placebo therapy, literally the replacement of the drug with a saline solution or vitamins (Ialovoi 1968). This was originally intended for patients for whom the drug was contraindicated, but the use of such placebo-therapy became increasingly widespread over the following decades (Fleming, Meyroyan, and Klimova 1994).

In a different attempt to manage this problem of treatment adherence, the method of implanting capsules of disulfiram subcutaneously was developed in France during the 1950s (Kline and Kingstone 1977; White 1998, 228). Here agency for adherence was shifted from either the patient or his caretaker and structured into the implant, which was meant to gradually release the chemical into the bloodstream. Significantly, clinical studies have shown that no disulfiram or ALDH inhibition is detectable in patients soon after the insertion of commercially available implants (Johnsen and Morland 1992; Brewer, Meyers, and Johnsen 2000). In other words, after the first week following the implantation of the disulfiram capsule, patients are highly unlikely to suffer from a DER. At the same time, since the early 1970s, researchers studying disulfiram implants have noted their effectiveness relative to unsupervised oral disulfiram, and most have agreed that such effects were due to a "psychological rather than a pharmacological deterrent" (Malcolm, Madden, and Williams 1974, 488; Kline and Kingstone 1977).

In the Soviet Union subdermal implants of the French Esperal' quickly became the most popular application of disulfiram: patients would have a capsule implanted behind their shoulder blades and warned of possible adverse effects from taking alcohol for a period from one to five years (Fleming, Meyroyan, and Klimova 1994). While other placebo therapies were also used, such as the tablet and the torpedo (these were represented to patients as oral and intravenous forms of long-acting disulfiram, respectively), implantation was by far the most popular (Chepurnaya and Etkind 2006). Among patients and relatives the therapy was referred to colloquially as an "implant" (*podshivka*), and patients would commonly say, "I was implanted" (*menia podshili*). Such treatment remained extremely common among patients I spoke to in 2004, and some returned regularly for repeat implantations.

In short, whereas clinical phenomena described as suggestion, placebo, or nonspecific effects have long posed an epistemological challenge for a somatically grounded biomedicine, many of the narcologists I spoke to in St. Petersburg emphasized precisely these aspects of disulfiram treatment. Narcologists such as Irina Valentinovna explicitly described khimzashchita as placebo therapy or as a treatment that depends on mechanisms of suggestion (*vnushenie*). As one physician working in a commercial addiction clinic put it, "In addition to the purely chemical effect [of disulfiram], there is an effect of suggestion [*Effekt vnusheniia*]."

However, clinical interpretations of disulfiram treatment had also shifted subtly throughout the Soviet period. Although the treatment had first been conceptualized in the Soviet Union as an aversive treatment like conditional-reflex therapy, its transformation into khimzashchita involved several key shifts. Whereas conditional-reflex therapy hinged on patients' bodily memories of past experiences, khimzashchita worked on their anticipation of potential future consequences. Moreover, while the former depended on a behavioral response to stimuli administered within the walls of the clinic, the latter transposed the source of this stimulus into patients' own bodies, in the form of implantations or injections. Underlying these was an even more fundamental conceptual shift: whereas conditional reflex therapy depicted the patient as a body responsive to inherently meaningless stimuli, khimzashchita assumed a subject replete with expectations, emotions, and beliefs. This way of thinking about khimzashchita foregrounded its similarities to the popular mode of treatment called kodirovanie—a treatment that had emerged from the same clinical styles of reasoning.

Kodirovanie: Dovzhenko's Gift

The direct antecedent to kodirovanie was emotional-stress psychotherapy, developed by the psychiatrist and medical administrator Vladimir Evgen'ievich Rozhnov during the 1970s.[10] Rozhnov wrote widely on psychotherapy and hypnosis. In two books aimed at an educated lay audience (*Prophets and Miracle-Workers: Studies of Mysticism* and *Hypnosis: From Ancient Time to Our Day*), he traced the familiar narrative of hypnosis and faith healing from Mesmer through Charcot but placed his own work on hypnotic suggestion in the line of objective research following the thinking of Pavlov and Bekhterev (Rozhnov 1977; Rozhnov and Rozhnova 1987). In his writings on psychotherapy for clinicians, Rozhnov argued that partly as a result of the research on trauma that emerged from the Great Patriotic War (World War II), physiologists had come to understand that "stress is not only negative, but may be positive as well" (Babayan 1985, 111).[11] In emotional-stress psychotherapy, "the physician, displaying a beneficial worry in his interactions with the patient, sets off in the latter a healing emotional reaction, at the basis of which lies stress as an exertion of the organism's adaptive strengths" (Rozhnov and Burno 1987). In practice, this "stress response," which Rozhnov was careful to distinguish from "fear," was induced in a number of ways, ranging from alternating hot and cold baths to treatment with emetics (along the lines of conditional-reflex therapy) to the words of the therapist (Rozhnov 1989). Much of Rozhnov's clinical research focused on applying this theoretical framework to the treatment of alcoholics (Rozhnov 1987).

The method that came to be known specifically as kodirovanie, however, was not Rozhnov's but a technique developed during the 1970s by Alexander Romanovich Dovzhenko (1918–95), a physician working in Feodosia, a town on the Crimean peninsula (Miroshnichenko, Pelipas, and Ivanets 2001). Dovzhenko described his technique as an "express" method of emotional-stress psychotherapy, which he claimed yielded positive results after a single session. The method was similar to khimzashchita in its structure and underlying assumptions about the person. Writing in the main Soviet psychiatric journal during the late 1980s, Dovzhenko and his colleagues stated, "It is suggested to patients [*bolnym vnushaetsia*] that the efforts of doctor, with the help of a set of "hypnotic" and physiogenic actions on their brains, will create a stable center of excited nerve cells, which from the moment of "coding" will block their craving for alcohol for a given length of time—1 year, 5, 10, 25 years or longer" (Dovzhenko et al. 1988, 94). Typically, patients were subsequently warned of the dire or deadly consequences of drinking before the end of the code and encouraged to come in for "decoding" if they decided to drink (Fleming, Meyroyan, and Klimova 1994).

Dovzhenko created a local following for himself in Feodosia during the 1970s and early '80s, with patients traveling there for treatment from throughout the Soviet Union. His method soon gained official sanction by the Soviet Ministry of Health, and it gained increasing popularity in the mid-1980s, particularly in the wake of the anti-alcohol campaign, when Dovzhenko claimed in print to have obtained over 68 percent efficacy (number of patients in remission one year after the therapy) (Dovzhenko et al. 1988). These claims did not go unchallenged. In medical journals Dovzhenko's method was dismissed as quick-fix quackery by proponents of Rozhnov's emotional-stress psychotherapy, while others came to the defense of the treatment (Voskresenskii 1990; Entin 1991; Lipgart, Goloburda, and Ivanov 1991). Despite these controversies, the use of Dovzhenko's method became increasingly common; during the early 1990s, nearly 10 percent of patients on narcological registers in Russia were counted as receiving a treatment of this kind—a figure that was almost certainly an underestimate (Entin et al. 1997). Dovzhenko also received ample official recognition: he was named a People's Doctor of the USSR, and after his death in 1995 a monument to his memory was erected in Feodosia. Since then a number of Dovzhenko's students (several of whom are also his family members) have plied their trade throughout the former Soviet Union, all making adjustments to the method while claiming authority through their association with the late master (Dovzhenko 1994; Grigoriev 2002).

A central reason for the success of Dovzehnko's method was its amenability to commodification at a particular moment in late Soviet history. Portraits of Dovzhenko often depict him in a clinician's white coat, embroidered with his initials, D.A.R., which, when read as a word—*dar*—means "gift" in Russian. As we shall see, this notion of the therapy as a gift from clinician to patient was central to the meanings ascribed to kodirovanie and particularly to the way that the clinician's will or agency was depicted as acting on or over that of the patient. However, the notion of kodirovanie as gift also has a highly ironic undertone, as the method was first popularized during the period of perestroika when cooperatives became the first officially sanctioned profit-generating entities in the Soviet Union since the New Economic Policy of the early 1920s. With its promise of a rapid and simple treatment for alcoholism, as well as one that could be applied to auditoriums of patients, Dovzhenko's method was quickly seized upon by pioneers of for-profit medicine and soon became closely associated with commercial narcology.

Narcologists have suggested that the early commercial success of kodirovanie was facilitated by the general fascination with mass hypnosis that flourished during the final years of the Soviet Union (Sofronov 2003). The most memorable representative of this period was the mass hypnotist Anatolii Kashpirovsky (also trained as a medical doctor), who conducted his séances in packed auditoriums (Lindquist 2005, 36). While some cultural critics and observers have interpreted this phenomenon as a case of elite-engineered distraction for the masses, others have regarded it more broadly as symptom of "an unstable time of apocalyptic expectations" (Etkind 1997a, 119).

Though a sudden interest in all things spiritual and esoteric is typically associated with the perestroika period, many scholars have shown that such practices had been slowly percolating for years under late socialism. Not only was interest in Russian folk culture and Orthodoxy slowly growing during the 1970s (often framed in terms of legitimate social movements, connected to ecological conservation and historical preservation), but interest in yoga and Eastern philosophies was also developing (in the former case, at least partly facilitated by the Soviet Union's strategic relationship with India). During the late 1970s several Soviet authors began to publish texts on such topics—an interest fed by officially sanctioned work on hypnosis, suggestion, and "autotraining" (Lauterbach 1984; Honey 2006; Lindquist 2005, 30–33).

In either case, even as such phenomena lost their luster of newness during the 1990s, they became increasingly institutionalized and rooted (forming into more coherent movements), and they had particularly profound effects on narcology as a social and discursive field. At the same time as the institutional basis emerged for the establishment of social movements based on these spiritual and religious worldviews, it became possible to commodify these practices—in the form of various healing services. Suddenly official narcology found itself competing with a variety of different practitioners. The anxiety that this combination of nonbiomedical healing and commercial medicine aroused in many narcologists is evident in this (entirely typical) excerpt from a professional article:

> A strong competitor to the state narcological service has appeared: in the guise of physicians in private practice, folk healers [*narodnykh tselitelei*], sorcerers [*koldunov*], shamans, psychics [*ekstrasensov*] and other enterprising agents, offering sufferers such services and guarantees that a serious doctor couldn't dream of: 100% curing [*izlechenie*] after one séance, "guaranteed by

a patent of the Russian Federation"; treatment without the knowledge or consent of the patient (which, by the way, is a breach of article 32 of "Legislation of the Russian Federation on the protection of citizens' health"); the fantastic "*narkodel*,"[12] and much much more. (Egorov 1996, 68)

Though more established Russian institutions such as the Orthodox Church have also begun to offer addiction counseling and rehabilitation, they have been much slower in doing so than the myriad of small spiritual groups and practitioners representing relatively new faiths and ideologies. It is important to note that throughout the 1990s a somewhat hysterical discourse surrounding the burgeoning number of "cults" and "totalitarian sects" was prevalent in Russia, driven both by a concern over the unscrupulous practices of certain religious groups and by the Orthodox Church's strong antisectarian campaign (Egortsev 1997; Borenstein 1999). The Church of Scientology, with its explicit antipsychiatric ideology and special drug addiction rehabilitation program, was a particularly strong source of anxiety for narcologists and public health officials alike.

Jean and John Comaroff (1999) have described a seemingly global upwelling of witchcraft epidemics, pyramid schemes, spirit possession, and moral panics as symptoms of what they called "occult economies"— inchoate articulations of discontent in postcolonial and postsocialist societies with the mysteriousness and immateriality of global capitalism by those who find the wealth produced in this process unattainable. Whereas these phenomena echoed earlier practices documented by ethnographers— through which people domesticated or resisted novel and threatening political economic forms, such as wage labor and money (Taussig 1980; Ong 1988; Parry and Bloch 1989)—occult economies emerged in "societies in which an optimistic faith in free enterprise encounters, for the first time, the realities of neoliberal economics" (Comaroff and Comaroff 1999, 294). Arguably, what unites these phenomena is not so much their supernatural or occult character as their evocation of a social world manipulated by invisible agents. It is in this sense that Katherine Verdery compared *talk* about mafia in postsocialist Europe (as distinct from the practices of using force to accumulate capital) to *talk* about witchcraft, as "a way of attributing difficult social problems to malevolent and unseen forces" (1996, 220).

Such discourses can be interpreted not only in this diagnostic mode but also, insofar as they articulate ideas about agency, authority, and social change, in terms of the way they shape the meaning of therapeutic methods and thus bear very concretely on the clinical setting. In this sense, debates about the ethical—and indeed political—significance of therapies become an important aspect of a broader therapeutic economy. Indeed, politically tinged ascriptions of agency have figured centrally in debates about the correct or incorrect uses of kodirovanie, as well as the ways in which different practitioners have transformed the technique. In short, while the flourishing of late and post-Soviet practices of mass hypnosis and interest in the occult fueled the popularity of kodirovanie for a certain time, it also created a problem of legitimacy for its practitioners, as we shall see.

Performing and Materializing Therapy

Though most narcologists who practiced kodirovanie or khimzashchita did not think of themselves as engaged in the same line of work as someone like Kashpirovsky, they were especially attentive to the performative elements of the clinical encounter and how the meanings that patients ascribed to clinical objects and substances shaped the effectiveness of therapies. For example, both khimzashchita and kodirovanie procedures began with the narcologist's describing the treatment to his patient. As Anton Denisovich made clear when he explained khimzashchita to me as he would have to a patient, delivering a compelling depiction of the treatment's physiological effects was particularly important. Of course, as Anton Denisovich himself acknowledged, his description of the treatment was often untrue in a referential sense, as he often used placebos in place of disulfiram. Like other narcologists, he treated such descriptions as means of fostering in the patient a particular belief (that a chemical agent in his body has made the consumption of alcohol potentially deadly), an accompanying affective state (that of fear, stress, or concern), and a consequent behavioral change (abstinence). Perhaps most important, a central idea implicit in such treatments is that clinical effectiveness depends on patients' belief in this "truth" about their bodies, a condition that the statements are meant to bolster.

Similarly, the forms that patients are subsequently asked to sign in order to acknowledge that they understand the procedure and its risks often function performatively, as props that aid the physician in delivering the intended effect as much as contracts meant to inform the patient and verify his consent. Thus, regarding these "signed papers warning patients about the health- and life-threatening consequences that can occur in the event of alcohol consumption during the duration of a 'code,'" the authors of an article defending narcological therapies explained that "one should not view these papers as fraud, easily unmasked by patients," adding that they have a "psychotherapeutic" character (Entin et al. 1997, 73–74).

After these key preliminary steps, the clinical interaction at the core of the treatment takes place. Many clinicians emphasized the significance of ritually marking the beginning of the patient's sobriety in a clearly defined manner. "To code a patient [*zakodirovat'*]," explained one narcologist, "is to bring him into a hypnotic trance and to build in [*provesti*] a certain stopping place [*ostanovochnyi moment*]." Such a temporal demarcation is particularly important in the case of kodirovanie, and a protocol for carrying it out was included in Dovzhenko's description of his method: "The doctor closes the patient's eyes with his hand, and pushes the patient's head back with his other hand. For 2–5 sec he presses on the supraorbital region until pain is produced, and then he sprays ethyl chloride into the patient's mouth, producing various somatic symptoms" (Fleming, Meyroran, and Klimova 1994, 360; cf. Elovich 2008, 14–15).

Alexander Sergeevich, a narcologist at the addiction hospital, explained in strikingly clear terms how such a clinical performance is key to that stage of khimzashchita and kodirovanie alike:

> Everything hinges on one short action, either in kodirovanie or in our methods of placebo therapy: in other words a small ritual [*malen'kii ritual'chik*]. Either a touching of hands to the head, some kind of words, the use of some substance that gives a sensation: maybe a local anesthetic is poured into the throat. This ritual just signifies a point in time when the period of sobriety begins. This exists in all versions of psychotherapy.

It is worth noting that, like others at St. Petersburg's addiction hospital, Alexander Sergeevich did not regard himself as an "alternative" practitioner but rather as a mainstream psychiatrist-narcologist. His account further highlights the degree to which the disciplinary assumptions of narcology attuned clinicians to view performance as part of their practice. Alexander Sergeevich emphasized the importance of ritual form over content (physical contact, words, and substance are interchangeable) in producing a meaningful temporal demarcation of a new period of sobriety for patients. Under this logic, narcologists' and patients' preference for implantations and injections over daily self-administered tablets takes on an additional significance, since such methods of application allow for yearly or half-yearly markings of "sober time."

Whereas kodirovanie relies on the charisma ascribed to the practitioner himself or herself, in the case of khimzashchita, the source of what Daniel Moerman (2002) has called the "meaning response" lies largely in the implant, injection, or tablet itself, or, more precisely, in the set of meanings given to the drug. Thus many of the patients with whom I discussed khimzashchita repeatedly spoke about the material aspects of the treatment: the size of the ampoules, the place on their bodies where Esperal' was implanted, the mode of administration—patients ascribed particular meanings to all these characteristics, which in turn mediated their assumptions about the potential efficacy of the therapy. "They have ampoules, about this size and bigger ones," Vyacheslav explained when I asked him to describe the treatment, indicating the size with his fingers. Torpedo injections were typically dyed a bright pink or blue to signify their chemical potency (Fleming, Meyroyan, and Klimova 1994, 360). The mode of administration was certainly important as well: the fact that patients and their families generally preferred implants to injections, which in turn they preferred to tablets, suggests that more physically invasive methods of administration may also have been associated with greater efficacy or potency. At the same time that they replaced disulfiram with vitamin C, saline, or other neutral substances, narcologists used various methods to reinforce patients' interpretation of the treatment as chemically potent. A narcologist interviewed by Chepurnaya and Etkind (2006) explained that he sometimes carried out sham surgery on patients—making and sewing up an incision without implanting anything—and then prescribed chemically active disulfiram tablets, telling the patients they were taking an antibiotic.

Patients also recognized the objects and substances used in khimzashchita as commodities, and they often linked the drug's potency and value to its geographical point of production. One such account came from Sasha, a patient in his late forties first described in chapter 1, who had spent the majority of his life imprisoned for acts (mainly burglary) committed while intoxicated. Sasha was a typical candidate for implanted disulfiram, the mode of treatment that was particularly popular for those categorized as noncompliant by their relatives or physicians. Sasha recounted how, after a drinking binge landed him in the hospital during the early 1980s, his mother had suggested that he try an Esperal' implantation. Obtaining imported pharmaceuticals (Esperal' was manufactured in France) during the Soviet period typically meant circumventing formal channels to draw on extensive networks of contacts—a practice known as *blat*—and Sasha's mother had ordered the implant through a physician friend (Ledeneva 1998). As was the case with many goods and services, the scarcity of such pharmaceuticals, the effort and access required to obtain them, as well as their place of origin, all added to their value—and in this case, their perceived potency.

By 2000 the availability of these substances had changed (typically the chief obstacle for patients was now a lack of money rather than a lack of access), but many patients and physicians continued to ascribe greater potency to implants imported from France or elsewhere than to their domestic equivalents. One patient recounted the choice he had heard a doctor offering an acquaintance: "[The narcologist] says: 'I can give you our domestic [*otechestvennaia*] khimzashchita—it costs 1,900 rubles [about $65]. I can't guarantee that it will work, if you drink that something will happen. Or I can put in the French one—that one costs [significantly more]. This is a 100 percent variant.'" In ascribing greater potency to imported disulfiram over the Russian-made variety, physicians and patients employed a common form of postsocialist consumer judgment that links material value to an object's geographical place of production (Patico 2002). Moreover, they implicitly translated commodity value into a judgment of potential clinical value or efficacy. This logic was encouraged by narcologists who spoke about the value and price of khimzashchita as a clinical consideration. Its cost was often linked to the length of time for which the patient was prohibited from drinking, and some physicians described the cost of a therapy as an important element motivating patients to take their sobriety more seriously (Chepurnaya and Etkind 2006, par. 32).

Professional Nuances

Among the therapies offered at the addiction hospital, khimzashchita was a particularly delicate topic for many narcologists. While some spoke about the use of placebo therapy without trepidation, in many cases bringing up the topic of placebos led to moments of doubt—during which physicians assessed whether I already knew about placebo therapy, or what I knew. These moments were repeated in many of my interviews. There were awkward pauses and pained glances. When the subject came up during one conversation with two narcologists who worked in the same ward, the younger of the two repeatedly tried to move the conversation on, explaining that the difference between chemically active disulfiram and placebo was a meaningless technical detail, telling me, "These are already professional nuances." His older colleague, however, explained that the difference *was* significant and that it depended "on the psychological particularities of the patient." Some patients, he went on, either were afraid of the treatment or for some other reason were not suited for it. "A better fit for them is emotional-stress psychotherapy, which is accompanied by the application of, essentially a placebo."

Indeed, narcologists offered a number of explanations for how they chose to give patients neutral substances in place of disulfiram, suggesting a subtle moral and social calculus that underlay their reasoning about clinical effectiveness. Decisions to administer neutral substances were underpinned by judgments of particular patients and their capacity for adherence. A strong disulfiram reaction could indeed be deadly to some patients, and narcologists often sought to mitigate risks to their patients, as well as their own potential liability, by using placebo therapy. Although most verifiable accounts of patients dying from a DER seemed to be clear cases of negligence of the part of physicians, narcologists at the hospital framed noncompliant patients as the primary source of risk.[13]

Judgments about patients' potential for adherence in turn drew upon a categorization of patients based on their familial resources as well as an ascribed level of "social decline." In a 2001 textbook, Russia's head narcologist, Nikolai Ivanets, recommends the use of disulfiram only for the small contingent of patients who remain "socially conserved" (*sotsial'no sokhranen*), and argues against its use for the vast majority, which he characterizes as "the asocial type [*asotsial'nyi tip*] of alcoholic" (2001, 113–14). Narcologists I spoke to articulated a similar logic. For the physicians, this way of thinking rendered their perceptions of respectability and social status clinically relevant, as indexes of a patient's potential adherence. Socially conserved patients included those who had not (yet) lost their jobs or contact with their family members; they were viewed as having greater motivation for sobriety but also as possessing greater social and familial resources to facilitate adherence. "The real medications have so many side effects," explained one narcologist. "We give it if there is a mother or a wife who strictly makes sure that the patient is taking the medication. Then we give it." In other words, the use of chemical disulfiram in the clinic was often seen as dependent on a complementary (typically gendered) arrangement for its management in a domestic space.

Therapeutic Legitimacy and the Management of Belief

Whereas using disulfiram entailed certain risks for a particular category of patients, the efficacy of both placebo therapy and hypnosis or kodirovanie was also seen by narcologists as highly variable. Some argued that these methods were more effective among certain types of patients, typically identifiable by certain psychological characteristics. For narcologists, patients' suggestibility could be conceptualized as either an individual disposition or a generational characteristic. Older patients, or "Soviet people," were often described as being more suggestible than younger people, an ascription that draws on a common stereotype of the *sovok* or Homo Sovieticus as conformist and prone to manipulation by political propaganda.

At times, such patients were described in terms of their tendency or capacity for belief or faith (*vera*). Indeed, narcologists partook of a particular concept of belief that, as Byron Good has argued, is central to the empiricist paradigm underlying the "folk epistemology" of biomedicine (1994, 5). Implicitly dichotomizing belief and knowledge, most narcologists cast themselves as rational actors who "know" in contrast to patients who merely "believe." The disciplinary assumptions and clinical techniques of narcologists may have fostered a particular attention to the relationship between this belief and the effectiveness of khimzashchita and kodirovanie.

Even further, some physicians characterized belief in particular therapies as a sort of nonrenewable resource requiring careful management. Alexander Sofronov (2003), a well-respected professor of psychiatry at St. Petersburg's Military Medical Academy, argues that the popularity (among patients) of modes of treatment such as khimzashchita hinders the advancement of methods accepted throughout the world, particularly the 12-step program and the therapeutic community model. Sofronov describes clinical technologies of khimzashchita and kodirovanie as "explanatory medicine" (*ob"iasnennaia meditsina*), in which the patient's only source of knowledge or information is assumed to be the physician: "The way we explain it is how they'll be treated" (4). When I asked him to elaborate on this notion, he evoked a trope of a premodern medicine dependent on belief, referring to a scene from *Don Quixote* in which two physicians argue over the days of the week on which bloodletting is effective. As he saw it, narcology's focus on explanatory medicine derived from the secrecy that had surrounded alcoholism during the Soviet period: "Because the stigma of alcoholism was high, no one would brag about going to see a psychiatrist or narcologist in the way they would about a famous heart specialist. Within this climate patients had little choice but to believe in what the physicians told them."

Despite his misgivings, Sofronov regarded methods such as khimzashchita and kodirovanie in a highly pragmatic way. During a conversation in his office, he posed a rhetorical question about the popularity of such treatments: "Should we undermine this belief? Absolutely not!" While Sofronov thought that explanatory medicine blocked the growth of more effective modes of treatment, he also worried that the latter were not yet adequately developed or available to patients in Russia. Not only was it unethical to undermine patients' faith in khimzashchita under such conditions, but, as Sofronov implied, belief in the efficacy of treatments needed to be carefully managed.

In other words, if the effectiveness of khimzashchita and kodirovanie hinged partly on narcologists' skills of persuasion and performance in their face-to-face encounters with patients, it was equally dependent—as the physicians saw it—on their successful management of the treatments' broader representation to various publics as a pharmacological therapy, and as an effective one at that. This work of building and maintaining the treatment's legitimacy took place not only during narcologists' bedside chats with their patients but also in conversations with family members, in debates on the pages of medical journals and newspapers, and in arguments or offhand remarks made to this ethnographer.

For example, when I asked Vyacheslav's physician, Anton Denisovich, whether he ever administered chemical disulfiram, he replied, "You understand that we can't give every single person the placebo, because we'll discredit the method that way." Not only did this answer suggest a widespread anxiety that khimzashchita might easily lose its effectiveness by becoming associated with placebo therapy among patients, but his statement was itself aimed at maintaining the legitimacy of the therapy. Whether chemical disulfiram was ever used or not, it seemed that it was important to tell me that it was, at least sometimes, lest I depict the entire therapy as a sham, as others had done.

In working to legitimate khimzashchita and kodirovanie, physicians used multiple strategies, ranging from quoting statistics of efficacy (typically percentages of patients achieving year-long sobriety) to constructing origin stories for treatment modalities that linked them to Russia and depicted them as culturally appropriate. For example, the argument was sometimes made that it was appropriate for physicians to employ their professional authority to frighten patients because this clinical relationship reflected a particularly Russian form of authority. Moreover, as narcology in 2003–4 was a thoroughly commercialized sphere of medicine, in which practitioners competed fiercely for patients, claims about the efficacy of one's methods and medications were often interspersed with disparaging comments about one's competitors as manipulators, cult leaders, quacks, or even mentally ill. "You know he's a schizophrenic," exclaimed one physician at the hospital when I told her of my visit to a psychiatrist who incorporated spiritual and occult imagery into his practice.

Moreover, as we have seen, narcologists saw the therapeutic legitimacy of their methods as closely tied to the historical and institutional associations of those methods. As numerous narcologists explained to me, a treatment modality could easily be "discredited" through improper use—as Grigorii Mikhailovich argued had been the case with conditional-reflex therapy. Of course there was a time-tested strategy for dealing with this problem: distinguishing oneself from one's competitors as the bearer of the true method. This is what one psychiatrist in private practice did when he explained to me that his use of subliminal suggestion methods represented one of the few clinical uses of the real technology. The attempts of others he described, ironically enough, as "placebo therapy at best." Such strategies were particularly evident in the use of kodirovanie, in part because of the method's association with commercial mass hypnosis and unscrupulous practitioners.

The Healing Vow

On a Sunday morning during the summer of 2004 I attended a therapeutic session hosted by Grigorii Grigoriev, a self-styled "Orthodox psychotherapist" and his organization, the International Institute for Human Reserve Potential. More than fifty people sat waiting for the session to begin in the auditorium of a children's music school rented for the afternoon by the institute. Most, though not all, of the potential patients were men in their forties and were, almost as a rule, accompanied by relatives: in front of me sat a mother and son, to my left a husband, wife, and little boy of about six. In St. Petersburg, Grigoriev is known as a student of Dovzhenko's who has blended the scientism of the original method into a performance that draws heavily on Russian Orthodox language and symbolism.

Grigoriev's session began with a preliminary lecture delivered by an assistant—Dr. Vladimir Bolt, a short and stocky physician wearing a white coat and name badge. In Dovzhenko's original protocol for kodirovanie this phase was identified as group suggestion, during which patients were told about the basis of the therapy they were about to undergo. Bolt, who spoke with the pitch and cadence of an untrained public speaker, reflected some of the subtle shifts that had been made by Grigoriev in the original coding technique. In a move that both distanced him from increasing attacks on the legitimacy of kodirovanie and branded his technique as distinct, Grigoriev had dropped use of the term "coding" several years earlier; he called his therapy "the healing vow" (*tselebnyi zarok*). This therapy, Bolt assured his listeners (in a refrain that would be often repeated that afternoon), was different from khimzashchita: this was a form of psychotherapy. Nor was the method based on fear, he continued: "We don't want to frighten you. The idea is not to scare you with the negative consequences of breaking the vow, although there have been negative consequences to people's health, even death, and there will be, among people who break the vow."

Having delivered this dubious assurance, Bolt launched into a speech that portrayed alcohol consumption and addiction as poisons to the Russian national body and signs of an overall post-Soviet "degradation." Perhaps intending to distract the audience from the commercial nature of the meeting over which he was presiding, Bolt blamed the thousands of yearly deaths from alcohol poisoning on "the industry of lies" (*industriia obmana*) that profited. Then there was a break during which patients paid for the treatment.

In her work on contemporary Russian magic, Galina Lindquist (2006) shows that practitioners often employ multiple strategies to legitimate their practice, simultaneously foregrounding their personal charisma, drawing on sources of official biomedical legitimacy (for instance, emphasizing their degrees as medical doctors), and emphasizing the roots of their authority in traditional Russian medicine or their association with "the occult." On stage in front of the audience of potential patients, Grigoriev used all these strategies to great effect. Unlike the stilted and mumbling Dr. Bolt, Grigoriev immediately entered into a dialogue with his audience, speaking fluidly and seemingly off-the-cuff (although in fact he stuck quite closely to the published version of his lecture). The reaction of the audience was clear: they laughed at the appropriate moments, answered when asked questions, and listened intently throughout. Grigoriev's presentation was literally divided into two parts: he gave one, which concerned the medical hazards of alcoholism, wearing a white coat; for the second lecture, in which he equated physiological craving with the "temptation of Satan," he emerged in an all-black suit that, along with his long beard of the type worn by Orthodox priests, suggested a religious persona.

After the lectures, patients lined up outside several rooms for the individual portion of the coding therapy. Grigoriev allowed me to sit in the back of the room where he saw patients: "We have nothing to hide!" he exclaimed. To transform the atmosphere of the room, which was used during the week for music lessons and was largely taken up by two grand pianos, Grigoriev burned incense, which thickened the air with pungent smoke. Through the haze, I watched his black-clothed figure as he stood above a patient, murmuring a prayer, carrying out his amended version of the coding ritual.

Grigoriev had preserved the structure of Dovzhenko's ritual but replaced the biomedical representations entirely with religious ones drawn from official Russian Orthodoxy. After a short consultation with each patient, he began by reading a prayer in Church Slavonic. He did this very rapidly, standing over the seated patient while pressing his or her temples with his fingers. When the prayer was finished, he intoned, "Now you are released from the craving for alcohol [drugs; gambling]. Now you have made an oath [*zarok*] not to drink for [a given length of time]." Many of the men had vowed not to drink for the rest of their lives. Grigoriev concluded this ritual by making the sign of the cross over the patient's face with a small pencil ("in the name of the Father, Son and Holy Ghost") and touching their heads lightly with an anointing brush.

A Clinical Cult of Personality

Grigoriev's adaptation of the technique was more than a hybridization of scientific and religious symbolism; it addressed commonly voiced and politically inflected concerns regarding how kodirovanie framed the agency of patients. In their original protocol for kodirovanie, Dovzhenko and his colleagues described one of the goals of the therapy as the "formation of a 'cult of personality' around the doctor-psychotherapist [and] the illustration of the unique capabilities of his will-power" (1988, 94). While he purposefully employed the term used by Khrushchev to denounce Stalin's rule, Dovzhenko did not draw attention to its pejorative connotations. Rather, he suggested that this structure of authority, based on a particular form of charismatic authority, could be harnessed for therapeutic purposes. It was a matter not only of convincing the patient of the physician's personal power but of structuring a clinical relationship that ascribed all agency over the illness to the therapist. "The semantic ground for this method is the formula suggested to the patient, which can be summed up as 'not your (the patient's), but my (psychotherapist's) will frees you of this ailment [*nedug*]'" (95).

Some psychiatrists, such as Eugene Zubkov, dismissed the claims of kodirovanie as irrational: "What kind of code can they put in your head? It was all nonsense [*Bred vsë eto bylo*]. But for some reason everyone bought it." Yet a more commonly heard criticism simultaneously concerned ethics and efficacy. For instance, in their trenchant critique of narcology a Russian and British team drew on Dovzhenko's protocol to suggest that kodirovanie manipulated patients, leaving them with no sense of personal responsibility for their recovery. While the immediate concern of this argument was the lack of patient autonomy in the clinical encounter, Dovzhenko's reference to the cult of personality (and its citation in such critiques) raised the political trope of hypnotist as dictator. In an article about late Soviet psychotherapy, the cultural historian Alexander Etkind (himself trained as a psychologist at the Bekhterev Psychoneurological Research Institute) signals the deep genealogy of this trope in European thought, arguing that "hypnosis is obviously akin to the psychological mechanisms used to implement totalitarian power. It was not without reason that Freud compared a leader's power over the mob to a hypnotist's sway over his patient" (1997a, 118–19). In post-Soviet Russia such anxieties about agency and images of persons controlled from without often clustered around the figure of the cult leader (antisectarian literature reinforced this link in condemning totalitarian cults). Some patients and newspaper articles also referred to kodirovanie as a form of zombification (*zombirovanie*), another term common in discussions of cults.

Responding to such arguments, post-Soviet proponents and adapters of kodirovanie and other forms of hypnotic suggestion often reframe the therapy as one that ascribes agency to patients as autonomous persons. Writing in response to the article by Fleming's group (which had been translated and republished in the journal *Questions of Narcology*), a Russian team argued that the late Dovzhenko had used "mistaken" language and that criticizing his clinical technology by reference the original protocol was like "describing a contemporary engine using as one's evidence the patent received by German engineer R. Diesel for his invention of an engine in 1892" (Entin et al. 1997, 73). Rather than undercutting the patients' agency, they suggested that the core of what they called "mediating psychotherapy" (*oposredovannaia psikhoterapiia*, a term encompassing *kodirovanie* and *khimzashchita*) was that "the patient himself sets the length of time the drug or 'code' will act, that is, in advance he 'programs' himself, so to speak, for a given period of time, against the use of alcohol, agrees to this voluntarily and is inclined to begin with to carry out the responsibilities he has taken upon himself" (72). Drawing on the metaphor of brain as computer, the authors conceptualized the patient's agency or willpower as separate from the hardware of his brain, allowing him to "program his sobriety" (73).

While they continued to employ methods based on suggestive hypnosis and trance, many of the practitioners I met in the early 2000s had gone a step further and removed any mention of coding from their practice. A psychiatrist with a successful private practice who treated addiction through "body-oriented psychotherapy," suggestion, and his own "extraordinary powers" made this point in strikingly clear terms: "We don't use hypnosis:

this person stays fully conscious. He is in a state where he can get up and leave at any time. . . . Hypnosis is placing the will of the patient under the will of the physician. The main postulate of our work is that you are a free, independent, autonomous person."

Grigoriev's adaptation of kodirovanie dealt with these issues of agency in a slightly different way, by reframing the technique to (have at least the appearance of) a form of pastoral care. In his book *Healing with the Word* (*Istselenie Slovom*) Grigoriev legitimates this retooling with a revisionist history of kodirovanie. Arguing that Dovzhenko was an Orthodox believer forced by Soviet ideology to frame his method in a scientistic register, Grigoriev traces kodirovanie to techniques used prior to 1917 in the Alexander Nevsky sobriety brotherhood (Grigoriev 2002; Herlihy 2002). In doing so, Grigoriev suggests that Dovzhenko replaced the sermon with a clinical conversation, the service with a general séance, the confessional with an individualized meeting with the doctor, and the vow (*zarok*) of sobriety on the cross with a voluntary promise of the patient to the doctor not to drink for a certain period of time. Grigoriev claims simply to have returned each element of this method to its original form. He writes that Dovzhenko considered alcoholism a disease of the will and that his method was meant to strengthen (*ukrepit'*) the will and reorient it from "serving Satan to penitence before the Savior" (Grigoriev 2002).[14]

Although these changing depictions of physicians' and patients' relative agency may have had some limited bearing on clinical encounters and relationships in practice, their effects were heavily mediated by the social and economic capital of particular patients. To examine the variation in these relationships it is worth returning to the statement made by Anton Denisovich in describing his rationale for substituting neutral substances for disulfiram: "So it's better to give him a placebo and give him the gift of several months of sober life than to inject the real medication." Many analyses of the clinical relationship have examined the meanings and effects of gifts given by patients to their physicians, particularly in Russia, where such practices as common (e.g., Salmi 2003). In this case, Anton Denisovich— echoing Dovzhenko's imagery of care as gift—reversed these terms in describing his care for some patients through the metaphor of gifting, and arguably evoked many of the ambiguities of power and authority in the narcological clinical encounter. Like many narcologists, Anton Denisovich depicted himself as operating under an ethics of benevolence that, at times, was explicitly distinguished from a bureaucratic ethical regime of informed consent.

Such a dynamic was particularly evident with the most "hopeless" cases—patients viewed as abject, "declassed," or socially marginalized. Although such patients' relationships with physicians could be characterized as beneficent, critics of khimzashchita were more likely to label them paternalistic or even clientelistic. As a psychiatrist who worked promoting Alcoholics Anonymous in Russia put it, "Under the conditions of the market, the job of the doctor is to attach the patient to himself [*privezat' k sebe bol'nogo*], to make the patient dependent on him. And underlying this is the market and financial situation." Indeed, physicians' relationships with certain patients could be characterized as having a quality of dependency. Narcologists often instructed patients that they would have to return to the same practitioner if they decided to end their sobriety early by having a code or implant removed. In the case of patients for whom the only alternative to the hospital was life on the streets and in shelters, such dependencies could become particularly strong. Narcologists allowed some patients to reside at the hospital, occasionally discharging and readmitting them in order to comply with official limits on periods of hospitalization. Many of these patients performed menial tasks around the hospital; they spoke about their physicians in deeply deferential and respectful terms. Such relationships of dependence and moral indebtedness stood in stark contrast to those that narcologists maintained with patients who had relatively greater social and economic capital. These clinical interactions were structured more like commodity relationships, in which there was an exchange of alienable services for money and each party walked away with no obligations to the other.

In St. Petersburg during the period of my fieldwork, there was a distinct tension between the extremes of clinical care as beneficent gift or as commercial exchange. This tension reflected the themes of agency and responsibility, framed in opposing terms of dependence versus autonomy, which underlay many debates about addiction treatments in Russia during the 1990s and early 2000s. More broadly, the clinical relationship between narcologist and patient can be viewed in the context of the complex Russian political and social order under Putin, in which self-responsibility, initiative, and personal sovereignty continue to be affirmed as necessary traits within the economic sphere, even as markedly illiberal relationships of beneficence and obligation are affirmed within the political sphere (Rivkin-Fish 2005; Matza 2009). At the hospital and in other therapeutic spaces, however, the distinction between gift- and commodity-like clinical relationships was largely mediated by patients' social and economic capital, itself linked to the—often downward—trajectories of their lives.

Rumors, Doubts, and Productive Uncertainty

While some narcologists spoke about belief as a resource that they needed to manage with care, uncertainty seemed equally, if not more, productive an affect in the workings of both khimzashchita and kodirovanie. For example, Gleb, a middle-aged working-class patient in Anton Denisovich's ward, explained that he had been given a torpedo in the past but had not been able to wait until it ran its course and had begun drinking. He added that nothing happened as a result of his drinking during the course of the torpedo. Yet the fact that he had, contrary to the assurances of his narcologist, survived this relapse without any consequences did not lead Gleb to doubt the potential dangerousness of khimzashchita: "Before you take it you sign a paper saying that if you drink, the doctors are not responsible for what happens to you. You get it for a year, then you have to wait it out for a year. If you do it, you want to live. It's fine if it kills you: better that than it paralyzing you or something. *We don't know with these drugs.* That would be worse. So each person needs to use his brain" (emphasis added). Gleb's description evokes the state of uncertainty experienced by many patients in regard to the risks of khimzashchita. Indeed, many stories circulated in St. Petersburg about deaths caused by disulfiram. Some of these were offered by narcologists as condemnations of the rapacious commercial practices of their colleagues. Others had the quality of rumors or warnings: accounts by patients or their relatives told about acquaintances who had died because of khimzashchita. It was well known that the popular Soviet singer Vladimir Vysotsky had undergone implantations of Esperal' in attempts to control his drinking, and several apocryphal stories attributed his death in 1980 to a particularly serious disulfiram reaction. Many patients also spoke about the importance of having an implant removed before beginning to drink (Chepurnaya and Etkind 2006). Whatever the intentions of people who circulated such rumors, the narratives themselves played an important part in reinforcing the idea of khimzash-chita's potency.

For every story about the chemical potency of the treatment, however, there was another that attested to its *ineffectiveness* as a technique for counteracting disulfiram's effects. Dmitri, a 12-step counselor, showed me the scars that implantations of Esperal' had left on his body and explained that he had never waited through the term of the implant and never had one removed. "I would just start to drink. And nothing happened. Besides that, I knew that nothing would happen: everyone was constantly talking about this. They'd say, 'Forget it, just drink a little lemon juice.' There were all of these means to counteract it that they'd give out right away, even while you were still in the ward, getting ready for the operation. Even though I would wave these ideas away, they would sink in somewhere." Physicians recounted their own stories (typically told in a comic mode) about patients who tried to manually remove or destroy their implants by tearing at their shoulders or striking their backs with sticks.

Other patients characterized khimzashchita and kodirovanie as "nonsense" and "fraud." Eduard, an unemployed man in his midthirties, whom I met at the hospital, was one such patient. During the late Soviet period Eduard had worked as a *fartsovshchik*, a black market dealer of goods from capitalist countries such as blue jeans, but he had been unable to maintain steady work for several years. When I spoke to him, his arm was bandaged from a burn he had received while cooking drunk. Eduard was doubtful of any therapies and described how he had become disenchanted with kodirovanie:

> I went to the hypnotist [*kodirovshchik*]. He seemed all right, his office very nice, Euro-standard. So, how did I figure out that this was all fraud? Because when we were doing the last séance, he says to me: "Remember: blindness, paralysis, death. Anything can happen [if you drink]. If you want, come back and I'll remove the code. Don't do anything on your own by any means. Now my assistant will help me." A nurse comes in. In her pocket she has a little flashlight—I immediately noticed this. So the doctor mumbles and mumbles and then grabs my throat. He pushes me back and forth, back and forth and then I see a flash in my eyes. "That's it, you're coded. You saw the flash?" I said, "Yes, I saw it." "That is your code." I wanted to say to him, "Did you see the flashlight in her pocket?" But I decided not to say anything.

All these narratives contributed to patients' pervasive sense of uncertainty surrounding khimzashchita. Moreover, as Olga Chepurnaya and Alexander Etkind (2006) argue, in this manner, khimzashchita—as well as kodirovanie—harnessed the informal practices central to Soviet society (e.g., rumors, networks of acquaintances) to bring deviant and unruly individuals voluntarily under the power of the party-state. Though the political stakes are somewhat different in post-Soviet Russia, the uncertainty produced by the circulation of such rumors—whether they depicted these therapies as potent and effective or as inert and powerless—allowed them to remain viable. And yet, for narcologists the possibility always remained that this productive uncertainty might dissipate and a therapy would become discredited.

Ironically, the patients like Eduard who received placebo therapy because they were categorized as noncompliant were the very ones who were least likely to give credence to the potential efficacy of narcology's treatments. It is particularly interesting to compare Eduard's account with that of Gleb, who did not doubt the potential dangerousness of khimzashchita, despite having experienced no physiological effects as a result of a previous torpedo. Unlike Eduard, who was living on the margins of homelessness, Gleb resided with his family. Like Vyacheslav, Gleb had integrated khimzashchita into his domestic life.

As the contrasting accounts of Gleb and Eduard suggest, patients' dispositions toward the efficacy of these two therapies may be more shaped by the overall contexts of their lives, their motivations and hopes for sobriety, and the legitimacy they accord to medical institutions than by specific experiences of efficacy or lack thereof. Indeed, though the standard account suggested that khimzashchita relied on patients' fear, which in turn depended on their belief in its potency, most narcologists also emphasized that the treatment worked only for patients who were, like Gleb and Vyacheslav, adequately motivated for other reasons.

For instance, Alexander Sergeevich explained how some patients used fear as a means of self-management. "The mechanism [underlying khimzashchita] is simply fear," he explained, but he added that one also needed a motivation to become sober. "If he doesn't have this then even fear won't hold him back." Part of the physician's work, as Alexander Sergeeivich saw it, was rendering this fear meaningful to the patient, making sure that it took hold. He added, "Many of [the patients], either openly or not, approach the doctor with the request, 'Put this fear of consuming [alcohol] into me.' Because many of them understand that nothing else will hold them back, only this kind of fear." It was not only physicians who made such arguments. Dmitri, the 12-step counselor, described to me how he had once voluntarily returned to a psychiatric hospital for a repeat of a sulfazine injection[15]—which he described as a "punishment" rather than a "treatment." "I said, do this thing to me one more time. I ask him voluntarily; I want to remember this state [*sostoianie*], this horrible state, I want to experience it and remember it, so that I'll always remember it." Such accounts suggest that the model patient for khimzashchita and kodirovanie is not the unknowing dupe of narcologists but the patient who successfully integrates these clinical technologies into a process of self-management and discipline.

Prostheses for the Will

Vyacheslav was the kind of patient narcologists saw as ideal for a method like khimzashchita. He was, as they put it, relatively "socially conserved." His ties with his family were intact, and along with his wife he had a routine for managing his compliance with the therapy at home. He was of a generation and class that was generally more deferential to the professional authority of physicians than were younger and wealthier patients. Narcologists' talk of motivation was perhaps the closest most of them came to speaking of volition or the will—and unlike those patients who spoke only of their losses, Vyacheslav had social ties motivating him to sobriety.

However, just as important were the ways that Vyacheslav spoke about himself—and how he did not speak about himself. Not surprisingly, he did not characterize his drinking problem as a chemical imbalance to be modulated. Nor did he articulate an illness-based addict identity—as advocated by 12-step programs—and speak of himself as "an alcoholic" or for that matter speak about "alcoholism" as an illness or all-encompassing category at all. Rather, to the degree that he wanted to speak about the treatment at all, Vyacheslav described himself simply as someone who was managing his drinking binges.

Though it would be easy to view such an attitude through the analytic of addiction as a disease of denial, I suggest that the fact that these therapies make such few claims on patients' selves or identities only increases their appeal to those post-Soviet people wary of totalizing frameworks of self-transformation. While some patients found methods such as the torpedo or kodirovanie useless as a means of achieving even temporary sobriety, and others passed through cycles of increasingly brief remission, at least for some, like Vyacheslav, narcology's methods worked as prostheses for the will: pragmatic aids that bolstered personal motivations for sobriety. The reason for these differences between patients had less to do with anything specific to the treatment protocol than with the broader configuration of institutions and relationships (both inside and outside the clinic) within which any particular instance of the treatment took place. Yet other patients, as we shall see in the following chapter, were attracted precisely to the self-transformative techniques of the 12-step program.[16]

The Red Feather

Early on in my fieldwork I was introduced to Boris Kalashnikov, a psychiatrist in private practice who specialized in treating addiction through subliminal suggestion on patients in a drug-induced state of relaxation.[17] In addition to this technique, which he called body-oriented psychotherapy, Kalashnikov treated patients using what he called "bio-energy" methods, which, he explained, were based on "my personal abilities" (*moi lichnye sposobnosti*). "I've had more experiences with the paranormal than should be statistically explainable," he told me, proceeding to describe his ability to "effect electricity from a distance." Dr. Kalashnikov seemed intent on building, proving, or legitimizing his charismatic authority in other ways as well. On his website at the time, visitors found two images of Dr. Kalashnikov. In the first, captioned "This is I, how I am," the doctor sits at his desk in a leather jacket; the second photograph, captioned "And for this you have to strive," shows him shirtless and tanned, standing on a sunny beach near a yacht. These images of wealth and success were bolstered by other claims to prestige, such as Kalashknikov's assertion that he appears in literary form in the prose of two well-known authors: Victor Pelevin and Mikhail Veller.[18]

As I prepared to leave, Kalashnikov asked me about my training in anthropology and then, to my surprise, eagerly explained that he had been heavily influenced by Claude Levi-Strauss's *Structural Anthropology*. In fact, he continued, he kept a copy of the book as bedside reading. "Yes, the bit about the shaman and the red feather . . ." he mused. As he was in a hurry to see his next patient, my conversation with Dr. Kalashnikov unfortunately ended there, and I was unable to meet with him a second time.

In the original text—the chapter "The Sorcerer and His Magic" from *Structural Anthropology*—the detail of the red feather is a key trope in a story about a Kwakiutl Indian who, skeptical of the reality of shamans' power, learns the arts himself. The red feather is a piece of bloody down that the shaman holds inside his mouth, and spits out and presents to the patient and others "as the pathological foreign body extracted as a result of his sucking and manipulations" (Levi-Strauss 1963, 175). Along with "The Effectiveness of Symbols," this chapter of Levi-Strauss is often cited by medical anthropologists and cultural psychiatrists as a forerunner of research on "symbolic efficacy" and "contextual healing" (Kirmayer 1993; Csordas 1993). And though this framework, with a particularly close focus on the healing ritual itself, might have served as my conceptual tool kit for understanding the clinical work of narcologists—including practitioners of kodirovanie—Kalashnikov's evocation of Levi-Strauss (both in our conversation and in print)[19] pointed to processes that transcended the clinical setting.

As he becomes an accomplished healer and increasingly has a stake in the effectiveness of his powers, the shaman protagonist of Levi-Strauss's narrative is unable to maintain his initial degree of skepticism. Moreover, his challenge to other shamans is interpreted as undercutting their particular curative abilities, not the possibility of shamanic healing as such. Similarly, in articles with titles such as "Why I am against kodirovanie," Kalashnikov (2001) repeatedly described the majority of his colleagues as frauds. "Ninety-five percent of the narcology market is a swindle [*moshennichestvo*]," he told me. Although these were statements made to strengthen Kalashnikov's own therapeutic legitimacy even as they undermined that of his rivals, they did not strike at the assumptions underlying the possibility for therapies like kodirovanie to be effective. This was skepticism that sought to advertise and market services, not to disenchant.

Additionally, the intended audience for such arguments was not exclusively (or even primarily) made up of potential patients, echoing Levi-Strauss's depiction of shamanism as "founded on a threefold experience"

(1963, 179): that of the shaman, that of the person experiencing the sickness, and "that of the public, who also participate in the cure, experiencing an enthusiasm and an intellectual satisfaction which produce collective support, which in turn inaugurates a new cycle" (ibid.). It is the significance of this reception of a therapy's procedures and representations—and clinicians' work to shape that reception—that I have focused on in this chapter. While such work is often not acknowledged by clinicians as falling within their professional purview, I have suggested that narcologists in Russia are particularly sensitive to such issues and that they view the effectiveness of their treatments as dependent on a number of factors, including not only individual patients' motivation for sobriety but also their belief or faith in these very techniques. As the following chapter will show, proponents of the 12-step program were also highly sensitive to the legitimacy of their method.

REHABILITATION FROM ABROAD

On a spring afternoon in mid-2004, I sat leafing through a photo album with Nikolai—an active member of the Alcoholics Anonymous (AA) community in St. Petersburg, who had, until recently, served as a substance abuse counselor at a rehabilitation center where I was conducting fieldwork. Nikolai had invited me for lunch at his home, a relatively spacious (by St. Petersburg standards) one-bedroom apartment in one of the city's socialist-built concrete-block northern residential districts (*spal'nye raiony*). However, my visit had coincided with a pediatrician's house call, and so we sat on the couch looking at photographs from Nikolai's trip to the United States, while his two-year-old daughter tottered between us and the bedroom, where her mother and grandmother spoke to the physician. An animated movie played on a wide-screen television, which, along with a DVD player and new stereo system, sat on a sleek cabinet system.

This might have been an unremarkable domestic scene—a snapshot of the rising middle class in urban post-Soviet Russia—but for the fact that Nikolai had, several years previously, been committed to a high-security hospital for the criminally insane after being found not responsible for a death that occurred while he was heavily intoxicated. His release and the subsequent radical transformation of practically every aspect of his life were both closely tied to his self-identification as an alcoholic, to the set of technologies that both afforded and demanded that identification, and to the network of associations this had opened for him. Moreover, the technologies and associations that allowed for Nikolai's successful rehabilitation (*reabilitatsiia*)—particularly AA itself—were more than simply local, in the most concrete sense. Nikolai corresponded over e-mail with an American AA sponsor from Florida, his travel to the United States had been for the purpose of receiving training as a substance abuse counselor, and the rehabilitation center where he had long worked was funded largely by an ex-tobacco executive from Connecticut. Yet to characterize the conditions that had facilitated the utter transformation of Nikolai's life as global or transnational is grossly inadequate. Similarly, narrating the story as one of traveling or circulating technologies—in which American techniques for recovery from addiction arrive in Russia—obscures the processes taking place largely in St. Petersburg, as well as the multiple crosscutting forms of movement taking place.[1]

However, more than simply a question of movement or circulation, or one of healing for that matter, technologies of rehabilitation such as those of AA carry a particular significance in that they explicitly aim to transform conduct and behavior and perhaps produce new kinds of people in the process (Cain 1991; Zigon 2010). That is, while many seemingly "selfless" technologies—particularly medical technologies—"inadvertently act as technologies of the self" by, for example, "modify[ing] embodied experience and chang[ing] the trajectory of an illness" (Lock and Nguyen 2010, 284), techniques like AA's 12-step program directly reference emergent milieus because they seek to rehabilitate those suffering from alcoholism *into particular kinds of people*—namely, recovering alcoholics. Specifically, AA and similar technologies foster association and sociality around illness status and employ this association as a means to transforming their members.

Scholars have offered contrasting arguments about the broader social and political meanings of these transformations. While some have categorized AA as a technology of the self that promotes the self-management and "responsibilization" of individuals (Rimke 2000)—and thus tacitly participate in a sociopolitical project of neoliberalism—others have suggested that the fellowship's emphasis on surrender, individual powerlessness, perpetual recovery, and mutual help puts AA in tension with an ethos of individual autonomy and personal enterprise (Valverde and White-Mair 1999).[2] Such questions are particularly pertinent in Russia, where the introduction of Alcoholics Anonymous coincided with a period of profound social and political-economic change, which demanded that people radically transform their everyday lives and practices, if not their inner lives. Moreover, while proponents of AA generally assume the universality of alcoholic experiences and depict their organization as a culturally neutral fellowship, AA is widely perceived in Russia as a US import, as Nikolai's story suggests, and this has bolstered its tacit associations with neoliberal forms of governance. Since the first groups were founded during the late Soviet period, various Russian critics have depicted AA as a cult or sect, a Trojan horse for Protestantism, or a threat to the professional sphere of addiction medicine.

Rather than framing AA simply as a set of confessional technologies of the self or a self-help program, as many arguments have done, in this chapter I emphasize it as what I call an "illness sodality"—an association for mutual help based on the common identification of members around their experience of suffering and addiction. I do so in order to focus on the ways that the transformation of subjectivity is tied up with shifts both in forms of sociality in which members engage and in the specific webs of association into which they are drawn. Indeed, I argue that it is these concrete associations between persons and institutions, some spanning significant geographical and social distances, and their articulation with older, more localized networks, that so radically open the horizons of possibility for members like Nikolai, even as they remain inaccessible to others.

Following their principal traditions, 12-step groups are not formally centralized organizations, and the international AA organization is careful not to impinge upon the institutional autonomy of the groups (Kurtz 1979; Mäkelä et al. 1996). For this reason, there is not a single narrative of the arrival of AA in Russia, as separate groups formed in different places under somewhat different circumstances.[3] Thus I make my argument by tracing the development of *one* particular AA network or community, at the center of which was the House of Hope on the Hill (HOH) (Dom Nadezhdy na Gore), a free-of-charge 12-step based alcoholism rehabilitation center located on the outskirts of St. Petersburg, where Nikolai once worked. Examining the story of the foundation of HOH, I focus here on the ways in which a motley group of wealthy American sponsors, Russian psychiatrists, Orthodox clergymen, and members of the cultural intelligentsia navigated the contradictions and tensions surrounding the 12-step program, working to domesticate Russian AA. I then return to the story of Nikolai, tracing his rehabilitation through a 12-step program based in a high-security hospital for the criminally insane and into the HOH community. Finally, I reflect on the rehabilitation of AA members like Nikolai in relation to more general issues of (self-)governance in contemporary Russia and consider the framing of AA as an illness sodality in light of anthropological work on biological and social citizenship.

In this chapter I explore AA in contemporary Russia (and beyond) as an illness sodality. In borrowing the term "sodality" from mid-twentieth-century American anthropologists such as Robert Lowie, I seek to highlight several aspects of the technologies and forms of sociality that so profoundly transformed Nikolai's life. Whereas Lowie used the term as a "convenient lumber room for a great variety of associations," ranging from the YMCA and bridge clubs to West African secret societies and Cree military organizations (1948, 294), here I refer more specifically to associations for mutual help based on the mutual identification of members around experiences of suffering and illness. I return to discuss AA as an illness sodality more thoroughly below, but here I mention several significant issues that this framing is meant to highlight.

First of all, my emphasis is on AA neither simply as a set of technologies of the self nor as an identity but as a concrete network of relations and associations held together through the work of these technologies and identifications. Mariana Valverde has aptly pointed to a tension at the heart of AA practice, between two forms of self-governance: (1) a set of pragmatic behaviorally oriented techniques for maintaining sobriety that she calls "a cobbled together, low-theory, unsystematic system for habit reform" (1998, 140), and (2) an identity-based form of self-governance linked to the notion of alcoholism as a disease.[4] These two modes of self-governance have distinct manifestations, and the techniques of AA and the 12-step program sometimes circulate independently of the addict or alcoholic as a kind of person or identity. Here I emphasize the ways in which such flows of technologies and categories of identification are linked to concrete associations of people.

Second, as I have mentioned, the notion of illness sodality foregrounds the idea that identification over experience of illness or suffering is meant to cut across or supersede other forms of identification—national, ethnic, class. It is important to note that in fact this is not always the case. Not only is it theoretically nearly impossible for *any* form of identification to supersede others in such a totalizing way, but, as my account of the efforts of Russian AA proponents to domesticate the fellowship should make clear, associations between the 12-step program and the United States are not so easily overcome. Interestingly, while numerous scholarly accounts have examined how processes of self-transformation in AA are linked to the construal and performance of autobiographical narratives, less attention has been paid to the processes of identification that such storytelling engenders (although see Kurtz 1979, 60–61).[5]

Robert Lowie argued that "by making cooperation a reality beyond the narrow confines of the blood tie they pave the way, in principle at least, for a wider integration, whether in the form of a state or of a supernational religion" (1948, 316, quoted in Boon 1982, 103). Setting aside his gesture to a developmental trajectory, here Lowie points to the imbrication of sodalities with other institutions, particularly the state. These are particularly significant in a setting such as contemporary Russia, where informal practices of exchange and highly personalized ties have long played a key role (Ledeneva 1998, 2006). As I discuss in greater depth below, the interpenetration of such networks and associations with the institutions of the Russian state complicates any interpretation of AA or other illness sodalities either as incubators of civil society (Critchlow 2000b) or as producers of neoliberal subjects (Zigon 2010).

Fieldwork and Identification in Alcoholics Anonymous

To get to the House of Hope, you have to travel half an hour by suburban train to a village on the city's outskirts. I first visited on a Sunday in January, and a crowd of downhill skiers disembarked at the station; a slope had recently been opened nearby, attracting more visitors to the once-sleepy station. From there the House is another forty-five minutes by foot (or longer in ankle-deep snow), past farm fields, traditionally styled Russian village houses, newer dachas, and several half-built minimansions. Though HOH's geographic location on the city's margins mirrors its position in the field of addiction medicine—compared with the addiction hospital's centrality—the material condition of its building reflects its relative youth and modest prosperity: an unremarkable red brick structure, newly constructed and well kept.

As I mentioned in the introduction, my first contact with the House of Hope community took place in New York, where I was put in touch with Eugene Zubkov, a Russian American psychiatrist who shuttled between the United States and Russia while serving as a director for HOH from afar. Zubkov expressed an enthusiasm for my project—and about my potential help in translating and fund-raising for the House—and arranged for my fieldwork at the House. Back in St. Petersburg, I was given extensive access to the center. I was allowed to interview patients, join them for their lectures and conversations, and sit in on meetings with the counseling staff. The only restriction was that I was not allowed to sit in on group therapy or closed 12-step group meetings. This restriction reflected the staff's efforts to protect patients' privacy, but it also reflected AA traditions, according to which closed meetings are limited to those who are already members or believe they "have a problem with alcohol" (Wilcox 1998, 48). As I soon learned, however, questions of my own identification in relation to AA and alcoholism extended far beyond the issue of attending closed groups.

The practices of AA and other 12-step programs require specific kinds of self-identification from participants. One longtime substance abuse counselor in St. Petersburg told me that for him self-identification as an addict was more than a prerequisite to rehabilitation: it was central to the entire process of the 12 steps. Not only does AA function as a technology of self-transformation, in which participants gradually learn to narrate their life histories in a way that enables them to self-identify as alcoholics or addicts, but it also encourages another sort of identification: that of individual members *with* one another through their common experiences (Rudy 1986, 18–42; Denzin 1987, 74; Cain 1991). These two types of identification are linked: telling one's story at an AA meeting is not only a means for the speaker to narrate his or her experience and receive support, but it also allows listeners—particularly new members—to reflect upon their own common experiences.[6]

Like the American rehab centers on which it was modeled, the House of Hope offered a program run primarily by recovering alcoholics and addicts. Some of the trained psychologists identified not as alcoholics but as codependent (*sozavisimyi*), a category that has entered Russia with the arrival of 12-step therapy. Originally a term from the 12-step movement that designated an illness in its own right—behavior by family members, typically wives, that supported or, in the language of the program, "enabled" their husbands' alcoholism—codependency has entered the discourse of North American popular psychology as, in its more extreme forms, a pathologization of almost any social relationships that abrogate individual autonomy or rights (Haaken 1993; Borovoy 2001, 98). At HOH codependency was a key category, ratifying the inclusion of a number of nonalcoholics into the therapeutic community. For instance, several members of the support staff, who at first had no particular affinity for the program, had gradually learned the language and culture of the 12 steps and had begun to think of themselves as codependent in the broad sense of the term (they did not have family members who abused alcohol). One had gone on to receive training as a substance abuse counselor. The category of codependency thus allowed members of the HOH community to constitute themselves as parts of a household or family unit linked by experiences of dependence and recovery.

Because AA groups are generally restricted to people suffering from alcoholism and because their definition of those individuals is based largely on self-identification and self-ascription, they present a particular challenge for ethnographic research. If several social positions are available for ethnographers to occupy in most clinical institutions, the legitimate options in groups such as AA are at once more limited and more flexible.[7] The structure of AA meetings, moreover, makes it very difficult for a visitor not to declare his or her relationship to the program and thus almost impossible not to get "caught up in it," as Jeanne Favret-Saada writes of her fieldwork on witchcraft in rural France (1990, 191). Indeed, on my very first visit to the House on the Hill I attended an open AA meeting, during which a visiting speaker presented his story of decline and recovery to the group. As we each introduced ourselves to the group, using the familiar formula—"Hello, I'm X and I'm an alcoholic"— I found I was the only person in the room to simply say, "Hello, I'm Eugene." Telling myself that a disingenuous identification would be patronizing to the patients and staff, I continued to introduce myself this way for a few months.

However, several members of the House community persistently refused to accept my disavowal of alcoholism. Eduard was particularly insistent. A burly man with a wide and friendly face, Eduard had spent a decade of his life drinking heavily and barely holding down a series of short-term jobs. When he had finally been persuaded by relatives to go through treatment at the House of Hope, he was so taken with the program that he eventually became a substance abuse counselor. He presented himself as a simple guy and enjoyed gently poking fun at the House's supporters among "intellectuals and bohemians." On several occasions when we rode the train together, Eduard asked me why I had decided to study alcoholism. I explained as best I could but found myself relying on what sounded like tired clichés (alcoholism represented such a profound public health crisis in Russia, etc.), especially when compared with his firsthand experiences.

As I spoke, I realized that I had never been asked this question at the addiction hospital. To be sure, the physicians there took for granted the importance of alcoholism as a problem in contemporary Russia, as did Eduard. What was strikingly different in these two field sites was how my interlocutors thought about the connections between personal experience and research interests. At the hospital, the physicians treated me as a kind of colleague, an emissary of "international science." If researchers agreed that alcoholism was an important topic for study, there was no further reason to question my choice; whatever other motivations I might have had, they were extraneous and irrelevant to many of the narcologists. Eduard, in contrast, was asking (indirectly at first) whether my (conscious or unconscious) motivation for choosing to research alcoholism treatment was my own (presumably unacknowledged) addiction. I thought I recognized Eduard's intention because I had already been asked this question, in the same way—not in Russia but in the United States, before my fieldwork began.

When I had told fellow anthropologists about my project, many initially asked whether I had experienced alcoholism in my family. At the time, I had assumed that the impetus for these questions was specific to anthropology (and its neighboring disciplines). For anyone socialized into the assumptions of contemporary academic anthropology, the notion that our research interests are shaped by biographical particularities has become something of a platitude. I was already, like many colleagues of my generation, carrying out my first project in a place where I had familial ties, so it was perhaps easy to extrapolate a similar personal connection to my thematic focus. In the field, as I attempted to answer Eduard's questions, my colleagues' questions took on a slightly different meaning. It was not only the anthropological creed of reflexivity that made a link between one's life's work and one's personal experiences seem self-evident: the same presupposition was woven through the amalgam of self-help techniques and pop psychology that makes up much of the American therapeutic culture. More specifically, this idea testified to the influence that the 12-step movement has had on North American assumptions, as illustrated by the familiar figure of the recovering addict turned substance abuse counselor. However, Eduard's questions were forcing me to encounter this idea in unfamiliar territory.

I was not mistaken about Eduard's intentions. After I collected his life story—over the course of several afternoons in his apartment—he confronted me directly: "Tell me, Eugene. Are you sure you don't have a problem?" There were many addictions, he explained; the dependence to which I was failing to own up wasn't necessarily on alcohol. I told him that no, everything was fine, he needn't be concerned; but I was irritated at his insistence. Over the following weeks, I increasingly felt that my behavior was being observed by people at the House, and I found myself disavowing an addict identification more deliberately and vehemently than I had done before. At a dinner for the House of Hope's American donors, I joined one other person at the table in ordering a glass of wine.

Late in the spring I accompanied Eduard and several other counselors to a celebration for a nearby 12-step group. At the registration for the event, everyone was asked his or her "status"—the appropriate response being one's illness identity (alcoholic, drug addict) and one's period of sobriety (e.g., sober for two years). As I pondered an appropriate answer, Eduard stepped in to explain, "He's codependent." I had never thought of introducing myself this way, but by this point considering myself codependent was beginning to have a certain logic. Could not my fieldwork relationships with Eduard and others at the House of Hope be understood in this way? I was, after all, getting pulled into relationships with my informants in ways I had not expected, and I was reacting to their demands in ways that I judged (from the standpoint of an imagined ideal ethnographer) to be at best withdrawn and at worst dismissive. More important, the notion of identifying me as codependent meant something to Eduard and other members of the HOH community: it placed me in a legitimate and understandable category and relationship to them. (Somewhat more troubling was the implication that my interest in the House of Hope, and my research itself, was pathological—that I was addicted to studying addicts and needed help.) Nevertheless, at the next open meeting I attended, I introduced myself as codependent.

Exporting Sobriety

The House of Hope and the community that surrounded it had its origins in a unique institutional and political economic conjunction that emerged from the mid-1980s anti-alcohol campaign on the one hand and the opening of Eastern European markets to American companies on the other. Although the overall emphasis of the campaign that became closely associated with Gorbachev's name was on supply reduction, it involved other measures, such as the development of a national temperance organization and the increased funding of narcology. The campaign also coincided with Gorbachev's shift to a policy of outreach toward the first world, and beginning in 1987 glasnost came together with the anti-alcohol effort in a series of joint Soviet-US conferences on alcoholism that brought experts on addiction from the United States to the Soviet Union.

Among these visitors were officials representing the General Service Office of Alcoholics Anonymous in New York as well as several clergymen who made a concerted effort to promote AA in the Soviet Union. These meetings led to the establishment of early Soviet AA groups such as the New Beginners in Moscow in 1987 and Almaz in Leningrad slightly afterward (Burke 1990). Although these early meetings were framed by the diplomatic trope of mutual learning and exchange, the flow of knowledge and technologies rapidly became one-directional. After touring Soviet treatment facilities and speaking to physicians and patients, most Anglo-American addiction specialists and 12-step proponents concluded that prevailing modes of long-term treatment offered by official Soviet addiction medicine were ineffective, backward, and unethical (A.B. 1991; Harris-Orffut 1995). Bringing 12-step programs to

Russia thus became part of a broader late 1980s and early 1990s project of importing various first-world institutions and technologies deemed more effective than state socialist ones. Underlying this project, for many promoters of AA in Russia, was a strong sense of moral righteousness born of the conviction that their method was the *only* way for alcoholics to be saved from imminent death.

The motives of Louis Bantle, the founder of HOH, were more complicated still. Bantle, the longtime CEO of U.S. Tobacco and a self-described recovering alcoholic, had been involved in the joint US-Soviet conferences on alcoholism. Significantly, Bantle was known in both business and public health circles for leading his corporation's successful effort to create a broader market segment for its so-called smokeless tobacco (Denny 1993; Wyckham 1999).[8] Over the following several years as his corporation began to develop business contacts aimed at opening Eastern European markets to its products, Bantle focused much of his philanthropic effort on propagating AA in Russia.

Setting aside the issues of Bantle's personal motives for pursuing this particular form of philanthropy, it is worth noting that his simultaneous promotion of an addictive substance and the technology for managing addiction is not simply a matter of differently conceptualized substances (in addition to smokeless tobacco, UST also marketed wine in Eastern Europe). Rather, it indexes AA's elective affinity with a particular type of liberalism as well as its historical origins in the post-temperance United States. According to AA's "disease model" of alcoholism, it is not alcohol as a substance that poses a moral problem or threat (as prohibitionist temperance movements in both the United states and Soviet Union argued) but the fact that a certain group of people suffer from a chronic illness that makes them incapable of drinking in moderation (Jellinek 1960; Gusfield 1996, 192–96). Such a model is clearly compatible with a liberal political and economic disposition in regard to alcohol and its consumption, as well as more broadly. Implicit in the steps, traditions, and practices of AA is the notion that the management of addiction is not the responsibility of a disciplining and prohibiting state but that of individuals banded together into a group of mutual interest and help (Kurtz 1979; Valverde 1998). Whether such assumptions would hold in the context of post-Soviet Russia would soon become the topic of numerous debates as Bantle moved ahead with his philanthropic project.

In 1992, Bantle hired Eugene Zubkov, who had recently emigrated to the United States, to manage this philanthropic operation. Zubkov was particularly well suited to play the role of cultural broker for 12-step programs in Russia, both because of his professional background and because of his network of acquaintances. Zubkov had worked for nearly a decade at the Bekhterev Psychoneurological Research Institute, specializing in adolescent and legal psychiatry. In addition to his professional ties, Zubkov had extensive contacts among the local cultural intelligentsia, particularly among St. Petersburg's informal art and rock music movements, and these contacts played a central role in his initial plan to promote AA in Russia.

Zubkov's approach to the project was informal and highly personalistic: drawing upon his own contacts, he hoped to knit various informal networks of post-Soviet society into AA's sprawling global illness sodality. He argued that three primary factors distinguished the social context of AA in the United States from that of Russia during the early 1990s: the respective roles played by professional medicine and religious organizations and the level of stigma associated with alcoholism. Consequently, Zubkov decided to target three groups—physicians, members of the Orthodox clergy, and well-known members of the cultural intelligentsia—by bringing representative members of each to the United States to tour rehabilitation centers and undergo training for substance abuse counselors. While Zubkov's plan was based on his analysis of the state of alcoholism treatment in Russia at the time, it also drew on the history of AA in the United States, where alliances between medical and religious figures were key in the development of the programs, and their endorsement by well-known public figures such as Betty Ford were important to their legitimation (Kurtz 1979). Zubkov hoped that his existing contacts among narcologists and in the St. Petersburg visual art and rock scene would help him bolster the legitimacy of AA among members of the medical establishment and cultural intelligentsia and thereby the general public.

Physicians, Clergymen, and Resistance to AA

By the time I met him in 2003, Zubkov was somewhat disappointed with the results of this early project in regard to physicians and clergy members.

A key sticking point with many physicians, and narcologists in particular, seems to have been a central characteristic of AA as an illness sodality— its nonprofessionalism and its ambivalent stance toward formally acquired expertise about alcoholism. Opposition to 12-step groups on this basis was evident among some prominent narcologists even in the first decade of the 2000s, at the same time as many other physicians praised the groups and directed their patients to them. For instance, in 2004 a well-known narcologist dismissed AA in a newspaper interview as "anonymous brotherhoods, where there are no doctors, as 'only a drug addict will help another drug addict.'" "In that case," he asked, in an aside that infuriated many local AA members, should we say that only "a schizophrenia patient will help another schizophrenia patient?" (Dyleva 2004b, 11). For his part, Zubkov emphasized the difficulties Russian physicians had in taking on the role of "wounded healer" expected of substance abuse counselors. "It's easier for a doctor to get drunk than to come to a meeting with his patients," he opined. "So they die, they drink themselves away [*spivaiutia*], they turn into idiots—but to tell a patient that he's an alcoholic and meet him in a group, that he can't do." AA's elevation of fellow-suffering experience over expertise and its requirement that physicians participate on a par with other members, if at all, struck at the particularly prominent role that physicians' authority played in narcology, at a moment when that authority was being threatened on several fronts. Though actual relationships between clinicians and patients varied widely, it is clear that AA's ambivalence toward expertise fueled some narcologists' sense of their profession as under threat.

If the overall level of enthusiasm for AA among narcologists was less than Zubkov and other promoters had hoped, support among clergy members was initially mixed as well. Although 12-step groups were officially blessed by Patriarch Alexei II in 1993, there was continued opposition from other clergy members. In addition to worries that AA was closely bound to American Protestantism and might be used as a cover for proselytizing was a more diffuse fear identification of it as a cult with the associated concerns about zombification and a loss of personal agency. In 1990s Russia such anxieties about agency and images of persons controlled from without often clustered around the figure of the cult leader (antisectarian literature reinforced this link in condemning totalitarian cults). Such worries surfaced in many media depictions of AA, for instance: "The formula, according to which AA group meetings take place (the preamble, a moment of silence, the repetition of the 12 steps and 12 traditions, reading from the textbook), already suggests zombification" (Kolomeiskaia 1999). This kind of anxiety was evident among laypeople as well, and several patients told me that their initial impression of AA had been shaped by the prevalent discourse about sects and cults. As one patient I met at St. Petersburg's Municipal Addiction Hospital, who had been through the rehabilitation program at HOH, put it, "This ritual: we weren't ready for it. . . . They invited me to come back . . . but I had a negative feeling about it."

More recently, 12-step and other therapeutic techniques have been taken up by rehabilitation programs run by the Orthodox Church (as well as by other religious groups)—in some cases adapted and imbued with specifically Orthodox content (Wanner 2007; Zigon 2010). Such adaptations infuriated many of the active members in the St. Petersburg AA movement, who argued, "There's no reason to change the steps!"[9] Zubkov argued strongly against such efforts to "make this program specifically Russian," explaining that "the format can change, but not the substance."

We Don't Want to Defeat Anybody

Zubkov and Bantle's efforts were more immediately successful with their contingent of cultural intelligentsia patients, perhaps in part because, unlike physicians and clergymen, these patients did not see AA as posing a threat to their professional status or cultural capital. Indeed, for some of Zubkov's intelligentsia patients, AA became a means of successfully transforming their rapidly depreciating Soviet cultural capital. While outspoken supporters of AA in Russia included the well-known rock musicians Yuri Shevchuk of DDT and "Dyusha" Romanov of Akvarium, this was particularly the case for members of the Mit'ki, an artists' group that had become well known in the 1980s as "anti-establishment" figures partly for their enactment of a heroic drunkenness.[10] In retrospect, Dmitri Shagin, one of the artists most central to the group, as well as the chief proponent of AA among them, argued that in the drunkenness of the Mit'ki "there was a kind of passive protest against everything that we didn't like about the Soviet style of life [*sovetskom obraze zhizni*]. We created the slogan: 'We answer to the Red Terror with delirium tremens'" (*Na krasn'yi terror otve-tim beloi goriachkoi*) (Nikitinskii 2004).[11]

Zubkov emphasized that the timing had been particularly successful. In his words, during the early 1990s "everyone was drinking and dying. To die from alcohol was considered a heroic act." In 1993 Zubkov brought Shagin and the painter and writer Vladimir Shinkarev (who had written *Mit'ki*, an unofficial manifesto of the group) to the United States for substance abuse treatment. After their return to St. Petersburg, the two went public with their alcoholism. Shagin became particularly closely involved in the AA movement, establishing an AA group that meets in part of the Mit'ki studio space and working on behalf of HOH once it was established. In his conversations with the press and in their own writings, Shagin represented what had previously been an ethos of heavy drinking as a disease and advocated Alcoholics Anonymous not only as a treatment but as a program for a new way of life (Shagin 1999). As Zubkov said of the Mit'ki: "They made a lifestyle out of this, a lifestyle which they propagandize. Of course, this was a commercial device. They kept their popularity and they helped us."

Indeed, though their initial motivations were certainly personal, the transformation of the entire artists' group into "sober Mit'ki," was arguably as useful for their adaptation to post-Soviet conditions as artists as it was to the goals of their American sponsors. The Mit'ki had crafted their particular artistic image and disposition firmly within the cultural politics of late socialism. In addition to their pseudonaive visual artworks and semiabsurdist writings, their drunkenness was at the core of their public image—as much performance as lifestyle. With the end of state socialism, the signifiers of Soviet respectability, in relation to which the Mit'ki defined themselves, were radically transformed as well. By transforming themselves in this cardinal way, the Mit'ki were able to reestablish themselves in the 1990s—precisely by capitalizing on the paradoxical nature of the sober Mitek image. Even in 2004, more than ten years after Shagin and others had given up drinking, articles in the mass media played up this irony with titles such as "Mitki without port wine" (*Mit'ki bez portveina*).

Moreover, the HOH and AA placed the Mit'ki and members of the St. Petersburg rock scene into some association—however tenuous—with a number of performers and celebrities who have publicly linked themselves to issues of substance dependence and its treatment. Most notably,

Eric Clapton visited HOH while performing in St. Petersburg in the early 2000s, an event that was fondly remembered by Shagin and the counselors at the center alike. Of course, there were limits to the degree to which an illness sodality like AA opened up such rarefied networks, and some members of the HOH community might have overestimated its potential for advancing their own ambitions. In my role as unofficial translator for Zubkov, I revised several letters written by a rock guitarist recently emigrated from Russia to the United States, who was unsuccessfully attempting to get himself included in a music festival organized by Clapton to benefit his Antigua-based Crossroads Centre for substance dependence.

Conversely, visible links with the Mit'ki helped to domesticate HOH's brand, as one counselor put it. Several patients at HOH explained to me that their initial fears about AA's being a sect were allayed by its local association with the Mit'ki. The Mit'ki did more than provide familiar faces to prospective AA members. A speaker at one of the AA meetings held in the Mit'ki studio space explained how her impression of the program was shaped by their involvement: "I thought to myself, 'These are alcoholics? These are intellectuals of the highest class!" (*Eto intelligentsiia vyshego klassa!*)[12] In other words, the Mit'ki served as objects of identification for prospective AA members who viewed themselves as members of the cultural intelligentsia and others who perhaps questioned the respectability of the program. That this artists' group, which earned its fame through something like a punk aesthetic, could become a source of respectability is only somewhat ironic: in middle age the Mit'ki—like many other artists—had reformulated and commodified their aesthetic—their drunken past providing a patina of authenticity to their new sober image.

The House and Its Family

During the midnineties, as sponsoring numerous individuals from Russia on treatment/study trips to rehabilitation centers in the United States increasingly looked like a financially unsustainable strategy, Bantle and Zubkov began to plan a rehabilitation center that would be based in St. Petersburg. After a false start in another location, in 1997 Bantle purchased a parcel of land located near a village about half an hour by suburban train from St. Petersburg. The twenty-eight-day inpatient residential therapeutic program established at what became the House of Hope was modeled on several rehabilitation centers in the United States and generally on a program known as the Minnesota Model.

Developed at several inpatient psychiatric and therapeutic treatment centers in Minnesota during the late 1940s and 1950s, the model is an institutionally based rehabilitation program with 12-step techniques and group meetings at its core (Anderson, McGovern, and DuPont 1999). Sharing the concept of chemical dependence as a chronic disease that cannot be cured, the Minnesota model aims to help patients develop a new lifestyle to live with their condition. Patients at the House of Hope take part in AA meetings and reading groups based on working through the 12 steps, as well as lectures on aspects of the program, mostly run by counselors who are recovering addicts or alcoholics. Unlike AA groups, however, which are restricted to fellow sufferers, institutions based on the Minnesota Model have a multiprofessional staff—which may include psychiatrists and psychologists who do not identify as alcoholics (Cook 1988). As I have mentioned, codependency worked as a category, ratifying the inclusion of a number of nonalcoholics into the therapeutic community, including several trained psychologists who ran the rehabilitation program.

An important part of the Minnesota Model, moreover, entails the constitution of a particular therapeutic milieu that is meant to contribute to patients' recovery.[13] At the HOH, patients participated in work assignments (preparing food, washing dishes, chopping wood, etc.), and patients and staff participated in a weekly community meeting at which interpersonal grievances were aired and logistical problems were discussed. Finally, as in other Minnesota model centers, HOH ran a family therapy program to which it invited the close family members of patients residing at the center.

Overall the aim of HOH's twenty-eight-day program is to acquaint its patients with the 12 steps and AA. It uses the 12-step program as a technology of self-transformation, aiming to teach patients to recognize, articulate, and manage their emotions and to gain insight into their conditions (e.g., Zigon 2010). A key goal of the program is to motivate patients to attend AA group meetings in St. Petersburg or elsewhere (a problem for those residing in some remote parts of Russia): indeed, these mutual help groups are meant to function as a sort of aftercare, and patients are encouraged to attend meetings daily for the first three months after finishing the inpatient program. When I conducted my fieldwork in 2004, HOH was the only center in the St. Petersburg area providing free-of-charge rehabilitation for alcoholism. Though the place it occupied in the local field of addiction treatment providers had long mirrored its geographic location on the margins of the city, the House was gaining legitimacy and attention.

Domesticating Russian Alcoholics Anonymous

Proponents of AA generally assume the universality of alcoholic experiences and argue that their program constitutes a social technology with equally universal effectiveness: the assumption is that AA is a kind of blueprint that can be enacted anywhere with only minor adaptations. This notion of AA as culturally neutral is paralleled by the program's spiritual ecumenism. In its official literature, AA is framed as a fellowship of self-identifying alcoholics that, although spiritual in its outlook, is not formally associated with any particular religion.

However, social scientists have long noted that the assumptions about self and sociality implicit in AA's practices and traditions are at least somewhat specific to the historical setting within which they were developed—namely, (1) a particular strain of Anglo-American Protestantism and (2) the social and intellectual context of the post-temperance Depression-era United States (Kurtz 1979; Antze 1987; Falby 2003).[14] AA was founded in the United States during the mid-1930s, and many of its concepts were developed on the basis of tenets central to the Oxford Group, an evangelical movement that focused on psychological interpretations of self, was committed to spiritual awakening through social interaction in a group, and was sometimes represented as a return to the ethos of early Christianity (Kurtz 1979; Falby 2003). As the fellowship gained in popularity in the United States during the 1940s and '50s, and later throughout the world, efforts to navigate religious and cultural difference decidedly shaped the program (for example, the ecumenicism underlying the emphasis on a "higher power"), although they typically emphasized cultural difference only as a barrier to the ultimate recognition of identity among fellow suffering alcoholics. Nevertheless, the international diffusion of AA occurred first to English-speaking and Nordic mainly Protestant countries and only subsequently to majority-Catholic states—particularly those in southern

Europe and Latin America—and non-Christian Asian countries (Makela 1991; Makela et al. 1996).

This tension between a claim to a cross-cultural identification based on fellow suffering and the perceptions of cultural particularity in the program was played out in the efforts of Russian AA supporters to promote the fellowship. Thus when I asked AA participants in St. Petersburg about local differences in their practice, nearly all argued that their shared identification as fellow sufferers trumped any national or cultural differences: "Alcoholics are the same everywhere," they invariably said. Or as one local AA participant told a journalist, "For alcoholism neither nationality, nor age, nor social position exists" (Fomenko 2002). Dmitri Shagin repeatedly made similar arguments in interviews with journalists: "As far as the famous 'Russian drunkenness' goes, this is also a myth, as you start to understand when you've spent some time with alcoholics from other countries. Alcoholics are everywhere alcoholics, whether in Russia, in America or in Africa. And we are all brothers" (Nikitinskii 2004). While such arguments emphasized the basis of the AA fellowship in identification with others over common experiences of being alcoholics, others compared the program more explicitly to biomedical techniques. "You want to say that a diabetic in America is ill in a different way [*po drugomu boleet?*]" asked one of the substance abuse counselors at HOH, evoking the commonly used reference of diabetes as a model of chronic illness. "The alcoholic is the same," she added. Another counselor made an even more direct comparison to biomedicine when I asked him about local differences in practice: "I try not to theorize. It works, that's what is important for me. When I take an Analgin pill, I don't ask what it's made out of. I don't take it apart under the microscope. I just put it in my mouth and that's it . . . it's the same here. It works, that's what matters to me." Here AA is depicted as another medical technology working on the "normal body" of biomedicine (Lock and Nyugen 2010, 32–33).

And yet at other moments AA was identified locally by many of its participants explicitly or implicitly as an American program. For instance, nearly every Russian speaker associated with the program in St. Petersburg pronounced the name of the program "Ay-Ay"—that is, in the English pronunciation rather than the Russian "Ah-Ah." This awareness of the program as American seemed particularly tangible at HOH, in part because of the close links that the center maintained with United States-based institutions.

Counselors working at the HOH had the opportunity to visit and train at several rehabilitation centers on the East Coast, and many described their journey almost as a kind of pilgrimage. When I first met Nikolai, he described how he had been asked about the purpose of his trip by a US consular worker during his visa interview. "I said to him 'I'm going to the homeland [*rodina*] of AA.' And the man asked me, 'What's the first step of AA?' and when I answered, 'We admitted that we were powerless over alcohol—that our lives had become unmanageable,' he stepped out from behind his desk, shook my hand and said, 'Welcome to the United States.'" As much as Nikolai's story suggested the personal significance that the United States held for him as the origin of AA, it also evoked the perception, held by many in Russia, that the program was particularly American. Nikolai also linked himself to the origins of the fellowship, proudly explaining that his sponsor—a more experienced member who provides guidance—lived in Florida (they communicated by e-mail) and that through the institution of sponsorship he was genealogically linked to Bill Wilson, one of the founders of AA ("He was my sponsor's sponsor's sponsor's sponsor").

These issues of whether AA was an American program or a culturally neutral one arose often in public discussions of the movement, with opponents often citing AA's origins to argue against its suitability for Russia. For example, one newspaper article quoted a psychologist who stated that "the model itself is a purely American invention which shouldn't have been carried over onto Russian soil without making various adaptations. This program doesn't work for the Russian mind [*mentalitet*]" (Kolomeiskaia 1999). Many early discussions of AA in Russia emphasized the difficulty that persons supposedly enculturated with official Soviet atheism would have with the notion of a higher power. In order to facilitate this transition, many AA proponents in Russia have used the common (rather Durkheimian) notion of identifying the higher power with the group itself. Dealing with such issues seemed to be a particular difficulty for some of the narcologists and physicians taking part in the program.[15]

Significantly, opposing arguments regarding the cultural or social appropriateness of AA were often made as well: arguments to the effect that AA was, for one reason or another, *particularly* suited to the Russian context. For instance, some media accounts have described AA as an "American in origin, but entirely Russian in spirit, technology of heart-to-heart [*po dusham*] conversations" (Bansovich 2001). Similarly, the head substance abuse psychiatrist for Moscow argued in an interview that "the first step is to understand one's powerlessness over alcohol or drugs. At its core it reminds one of the Orthodox confession and in this sense it successfully translates to the Russian mentality" (Fomenkova 2000).[16]

At HOH the association with the United States cut both ways. Whereas the perceived Americanness of AA lent the therapy legitimacy in the eyes of some patients, others were suspicious of the foreign connection. Aside from patients, Zubkov felt that the perception of the center as American by local administrators and bureaucrats was not particularly conducive to its long-term survival in Putin's Russia. An important part of domesticating AA had to do with associating the program with Orthodoxy while respecting its formally nondenominational character. In addition to fostering informal links with local Orthodox clergy, this meant introducing certain explicitly religious elements to the House's program, such as an Orthodox chapel where weekly services are held. At the same time, the program continued to be practiced according to its international nondenominational precepts, and it was emphasized that religious services were formally optional for patients undergoing rehabilitation at the center.

Additionally, Zubkov was on a continual, and somewhat futile, hunt for Russian sources of funding, which he felt would bolster its standing as a domestic institution. Local businesses, he argued, were not interested in donating money to and thus becoming associated with a rehabilitation center for alcoholics. A newspaper report on HOH quoted a businessman stating, "I'd sooner flush my dough down the toilet than give it to the alkies" (Barabash 2006). In fact, when Zubkov was able to secure funding from a Russian businessman in 2003, it was only on the condition that he remain anonymous (Barabash 2006). Significantly, even this was possible only through the cultivation of personal ties: a friend of Zubkov's with a relatively high position in Putin's administration had apparently directed the businessman to make the donation.

A Psychiatric Hospital of a Special Type

I first met Nikolai at St. Petersburg's Psychiatric Hospital of a Special Type under Intensive Surveillance, where he was once interned. The institution is located on the Vyborg bank of St. Petersburg, several minutes on trolley bus from the Finland Station. A century ago this was a solidly working-class district as well as home to a significant number of factories, some of which have left their names to neighborhood streets. The hospital sits on Artillery Street (former patients often refer to the hospital itself as Arsenal'naia), down the block from a former asphalt and concrete factory and across the way from a women's prison (*zhenskii izoliator*). From its construction in 1913 until the establishment of the special psychiatric hospital in the early 1950s, the forbidding beige brick building also housed female prisoners.

I had been invited to visit the special hospital through Zubkov. The hospital's director, Victor Styazhkin, had a long-standing relationship with HOH, and his hospital housed a unique program that Zubkov encouraged me to visit: a 12-step-based rehabilitation program for men convicted of having committed violent crimes, all of whom had major psychiatric diagnoses. Though wary of the sensationalistic terms Zubkov used in describing the hospital—"He's got a hospital full of maniacs, serial killers, and psychos!"—I made an appointment to meet with Styazhkin.

A brick wall topped with barbed wire surrounding the hospital compound was the first sign of a total institution that, to a visitor expecting closed-circuit cameras and radio-monitored ankle bracelets, seemed both overtly menacing and deceptively quaint. I found my entrance to the hospital slowed not by computer scans of my passport or even metal detectors but by the dulling familiarity of queues and paperwork (and this with an invitation from the hospital's director). Having spoken to Styazhkin earlier that morning, I made the mistake of entering the hospital directly through the main door. An older woman, dressed in the requisite green smock of a hospital attendant (*sanitar*) stopped mopping the concrete floor to tell me I'd need to get an entrance pass (*propusk*). To obtain this document, I had to leave the main entrance and reenter the building through an unmarked side door that, though it looked as if it might lead to a toolshed, opened onto a waiting room painted an incongruous dirty pink. Here visitors to the hospital sat on benches or milled about as an attending guard, a young woman, filled out the paperwork allowing them to enter the hospital or give food and gifts to patients. A gendered division of security labor in the hospital seemed to place women behind glass windows, checking passes and interacting with visitors, while young men were assigned to guard entrances and exits and escort patients and visitors through the grounds. Next to the guard's office hung a notice (signed by Styazhkin) listing items forbidden to patients: powdered mashed potatoes, hot soups, glass containers. The text of a nearby form revealed the range of expected relationships between patients and visitors: "I am bringing _____ for my (circle one) husband/son/brother/relative." A middle-aged woman ahead of me in the queue handed items for a patient through the small window to the guard, who checked them off a list and placed them in a burlap sack: cheese, crackers, bread, jam, and three address books. "Why so many?" asked the guard. "I don't know," the woman replied, visibly flustered, "I've had it up to here with his requests." An old man meandered around the room, waiting for a discrepancy with his passport to be cleared up. It took another call from my cell phone to the hospital director to get the necessary pass.

Several minutes later, having left my passport at the main entrance and been escorted across the hospital grounds by a young uniformed conscript, I sat in one of the modernist leather armchairs in Victor Styazhkin's well-appointed office while he chain-smoked and told me about the hospital and its role in the Russian criminal justice system. The special hospital is one of seven institutions for the criminally insane in Russia, which, he explained, belong to the highest of four categories of security—categories that match the severity of both the crimes committed by its patients and the mental illnesses with which they are diagnosed. Styazhkin described the criteria by which patients ended up in the hospital in comparative terms: "They must be mentally ill and not responsible [*ne otvestvennyi*], nonculpable [*nevmeni-aemyi*]. The system here is a little different from the US. Here if a person carries out a crime in a state of nonculpability [*nevmeniamosti*]—he goes free of punishment. In the US he might be punished; here he is freed from punishment and goes for compulsory treatment [*prinuditel'noe lechenie*]. And depending on the severity of the crime and the severity of the illness, these are the four levels of security."[17]

When I later told friends and acquaintances in St. Petersburg (who had nothing to do with addiction treatment) about by my visits to the special hospital, their reactions most commonly assumed that the majority of patients did not belong there—although for two completely different reasons. Most of my friends immediately speculated that the patients were malingering in order to avoid prison—an assumption that drew upon the common knowledge of young men simulating psychiatric symptoms in order to avoid conscription into the army, during both the late and post-Soviet periods. Zurab, a heavy metal guitarist, even described his own brief stint under observation in a psychiatric hospital: "It was great. We would go outside wearing our patients' robes and we could do anything without any consequences. You could scream in a policeman's face and he couldn't do anything to you. You're a *psikh!*" Paradoxically, the other association that many acquaintances had with the special hospital had to do with another nonclinical use of diagnosis—in this case, the commitment of political dissidents during the late Soviet period.

During the 1970s and early '80s, the special hospital in what was then Leningrad became somewhat notorious for its involvement in the story about Soviet psychiatry most widely known in the Anglophone world: the use of forensic psychiatry against prominent political dissidents. This practice of diagnosing political nonconformists as mentally ill and committing them to psychiatric hospitals seems to have emerged specifically as a late Soviet phenomenon that accelerated during the Brezhnev years (Etkind 1994). (Indeed, during an earlier period, commitment to a psychiatric hospital may have been seen by legal officials as a means of evading much harsher forms of punishment.)[18] Most of the dissidents diagnosed as mentally ill and thus nonculpable were accused of violating articles 70 and 190–91 of the Soviet Penal Code, which forbade anti-Soviet agitation and dissemination of propaganda defamatory to the state (Gordon and Meux 1994). Though courts were required to specify a period of imprisonment, commitment to one of the special hospitals was open-ended, left to the discretion of psychiatrists.[19]

The overriding focus that the Cold War debates placed on the political abuse of psychiatry arguably removed attention from the increasing levels of normal institutionalizations taking place at the time (Joravsky 1989, 418). Indeed, between 1955 and 1975, a period marked in the United States by massive deinstitutionalization and decrease of inpatient services for the mentally ill, the number of Soviet psychiatric hospital beds grew from 106,500 to 312,600 (432). Additionally, the same legal frameworks and diagnostic categories that facilitated the commitment of political dissidents also made it easier for ordinary citizens to lock away unwanted relatives—sometimes after paying off a psychiatrist (Field 1991).

Yet, as is once again the case today, accounts of politically motivated commitments trumped any interest in more systemic or everyday problems of inpatient psychiatry in Russia. Starting in the early 1970s, first-person accounts of Soviet political dissidents who had been declared mentally ill and committed began to circulate widely outside the Soviet Union, along with writings by dissident psychiatrists such as Semyon Gluzman, who provided counterdiagnoses. Taken up into the polarizing logic of Cold War politics, this issue quickly reversed the generally respectful and interested disposition that North American and British psychiatrists had held toward their Soviet counterparts over the previous two decades (Belkin 1999).[20] Repeated condemnation by the international scientific community led the Soviet All-Union Society of Psychiatrists to withdraw from the World Psychiatric Association (WPA) in 1983 rather than risk being expelled. Five years later, with perestroika under way, a number of reforms were made, including the shift of the high-security psychiatric hospitals from under the aegis of the Ministry of Internal Affairs to that of the Ministry of Health, and the Soviet psychiatric society was provisionally readmitted to the WPA the following year (Smith and Oleszczuk 1996).

During this period Styazhkin, who had worked at the hospital since the late 1970s, had been one of the first psychiatrists to make public his hospital's dossiers on several prominent political prisoners, and he had participated in international conferences on Soviet psychiatric abuse. Indeed, because it was situated in what was then Leningrad, the special hospital housed a disproportionate share of prominent political prisoners, and by the late 1990s newspaper articles about the hospital would quote Styazhkin listing the dissidents who had passed through the hospital almost as a badge of honor: Victor Bukovsky, General Pyotr Grigorenko, Vladimir Borisov, Victor Fainberg, Esenin-Volpin:

"By the way, many of them remember their stay in the hospital with great warmth," says Victor Styazhkin, and as proof relates the following story. In 1992 Victor Dmitrievich went to New York for a conference of psychiatrists. There, a friend introduced him to the wife of the general-dissident [Grigorenko]. She invited Styazhkin home and fed him a hearty borscht. And then she gratefully said, "Pete never said anything bad about your hospital. He said that everyone there treated him benevolently enough. Of course, that's compared to other similar institutions." (Orlov 2005)

When I asked Styazhkin which diagnoses patients in the hospital tended to have, he explained, "Seventy to 78 percent are schizophrenia." "That's by the old classification," he added, referring to the Soviet nosological system that had, several years earlier, been officially replaced by the WHO's International Classification of Diseases. Schizophrenia was the diagnosis given to the majority of people committed to Soviet psychiatric hospitals, and indeed Cold War critics argued that Soviet categories of mental illness—particularly a "transitory" variant of schizophrenia that could be diagnosed in the absence of any presenting symptoms—facilitated the purposeful misdiagnosis of political dissidents (Joravsky 1989, 429–31).[21]

"According to the new [nosology]," Styazhkin explained, these formerly schizophrenic patients were diagnosed with schizo-type or schizo-affective disorders. And the rest are about the same [proportions]: oligophrenia, psychopathy, epilepsy, organic illnesses of the brain, traumas." However, as he continued, 80 percent of the crimes committed by patients in the hospital were committed in a state of drug or alcohol intoxication, and 52 percent of these patients suffered from substance dependence (Kazakovtsev, Styazhkin, and Tarasevich 2002).

This had been the initial justification for the program that was the original purpose of my visit: the 12-step-based rehabilitation program housed in the hospital's Ward 12. As Styazhkin explained, the program had not simply been created at the instigation of 12-step activists in Russia but had been modeled after one in a corrections system undergoing a drastic neoliberal transformation of its own: "At the origins of our 12-step program was Bob Kennington from CCA [Corrections Corporation of America]. [There is] a large private prison in Nashville and about half of the prisoners are in the program—I've been there myself. We liked the program a lot—I was there with the prosecutor, who in his time oversaw the carrying out of the law here. [Kennington] was then invited here and he worked with our coworkers."

Like HOH, this program was based on the Minnesota Model, which meant that the entire therapeutic milieu was understood as key to patients' recovery (J. Spicer 1993). While the program includes medication, social work, psychotherapy, and work therapy (the ward maintains a small computer cluster and woodshop for patients), the weight of therapeutic work is placed on the 12-step group meetings that take place in the ward. The group itself, called Mirror (Zerkalo) meets three times a week—of the hospital's 650 patients, approximately 75 take part. In a program based on patients' self-identification as addicts, Styazhkin emphasized the importance of employing addiction counselors who not only identified as recovering addicts but had been inmates as well. "What we found useful in Kennington's [CCA] program is that he attracts former patients—people who've been freed—to participate. . . . This makes the work more effective. Because when the doctor says that drinking is bad for you, then inside the patient the thought arises: 'Have *you* ever tried drinking like this?' At the meetings I've attended—I think this is very useful."

It was precisely this aspect of the 12-step program—its autonomy from the practices and knowledge of biomedicine and psychiatry—that created the greatest obstacles for Styazhkin. The resistance of medical personnel to a program that to some degree placed the authority of physicians below that of fellow sufferers and overtly blended techniques seen as psychotherapeutic with those seen as spiritual was perhaps fueled more by a strong and increasingly embattled ethic of professional authority and expertise than by any Soviet legacy of atheism or materialism. Yet Styazhkin seemed to have prevailed whether by persuasion (he had organized a series of lectures on addiction treatment for the hospital staff), example (his own involvement with the House of Hope included presiding over the dedication of the chapel), or the exercise of his authority (he emphasized that he had no superiors at the hospital and answered directly to the Ministry of Health), and the hospital was now regularly visited by addiction counselors.

Stayzhkin and the physicians who ran the program emphasized the successful rehabilitation to society of the patients who had completed the program and been released from the hospital (a psychologist on the ward referred to them as "our alumni" [*nashi vyipuskniki*]): many of them were working now. Often patients were released from the hospital and transferred to another rehabilitation program: more than forty had been transferred to the House of Hope. Others lived for a while in a halfway house established by the doctors and counselors. Unlike the general population of patients, who tended to be released in three years, patients from the program were released in half that time.

The link between the addiction-oriented 12-step program and the patients' presence at the hospital was not entirely straightforward in that neither a diagnosis of alcohol nor one of opiate dependence would render a defendant in a criminal case nonculpable according to the Russian Federation's Criminal Code. (If anything, intoxication and addiction are treated as aggravating circumstances.) Rather, nonculpability usually depended on having carried out a crime in a psychotic state, and more than 70 percent of the patients in the hospital were diagnosed with either schizophrenia or a schizoaffective disorder.[22] And yet one of the psychiatrists argued that "very few people commit their crime in a state of psychosis," and Styazhkin explained that 80 percent of the crimes committed by patients in the hospital were committed in a state of drug or alcohol intoxication, and 52 percent of these patients suffered from substance dependence (Kazakovtsev, Styazhkin, and Tarasevich 2002). The psychiatrists viewed many of these patients' addictions as precipitated by self-medication. "They tell us, 'When I drink the voices in my head stop,'" explained one clinician on the ward.

In order to allow release from the hospital, the law required that there be an "elimination or lowering" of patients' social dangerousness, yet both Styazhkin and the ward psychiatrists emphasized that what they looked for was "a more or less critical relationship to the illness." "This is an important part of the program," Styazhkin explained, "A critical relationship to the illness, a critical relationship to his own social status. For us, it's a good sign if a patient enters the program. As a doctor, then I understand that he is beginning to understand his own problems." However, he added, "We always tell the participants—that participation in the program is good for you, but it won't be the main reason for your release [*vypiski*]. This is a program for you, your life." One of the ward psychiatrists added, "The 12-step program creates a conscious relationship to oneself [*osoznannoe otnoshenie k sebe*] and [the patients] see that they are not alone or unique. The patient is active."

Here, the 12-step program was viewed instrumentally by the clinicians as a means of managing the stigma of severe mental illness by replacing it with alcoholism as a kind of proxy illness or form of self-identification. As Styazhkin put it in a journal article about the program, "It is often easier for the patient to acknowledge that he is an alcoholic or drug addict than a mentally ill person, and in this way to carry over all of his psychological problems onto the plane of alcoholism or drug addiction" (Kazakovtsev, Styazhkin, and Tarasevich 2002, 17).[23] Self-identifying as an alcoholic was meant to be the first step in a general process of self-reflection, insight, and improvement, which for the psychiatrists and the hospital director had as its end an ideal of rehabilitation—of reintegration of the patients into a particular vision of the social. According to this logic, the seeming lack of fit between diagnoses and methods of rehabilitation—the fact that no one was sent to the hospital because of a diagnosis of alcohol dependence—was no incongruity at all but a technique for managing the effects of stigma. And yet this framing of addict self-identification was deeply in tension with the way that this identification was understood by Nikolai and other counselors and participants in the program.

Psychotherapy with God

Nikolai was often described as the ultimate success story of both the program in Styazhkin's hospital and HOH. He had been committed to the hospital after years of arrests and hospitalizations related to his drinking. He had been one of the first patient-inmates through the 12-step program at the hospital, and like those who followed him he was transferred upon discharge to the House of Hope. Over the following five years, he had gradually risen to become one of the head addiction counselors there and had completed a training course in upstate New York.

For Nikolai, embracing the 12-step program was inextricable from trying to live "a Christian life." While this meant a certain level of involvement with organized Orthodox Christianity, the AA movement and its practices seemed to figure as the central source of religious institutionalism in his life. Like other St. Petersburgers I met who were involved in AA, Nikolai spoke about having a spiritual (*dukhovnyi*) outlook and approach to life rather than a religious (*religioznyi*) one. When I asked him what living a Christian life meant, Nikolai emphasized that it was more than simply "re-entering society"—something that might be seen as a basic goal of rehabilitation programs. As he put it, "Everyone has a purpose, a God-given purpose, that's more than just working, getting married and having children." At this point, while describing the fourth step—which requires members to make a "fearless and searching moral inventory" of themselves—Nikolai evoked the hybrid therapeutic and spiritual character of AA's practices, explaining, "It's like the most amazing psychotherapy, but where the psychotherapist is God."

Within the network surrounding the House of Hope, Nikolai served as both a charismatic leader and a model of recovery—a "miracle" in the words of an American donor. The hospital director emphasized Nikolai's transformation: "Of course when he first came to us, Nikolai was more an animal than a person." While no longer working as a counselor, Nikolai continued to lead AA group meetings in the city and work as a social worker at the special hospital. Along with his friend Andrei, he organized a series of concerts that brought musical performers in HOH's social network to the hospital. Nikolai also acted as an unofficial liaison between the rehabilitation program at the hospital and HOH, arranging for patients to be admitted to the rehabilitation center and shuttling them to the center on the outskirts of St. Petersburg. Moreover, Nikolai's close involvement with these groups brought him into contact with the American sponsors of HOH, as well as with the Mit'ki and other cultural figures associated with the center, in a set of relationships that blended friendship, recovery, and business. This network also provided Nikolai with the resources to reconstruct a family. I knew that he had been married before and that his teenage son was addicted to drugs. He had met Vera, his present wife, after his release at a 12-step group meeting in the city; she was a recovering drug addict at least ten years his junior.

What did it mean for Nikolai to identify as an alcoholic? Within the social network of 12-step programs and their adherents, this identification provided him with a valuable source of symbolic capital. In addition to being released from the hospital, he gained access to a set of therapeutic techniques in which (despite a lack of formal higher education) he could claim not only expertise but a privileged position (in relation to sober psychiatrists) as a "fellow sufferer." And though he was certainly not accepted as an equal by intelligentsia members of AA, he was able to circulate among them and to benefit from a network of contacts that spanned class distinctions as well as national borders. Despite all of this, Nikolai and other patients did not frame their identifications as means to other ends but as ends in themselves.

Rehabilitation, Citizenship, and Sodality

In radically extending the parameters of Nikolai's life by means of his identification with an illness, AA's rehabilitative techniques have a family resemblance to the numerous phenomena anthropologists have lately described under the rubric of "citizenship." Building on Paul Rabinow's (1992) notion of a sociality constructed around a now technically manipulable biology, which itself of course was an elaboration of Foucault's concept of biopower, scholars have described varieties of "biological citizenship" (including "therapeutic" and "pharmaceutical" citizenship)— claims to rights and privileges made to state and nonstate organizations on the basis of illness status or biological fact. A particular set of conditions underlies the otherwise varied cases described under the rubric of biological citizenship—whether in the case of Ukrainians claiming disability status due to their exposure to radiation during the Chernobyl disaster (Petryna 2002), AIDS activists in Brazil or Burkina Faso working to access antiretroviral medications (Biehl 2007; Nguyen 2005), or refugees from North Africa claiming asylum in France on the basis of marks of torture and trauma (Fassin 2007; Ticktin 2010). In Vinh-Kim Nguyen's felicitous phrasing, underlying all these cases are the conditions of "a neoliberal world in which illness claims carry more weight than those based on poverty, injustice, or structural violence" (2005, 143). While such concepts of citizenship illuminate significant ways in which illness and health increasingly mediate the claims people make on various governing institutions, there are a number of compelling reasons for developing a more differentiated terminology for thinking about the politics of life and health in the contemporary world.[24]

In this chapter I have proposed the notion of the illness sodality as one step in this direction. Cases such as that of AA in Russia highlight several phenomena that a language of citizenship deemphasizes or even fails to capture. These include the hybrid secular-spiritual character of associations such as AA and their deliberate dissociation from any projects of institutional governance, welfare provision, or claims to rights or resources. This does not mean that such associations are in fact unrelated to such projects. Illness sodalities such as AA may overlap with projects of citizenship, but unlike these—and unlike patient advocacy groups—they are not explicitly concerned with any projects of institutional governance, whether carried out by the state, NGOs, or other transnational actors.

Conclusion

This book has examined the ways in which the clinical management of alcoholism has changed over the critical period of post-Soviet transformation in Russia, focusing on the implications of these changes for practitioners and patients. Taking narcology as a domain of knowledge, ethics, and intervention, it raises a number of questions regarding the place of truth and ethics, responsibility, personal autonomy, beneficence, and obligation in the processes that make up this domain. In what follows I bring together a number of the themes and arguments developed in the book.

First, the book examines the translation of clinical ideas and technologies along several vectors: (1) interventions and institutions developed during the Soviet period are retooled for post-Soviet times; (2) clinical technologies originating in the United States are translated into a Russian setting; (3) a constant translation between expert and lay spheres of knowledge takes place; and (4) social and political meanings and processes are translated into clinical and commercial value.[1] I argue that since the late 1980s, the field of clinical and public health addiction management has undergone two distinct but closely related shifts. The more remarked-on of these is the shift from a state socialist political economy (characterized by competition among firms for scarce resources and exchanges of favors [*blat*]) to an unevenly regulated market in which state, commercial, and nongovernmental clinical institutions compete for patients (Verdery 1996; Ledeneva 1998; Salmi 2003). The second shift took place in the political economy of knowledge regarding addiction and its treatment. Late Soviet narcology was based in a very particular biomedical model, which claimed its origins in Ivan Pavlov's physiology of reflexes (Babayan and Gonopolsky 1985; Joravsky 1989). Though by the 1970s and '80s, the actual research and treatment conducted under this banner often ignored Pavlov's work, late Soviet medicine defined addiction in overwhelmingly biological terms and made heavy use of behavioral treatment methods, such as the alcohol antagonist disulfiram and emotional-stress psychotherapy (Ivanets 2002). At the same time that Russian narcology has developed closer ties to the international medical and scientific communities, its practitioners have increasingly found themselves competing with imported methods and movements, ranging from Alcoholics Anonymous to Scientology.

In tracing these translations, I have focused on the practices through which clinicians and other practitioners produce and manage what I call "therapeutic legitimacy." As Margaret Lock and Vinh-Kim Nguyen have written, "in addition to the mastery of biomedical technologies, practioner-selfhood encompasses the political and social processes that confer therapeutic legitimacy. The power to heal is not only a result of individual prowess, but the social relations that accrue to those endowed with therapeutic authority" (2010, 291). As I have suggested throughout this book, such social relations and processes extend far beyond formal criteria of training and credentialing. Indeed, highlighting therapeutic legitimacy draws our attention to the diffuse and informal processes through which efficacious healing is enacted. Throughout this book, but particularly in chapter 4, I have thus traced how therapeutic legitimacy is produced and managed in face-to-face interactions between clinicians and patients, as well as in the broader discursive arenas of the media and in the slippery domain of rumor.

One of the aims of this argument is to move away from using analytic frameworks that narcologists (and their non-Russian colleagues) typically deploy in their own discourses: biomedicine versus alternative or complementary medicine, manipulative methods versus humane ones. Aversive treatments were often depicted by their detractors as Soviet, authoritarian, and manipulative, and depicted as fostering dependence, by contrast with 12-step programs and psychodynamic therapy, which were cast as humanistic and depicted as fostering autonomy and independence. In response, proponents of khimzashchita and kodirovanie argued that these therapies *did* confer agency onto patients and that they were more appropriate to the Russian culture and mentality. Although I am not suggesting any substantive relationship between modes of political authority and clinical techniques, attempts to create or bolster such associations were clearly an important strategy used by practitioners in building or undermining the legitimacy of various therapies. In other words, I have examined how these very labels are employed in the process of building legitimacy for certain methods over others. Thus contemporary Russian debates about and struggles over appropriate interventions into the problems of addiction evoke the broader institutional, political, and historical contexts within which these therapies and interventions are embedded.[2]

This book gives attention not only to the accounts of physicians but also to those of patients, specifically arguing that while many narcologists have an interest in portraying hypnosis as a powerful and authoritative technology, patients undergoing such treatments do not experience themselves as controlled by some external agency or by something akin to political persuasion. Rather, many patients see treatments such as hypnosis as actually affording them relatively more autonomy—both in their everyday lives and in their self-conceptions—than 12-step methods, which require of adherents a full self-transformation, somewhat like a religious conversion. While relationships of dependency do develop between physicians and their patients, these have less to do with any particular clinical methods than with the overall social trajectories of patients' lives.

Patients have been caught in a web of institutional and discursive practices—the forensic, the legal, the rehabilitative, the spiritual. The figures of personhood and responsibility that inhered in those practices differed from, and at times clashed with, one another. Whereas some of these practices were enacted by psychiatrists, narcologists, counselors, and healers ascribing certain forms of personhood (and certain claims about responsibility) to patients, others were taken up, rehearsed, struggled with, modified, and sometimes claimed by the patients themselves. Indeed, I have suggested that one key distinction between the therapeutic methods I call prostheses for the will and 12-step methods is the degree to which the latter are part of an ongoing process of acting to become a person of a certain sort. This is a process not without a potential for irony, tension, and failure, yet one that has an elective affinity with the cultural logic of neoliberalism.

Ultimately, I have suggested that patients' different experiences and understandings of therapeutic modalities had as much to do with the broader configuration of institutions and relationships (both inside and outside the clinic) within which any particular instance of the treatment took place as they did with the particularities of the therapies themselves. The addiction therapies discussed here highlight how the efficacy of *all* treatment is shaped by elements, including chemical effects and patients' interpretations of those effects, clinical performances and relationships, clinicians' styles of reasoning and local research traditions, and the institutional and political economic settings of treatment. Moreover, such a perspective suggests how partial and incomplete an understanding of any clinical intervention is when it is reduced to a therapeutic protocol, a reduction that depends on the assumption that clinical technologies are discrete, portable, and transposable between contexts with little transformation. As the movement of clinical knowledge, substances, and techniques becomes ever more ubiquitous and far-reaching, it is increasingly important for anthropologists of medicine and psychiatry to explore the processes and mechanisms that link patients' treatment experiences to the material, discursive, performative, and institutional elements of which all interventions are composed.

Notes

Introduction

1. Much Foucault-inspired literature on health focuses on medicalization, understood as a particular mode of knowledge and intervention underpinned by the specialist authority of the medical profession (Foucault 1980; Petersen and Bunton 1997). This literature typically examines the ways in which the framing of human experience (particularly experiences of suffering) by the dominant paradigms of biomedicine tend to obfuscate or erase social and political meanings and implications, thereby shaping and reinforcing existing arrangements of power and distributions of resources. The conceptual key to such analyses is precisely not that physicians act as puppets for a *repressive* power of the state or a particular class (as Marxist analyses would have it) but that medicalization functions as a form of *productive* power underwritten by the professional autonomy, expertise, and knowledge of physicians. Medicalized discursive and institutional practices are thus one particular form of biopower—that is, they are a form of political rationality and practice focused on "fostering life" and regulating populations (Foucault 1980).

2. As historians of science and medicine have shown, today's chronic, relapsing brain disease model is just the most recent in a long series of attempts to conceptualize addiction to alcohol, opiates, or other drugs as a disease (Acker 2002; Campbell 2007; Valverde 1998). While these models share certain characteristics, they invoke distinct loci and mechanisms of addictiveness and privilege different forms of intervention and lines of scientific research; in addition, all have been shaped both by their contemporary political and social milieu and by the styles of thought prevailing in contemporaneous scientific communities (Berridge 2013; Courtwright 2005; Gusfield 1996;

Vrecko 2010b). If there is one red thread running through this literature, it is the idea that experts arguing for disease models have, since the nineteenth century, represented themselves as "'moral entrepreneurs' or 'moral pioneers' [seeking] to change public policy and shift popular perceptions" (Campbell 2013, 239) of addiction as moral failing or deviance. While some of this research emphasizes continuity—tracing a process of medicalization, an expansion of the addiction concepts' applicability, or a genealogy of "the disease model"—much of the recent literature highlights the divergent ways in which addiction (as well as its objects and subjects) has been framed in medicalized terms.

3. In a set of observations that can be generalized to other clinical settings, Van der Geest and Finkler (2004) note the widespread perception of hospitals as spaces where the practices of contemporary biomedicine are conducted and reproduced in a relatively uniform manner, regardless of local context. However, as work conducted on the anthropology of biomedicine over the past twenty-five years has shown, this perception of uniformity and relative homogeneity is better understood as the ideology of biomedicine.

4. Most of the names used in this book are pseudonyms. In order to simply demarcate the roles of different informants, I use first names (such as Vyacheslav or Pavel) to indicate patients and 12-step counselors and first names along with patronymics (Anton Denisovich, Alexander Sergeevich) to mark most physicians. Because the first name/patronymic combination is a relatively formal type of address, typically used to mark respect or social distance in Russian, its use runs the risk of essentializing the distinction between physicians and patients; but this naming system also gives a sense of the interpersonal hierarchy at play in most St. Petersburg clinics. I have used the actual names of those few figures who have already been written about in the media; they are identified by their first and last names (e.g., Sergei Tikhomirov).

5. Given physicians' generally high level of authority in the hospital, relative to patients, this selection of interviewees led me to question patients' capacity to give consent under such conditions. See Vieda Skultans's discussion of a similar quandary during her fieldwork with psychiatrists and their patients in Latvia (2005, 496).

6. While anyone is allowed to attend AA meetings designated "open," "closed" meetings are restricted to those who are already members or believe they "have a problem with alcohol" (Wilcox 1998, 48).

1. States of Crisis

1. This slippage is somewhat masked for English readers by the fact that both *russkii* (which refers to the language and nationality) and *rossiskii* (which refers to the Russian Federation) are translated as "Russian."

2. As I discuss in chapter 2, such use of antipsychotics has been justified by the theory, influential in Russian narcology, that understands addictive craving as a kind of "over-valued idea" or even a phenomenon approximating a delusion (Mendelevich 2013).

3. It is important to note that shifts between formal and familiar registers—primarily marked through the second-person pronouns *ty* and *vy*—can have a range of meanings and effects, depending on the situation and the relative social position of the speakers. Thus the familiar *ty* can be used not only to convey a closeness of relations but also to demean someone or highlight his or her subordination.

4. The legal category that most closely approximated these colloquial and quasi-clinical categories of abjection, was BOMZh, which stands for "Without a Fixed Place of Residence" (*Bez Opredelennogo Mesto Zhitelstvo*) and refers to persons who lack a residency registration. The contemporary Russian residency registration—still referred to by most people as *propiska*, its Soviet name—is often described as the latest version of a state technology for the surveilling, managing and restricting the mobility of populations that dates to Peter I's introduction of internal

passports during the early eighteenth century. Reestablished in 1932, the propiska system became the linchpin of the Soviet "mobility regime" and the means by which the party-state sought to settle nomadic populations, organize labor power, enforce military conscription, control urban in-migration, and deliver social services (Stephenson 2006). While most of the punitive elements of this system—including various laws aimed at "vagrants" and "parasites"—were abolished in the early 1990s, the Russian registration system continues to link social citizenship—in the form of access to health care, legal employment, education, and pensions—to residency. There is, of course, some flexibility to the system—as many of the patients in the narcological hospital lacked registrations but were still allowed to access its resources. Yet on a day-to-day basis, the administrative category BOMZh was perhaps less salient to these patients than the everyday notion of *bomzh* and its associations with dirt, disorder, and moral bankruptcy (Höjdestrand 2009).

5. In Russia, rates of HIV/AIDS remained relatively low until the mid-1990s, when highly processed heroin began to displace various types of opiates made from poppy straw—in a pattern that directly followed the spread of "hard currency" markets throughout the country (Paoli 2002). For the first fifteen years of the epidemic, injection drug use was responsible for the vast majority of HIV transmission in Russia. For example, public health researchers estimated that in 1997 between 74 and 90 percent of new HIV infections in the Russian Federation originated in injection drug use (Atlani et al. 2000). By 2012 this figure had dropped to below 60 percent (Federal AIDS Center 2012). Heroin remains the most commonly used drug in Russia, with some recent estimates putting the number of injectors at 1.5 million or even higher; over one-third are likely to be HIV-positive (Goliusov et al. 2008; UNODC 2011).

6. Such sweeping culturalist arguments (made by Russian elites as often as by visitors) were one of a number of Orientalizing (and self-Orientalizing) discourses that, as Larry Wolff (1994) has argued, served to demarcate Eastern Europe as a space of backwardness.

7. While contemporary accounts are generally more astute, many tacitly employ the accounts of early European travelers to Russia as evidence of the timelessness of Russian heavy drinking practices. Indeed, as Simpura and Levin have argued, two basic mythic narratives have prevailed in many discussions of Russian drinking and alcohol. According to one, "the Russians and alcohol, and vodka in particular, have lived in a harmony where the benefits have been rich and the damages negligible. . . . A side-plot in that story consists of the efforts of evil rulers to bring discipline into this inherently harmless relationship" (1997, 13). The opposite (but closely linked) mythic narrative assumes that "Russians are particularly prone to excessive drinking, with particularly detrimental consequences in production and reproduction" (ibid.). Yet even this narrative has another shade of meaning, for, as Simpura and Levin point out, it is often assumed that "that excessive drinking is but another of the hardships the Russians have to undergo," and that "these hardships also refine the Russians into a deeper understanding of life, into spheres that are inaccessible to those more blessed with well-being" (ibid.).

8. Significantly, the popular perception of narcotic drug use as a solely post-Soviet problem overlooks the fact that the USSR experienced a significant epidemic of drug use during the 1920s and '30s (Latypov 2011; Vasilyev 2012).

9. By the mid-1990s some of these groups had transformed from their emergence several years earlier as protection rackets into semilegal and legal security organizations and had come to be widely perceived as agents of much-needed social order (Yurchak 1999).

10. As Dale Pesmen eloquently puts it, in the process of sitting and drinking together "work was transformed into rest, business into community, exchange into help, and vice versa through fluidity, leakage, and formal similarities between economic and emotional solidarities" (2000, 181). But see Doug Rogers 2005, 69, on women in his rural field site in the Urals who distinguish between drinking that has some instrumental or productive aspect and spur-of-the-moment carousing.

11. As some observers have argued, this campaign demonstrated the ideological and dispositional kinship of Gorbachev with his sponsor, the late general secretary Yuri Andropov. It was during Andropov's brief rule during the early 1980s that various campaigns had been spearheaded against corruption, theft from the state, and other crimes against the Soviet state and society. It was also during this time that a new discussion about alcoholism was initiated in the press (S. White 1996; M. Levine 1999).

12. As two Soviet educators wrote during the late 1970s, "Boys being raised without a father either internalize 'female'-type behaviors or create a distorted notion of male behaviors as antagonistically opposed to female behaviors and reject everything that their mothers try to instill into them. In both cases, there forms a vulgarized notion of male behaviors as aggressive, uncouth, harsh, and cruel . . . in an expressly belligerent sense" (Isaev and Kagan 1979, 29; quoted in Zdravomyslova and Temkina 2012).

2. Assembling Narcology

1. As many anthropologists of postsocialism have shown, expressions and enactments of nostalgia for various aspects of the socialist past have been commonplace—if not ubiquitous—over the past twenty years (Berdahl 1999; Boyer 2006; Todorova and Gille 2010).

2. In what follows, I will focus primarily on "official narcology," the branch that predominates in the state-funded addiction treatment service, central research institutes in Moscow and St. Petersburg, and the Ministry of Health. Because of the high level of centralization in Soviet medicine, much of this account may serve for former Soviet republics other than Russia as well.

3. Throughout this book, I use the notion of "style of reasoning" drawn from the work of Ludwik Fleck (1979) by Ian Hacking (1992). As Allan Young describes it concisely, a style of reasoning "is composed of ideas, practices, raw materials, technologies and objects.... It is a characteristically self-authenticating way of making facts, in that it generates its own truth conditions," (2000, 158).

4. Foucault wrote about problematization as "the ensemble of discursive and nondiscursive practices that make something enter into the play of true and false and constitute it as an object of thought" (1966, 670, quoted in Rabinow 2003, 18). Paul Rabinow adds that "a problematization . . . is both a kind of general historical and social situation . . . as well as a nexus of responses to that situation. . . . The domain of problematization is constituted by and through economic conditions, scientific knowledges, political actors, and other related vectors" (2003, 19).

5. Such accounts typically begin with the establishment of kabaks (taverns that distilled their own vodka) by Ivan IV during the 1540s (Christian 1990). From the institution of the state-run kabaks in the sixteenth century, the Russian state employed a number of institutional arrangements to extract value from the production and sale of vodka. (These were paralleled by the restriction of production or trade outside state-regulated circuits; from 1660 non-nobles were prohibited from distilling for private use.) By the early eighteenth century taxes on the production and sale of vodka accounted for 10 percent of state revenues; by the nineteenth century vodka had become the largest single source of income for the Imperial Treasury, bringing in up to one-third of ordinary revenues. Such levels were, to some degree, connected to the fiscal structure of the imperial state: vodka was not the only substance that was taxed. Until the mid-eighteenth century, the taxation of salt provided comparable levels of income. As Christian and others have argued, the state's increasing fiscal dependence on revenues from vodka in particular played a significant role in transforming the drinking practices of villagers, peasants, and serfs. Since kabaks were able to generate a higher profit from distilled liquor than from beer or mead, they promoted the consumption of vodka over lighter alcoholic drinks through pricing (Christian 1990; Takala 2002).

6. A campaign to revive what Stalin called "the fashion for money" accompanied this shift. While the new policy was interpreted by the sociologist Nicholas Timasheff and others as central

evidence of a "great retreat," later accounts of the Stalin period have rejected this argument and have taken the statements of the regime more seriously. Thus David Hoffmann argues that the shift in the mid-1930s was tied not to the abandonment of socialism but to its supposed realization. Noting Stalin's declaration at the seventeenth party congress that socialism had been built and the vestiges of capitalism "rooted out," Hoffman argues that institutions and values that may previously have been suspect as bourgeois were now available to bolster socialism. "No longer was it necessary to use iconoclasm to attack bourgeois culture, now that the economic basis and social classes that had spawned that culture had been eliminated in the Soviet Union" (2003, 6).

7. While I discuss the distinctions that specialist discourses on narcology drew between such categories as alcoholism and chronic alcoholism in the following section, popularizing texts of the 1960s and '70s (even those authored by physicians) often failed to distinguish between drunkenness and alcoholism altogether (Zenevich 1967).

8. Susan Gross Solomon (1989, 1990) argues that while social hygienists avoided making the kinds of broad social critiques that their researches may have facilitated, their emphasis on gradual adaptation, moderation, and voluntary resocialization clashed with the ethic of impatience and speed, as well as the belief in the unlimited possibilities of sheer willpower championed during the 1930s industrialization. At a more fundamental level, whereas hygienists' depiction of alcoholism as a social disease conferred primary responsibility on the Soviet state, psychiatrists' definition of it as a mental pathology placed this responsibility more fully on the patient.

9. This sentiment epitomized the affinities between Pavlov's theories and the Bolsheviks' dispositions regarding materialism, mind, and consciousness. David Joravsky argues that party leaders simply persisted in the unexamined assumption (by then prevalent in radical circles for some fifty years) "that reduction to physiology was the only way for psychology to become a science" and added to this the assumption "that Pavlov's school was leading the way" (1989, 212). All of this discussion was very general and unspecific: there is no evidence that any of the Russian Marxists were aware of the actual arguments underlying the early twentieth-century rejection of the concept of mind (185). This of course is hardly surprising. Given their practice-oriented dispositions and consumed as they were with the tasks of building a revolutionary organization, seizing state power, and reconstructing the institutions of governance, even the more thoughtful Bolsheviks had little time for squaring their theories of human action with those being developed in the human sciences.

10. Following a longitudinal approach, Soviet psychiatrists were more likely to base their diagnoses on the changing course of a patient's symptoms over time than they were to examine only those symptoms presented during a single clinical encounter. Calloway (1992) notes that the preference for longitudinal diagnosis was facilitated not only by theoretical factors but also by institutional ones: namely, the fact that mental illness care was coordinated through dispensaries, which were responsible for overseeing territorially bounded patient populations. A dimensional approach to mental disease in turn assumes a continuum of possible states, ranging from relatively healthy ones through different forms marked as pathology. Such an understanding of illness has been described as fitting well with a nominalist conception of disease generally.

11. Snezhnevskii was vaulted to power from relative obscurity in the late 1940s, during the midst of a xenophobic campaign to create a Soviet Russian psychiatry and root out cosmopolitanism (code language for Jewishness). In 1950 he was appointed director of the Serbskii Institute and soon afterward chief of psychiatry at the Central Institute for Postgraduate Medical Training. Rival schools of thought avoided publishing overt criticisms of Snezhnevskii's concept of schizophrenia (Joravsky 1989).

12. The dominant argument was simply that alcoholism was one of many social ills (poverty, prostitution, and crime among them) that were inevitably fostered by capitalist relations of production (Galina 1968, 6). By radically transforming these social roots of alcoholism, many

texts argued, the construction of socialism would, by definition, eradicate such phenomena. While such claims were patently absurd by the 1950s and '60s (after more than two decades of life under socialism, according to official definitions), the questions that they raised were avoided in public discourse.

By the 1970s and '80s some Soviet commentators were distinguishing the "primary social roots" (exploitative relations of production), which fed alcoholism under capitalism, from the "secondary" ones, which explained its persistence under socialism: "people's habits and norms" (*privychki i nravy*) (Beisenov 1981, 12). Thus, perhaps it was not surprising that the broad conclusions reached by these researchers were similar to those of the social hygienists: heavy drinking, or alcohol abuse, was depicted as a learned behavior or habit born out of the drinker's relationships in his "microsocial environment" (*mikrosotsial'naia sreda*) (Zenevich 1967; Galina 1968, 50–58; Tkachevskii 1974, 37).

13. Despite its somewhat confusing name, many Russian narcologists refer specifically to alcohol abstinence syndrome rather than withdrawal, indexing the Soviet scientific origins of the former. As described during the late 1920s and early '30s by the Soviet neurophysiologist S. G. Zhislin (1959), "abstinence syndrome" (*abstitentnyi sindrom*)—sometimes referred to as "hangover syndrome" (*pokhmel'nyi sindrom*)—is characterized by tremors, sweats and difficulty sleeping. Ivanets (2001) argues that Zhislin's work went unnoticed overseas, until it was essentially replicated as withdrawal syndrome by American researchers during the 1950s.

14. The crime of "hooliganism" had been created in 1922 primarily to address the "consequences" of intoxication such as brawls and disturbances of the "public order" (Solomon 1978, 91). This labile category, which was applied to acts ranging from public swearing to fighting to destroying state property, was defined in the criminal code as "intentional actions violating the public order [*obshchestvennyi poriadok*] in a coarse manner and expressing a clear disrespect for society [*obshchestvu*]" (Kirichenko 1967, 5; Solomon 1978, 194). Although discussions of hooliganism often related it to intoxication, this legal category encompassed only "public" spaces, excluding similar disturbances in domestic spaces or even communal apartments (Solomon 1978). This is one of many seemingly minor ways in which new public-private distinctions were being drawn in the Soviet Union during the 1950s and '60s. An increasingly important theme in the historical and ethnographic literature on socialism and postsocialism is the question of how spaces or practices outside the purview of the party-state (or indistinguishable to its gaze) emerged (Yurchak 2006).

15. In fact, the initial legal basis for giving compulsory treatment to addicts categorized as "socially dangerous" had been laid by a 1927 decree. However, the specific provisions and institutions for carrying out such treatment were not developed until this point in the post-Stalin period (Babayan and Gonopolsky 1985; Solomon 1989).

16. As Solomon explains, the planned campaign against the "roots" of heavy drinking was preempted and scuttled by a campaign against hooliganism initiated by the Ministry for the Defense of the Social Order (MOOP). Since the anti-hooliganism campaign was perceived by security officials as a "repressive measure," the call for extending compulsory treatment to noncriminal alcoholics was the only recommendation that fit into the goals of this campaign. Solomon suggests that this turn of events may have reflected the strength of MOOP (and related security ministries such as the MVD) relative to other organs of the Soviet state, such as the supreme court (1978, 88).

17. The broader anti-alcohol measures (cuts in production, propaganda) were initiated five years later, in 1972, with a joint decision by the Communist Party's Central Committee and the USSR Council of Ministers: "On measures to step up the drive against drunkenness and alcoholism." A nationwide network of commissions was established to oversee the campaign (Tkachevskii 1974, 30).

18. During the 1990s the number of sobering-up centers decreased rapidly. The system was shut down entirely in 2011.

19. Field attributes the creation of "medical microdistricts" and a system of care based on these districts as the ground-level unit of organization to the zemstvo reform of 1864. "A microdistrict (*uchastok*), a territorial or geographic unit for the delivery of medical care, was designed to provide complete and comprehensive medical coverage for the population. The basic organizational medical nucleus was an outpatient clinic to which was added, later, a small hospital" (1967, 22).

20. For accounts of the genesis and use of the propiska system by the Soviet party-state, including its role in "fixing" national identities see Matthews 1993; Kotkin 1995; Popov 1995; Shearer 2004. On the post-Soviet effects of the system, particularly for those left without documents or housing, see Höjdestrand 2009.

21. *Zona* is a Soviet term used to denote detention and prison colonies, often located in Siberia, the Far East, or the circumpolar regions of Russia; it is often used more or less interchangeably with the term "gulag."

22. For a statistical breakdown of LTP inmates during 1989 by age, education, criminal record, and diagnosis, see Bondarev and Karetnikov 1991.

23. See http://верхотурье-сити.рф/publ/21-1-0-47 (http://72.fsin.su/strukturnye-podrazdeleniya/fku-sizo-2.php).

3. Selling Sobriety

1. Similarly, the funding of hospitals according to their ability to fill a given number of beds and polyclinics according to their capacity created an incentive for specialists to carry out more procedures than they might have otherwise. Thus, during the 1980s the USSR had an average of 2.8 days of hospital stay per person annually, as opposed to 1.2 in the United States (where the deregulation of medical insurance was simultaneously promoting the opposite effect) (Twigg 1998).

2. Other systemic tendencies of the planned economy affected the healthcare sector as well. Like other units or firms within the socialist economy, hospitals and polyclinics operated under what Janos Kornai (1992) and other economists have called "soft budget constraints": that is, conditions under which a fiscal failure leads not to bankruptcy but to a firm's being bailed out by the state. Simultaneously, socialist managers were pressed to fulfill and overfulfill quotas and goals of the plan, a task that placed them in competition with other firms for limited material resources. These two conditions combined to create an incentive for socialist managers to hoard supplies, pad their budgets, and request more than they needed from the center, as well as to circumvent official channels of distribution by exchanging directly with other firms. These dynamics created shortages throughout the socialist economy, which only fueled the same dynamic (Berliner 1957; Kornai 1992; Verdery 1996, 21–22). Moreover, such practices of hoarding extended to human resources, as managers (anticipating no-shows or underqualified employees) often requested more specialists than they needed from the centralized system that assigned university graduates to jobs (Solnick 1998, 135–36).

3. Additionally, the share of the national budget allotted for health dropped from 6.5 percent in 1965 to 4.6 percent in 1985; translated into a percentage of estimated GNP, this amounted to something in the range of 3 to 2 percent (Davis 1989, 246; Rivkin-Fish 2005). Physicians' salaries were typically only 70 to 80 percent of an average manual worker's pay, one of the factors that led to the increasing feminization of the Soviet medical labor force: women accounted for 76 percent of the labor force in this sector in 1950, a figure that had climbed to 80 percent by the late 1990s (Ryan 1978, 42, 1990, 22; Schecter 2000, 89).

4. Soviet laws mandating employment also fostered a brisk market (which has also persisted into the present day) in the "sickness certificates" that provided a legitimate excuse for missing work (Ryan 1978, 117–25; Field 1991). Universal male conscription and ubiquitous practices of hazing (*dedovshchina*) created a similar market in physicians' statements attesting to a young man's physical or mental lack of fitness for military duty (Solnick 1998, 181; Elkner 2004).

5. The eighty-eight regional funds and the single federal fund were to receive their primary financing from income-based contributions made by employers: 3.4 percent for a regional fund and .2 percent for the federal one (Sheiman 1994). In most cases the funds were meant to act not as insurance providers but as independent regulators of the insurance system; they would finance commercial insurance companies, which in turn would develop contracts with local hospitals, clinics, and medical practices. Competition in this system was to take place at two levels: consumers would have a choice of insurance companies vying for their business, and hospitals and clinics would compete for contracts with insurance companies. Additionally, the system retained a strong element of state support: the health care of those citizens who were unemployed or retired would be financed by the federal fund or by municipal governments' contributions to the mandatory funds. The federal fund was meant both to equalize funding across regions and to support medical care that was deemed particularly significant—including oncology, tuberculosis, and some STDs (Sheiman 1994; McKeehan 1995; Twigg 1998).

6. Moreover, the rapid decentralization of health care has arguably resulted in eighty-eight separate healthcare systems—each structurally and functionally different from the others. Critics have argued that this has to do both with the inadequate regulation of the market in some areas and with an excessive devolution of authority in others (Twigg 1998). One essential problem lay in the fact that much of the money meant to finance clinics and hospitals never reached them; rather, it disappeared or remained in the insurance funds. Thus throughout the 1990s, only 30–35 percent of healthcare financing came from the mandatory insurance funds (Balabanova, Falkingham, and McKee 2003; Rivkin-Fish 2005). At the same time cash-strapped municipal governments, expecting that these payments would be forthcoming, began to slash their health budgets, leaving hospitals and clinics in a financial bind.

7. By 2000 the number of beds had further declined, to 30,233 (Ivanets 2001). In 2012 there were only 101 narcological dispensaries left and 24,250 beds (Narcology Research Institute 2012).

8. For instance, a local movie theater catering to middle- to high-income people offered VIP viewings of films for about three times the price of regular tickets. They were screened in a small hall containing only five pairs of plush seats, each of them equipped with a button allowing viewers to silently summon a waitress.

9. Many thanks to Daniel Alexandrov for suggesting this interpretation of anonymous treatment and the register.

10. The lack of protection of privacy was linked to a number of concrete factors, including the conduct of medical consultations. Vieda Skultans writes that in Soviet Latvia psychiatric consultations "lacked the privacy with which they are associated in the West. Access to consulting rooms is seldom restricted to a doctor and her patient. Besides the prescribing nurse who shares the consulting room, other staff and, indeed, patients frequently interrupt an ongoing consultation.... Patients were, until recently, in charge of their own notes. In such contexts, problems are publicly shared" (2003, 498).

11. Dreizin had also had a sordid past—in 2002 his clinic lost its license when the head of the city's licensing bureau was accused of receiving bribes from him. A bomb subsequently went off near this official's home.

12. The man who had held the position of head narcologist for the northwest district prior to Tikhomirov, Leonid Shpilenia, was attacked several times, in his account because he refused to sell licenses. Shpilenia had been in the post of head narcologist for only two months when in March 2003 he was severely beaten; in June of that year, two attempts on his life were made by

bomb. Upon Shpilenia's resignation, the post went to his deputy, Tikhomirov. Other attacks and intimidations surrounded the doctor. Originally when Shpilenia was appointed head narcologist, a Natalia Kulikova was named his deputy. However, days before she could assume the post, she had been attacked by an acid-wielding assailant as she approached her home. Tikhomirov was named to the post instead. Soon thereafter, two other narcologists resigned from the addiction hospital after receiving death threats (Andreev 2004; Bezrukova 2006; Tumakova 2004).

13. The seminar, "Propaganda for a Healthy Lifestyle and Drug Use Prevention: Different Understandings, Common Interests?," was held on December 9, 2003, at the Center for the Development of Noncommercial Organizations in St. Petersburg.

14. Article 55.2 in the Federal Law on Narcotic Drugs and Psychotropic Substances, 1–8–1998.

15. The argument is not that the state has been taken over by the mafia but that it has lost its monopoly on legitimate violence and become one of many actors providing similar services (Volkov 2002).

4. Prostheses for the Will

1. In the case of pharmaceutical interventions, patients' self-identification and their conceptualization of their illness play a somewhat different role in the treatment process. While it is not intrinsically necessary for patients to conceive of their problems as originating in their brains in order for psychopharmaceutical interventions to work effectively, they are in fact encouraged to think this way for several reasons: to produce demand for pharmacological products, to increase compliance with pharmacological treatment regimens, and to ensure a relationship of trust and mutual understanding between physician and patient under an ethical regime of patient autonomy. Thus while many actual patients may continue to think about themselves and their distress in a variety of different terms, it might be fair to say that the ideal patient implicit in the imagination of many biologically oriented psychiatrists is one who conceptualizes her symptoms as stemming from a neurochemical imbalance (Dumit 2003).

2. As practiced in the Soviet Union, "rational psychotherapy" emphasized the role of the physician as a mentor-like figure who explained to the patient the ways in which his thinking was illogical. Alexander Etkind suggests that the belief in the rationality of the mentally ill underpinning this branch of psychotherapy leads to a displacement of responsibility onto the patient, and therefore something close to a "punitive psychiatry" (1994, 70). It is worth noting that while such an approach may be deeply divergent from psychodynamic ones, it is not so different from cognitive-behavioral therapies so popular in the United States. More important, Soviet writers argued that the effectiveness of rational psychotherapy depended on an unequal relation of authority between physician and patient, often emphasizing the requirement that the former be "intellectually superior" (Lauterbach 1984, 61–69).

3. During the 1930s, Walter Voegtlin, a gastroenterologist who had studied with Pavlov, established a sanitarium in Seattle for the treatment of alcoholism by conditional-reflex therapy. Along with several other self-styled "alternative clinics" throughout the United States and United Kingdom, this institution—now known as the Schick-Shadel Hospital—continues to treat addiction using aversion therapy (Lemere 1987; White 1998, 106–8).

4. This was the term used by social hygienists to describe those patients whose illness was primarily explicable by reference to "social factors" and who would benefit from the outpatient treatment they advocated (Solomon 1989).

5. Indeed, even textbook protocols suggest the punitive character of the technique. A course of treatment with procedures like the one described above included "15–20 daily sessions" (Babayan and Gonopolsky 1985, 221). The fact that the effectiveness of the therapy was thought to hinge on the extreme unpleasantness of the experience meant that narcologists were effectively

encouraged to place the health of their patients in danger (at least temporarily): "Nausea and vomiting begin about ten minutes later, but the patient must be compelled to take additional portions of alcohol, which in turn causes repeated painful retching spasms. . . . It should remembered, however, that each session may end in pronounced, and at times severe, states of cardiovascular insufficiency, occasionally even reaching the state of collapse. Hemorrhage from the esophagus and stomach due to the rupture of small vessels and epileptic seizures are also possible. Therefore, a first-aid kit should be fitted with all the essential drugs and kept at hand" (224).

6. Derived from the full chemical name—Tetraethylthiuram disulfide—*teturam* or *tiuram* is a name used for disulfiram in Russian (Sereiskii 1952; Eneanya et al. 1981). Antabuse is the trademarked name of disulfiram. Esperal is a brand name for disulfiram produced by the French pharmaceutical company Sanofi-Aventis, but in Russia "Esperal'" typically refers specifically to disulfiram implants.

7. When it is used, disulfiram is typically recommended as an adjunct to psychosocial treatment programs, used to facilitate periods of sobriety during which patients can develop a "sober life-style" (Brewer, Meyers, and Johnsen 2000, 329).

8. Anne Harrington has argued that the roots of twentieth-century skepticism toward placebos emerged when epistemological concerns regarding the existence of invisible forces such as "animal magnetism" intertwined with moral anxieties provoked by the notion of "a weak and impressionable mind (i.e., the patient's) [coming] under the thrall of a strong and persuasive personality [i.e., the doctor's or healer's]" (2006, 185; 2008). Harrington argues that the epistemological and moral anxieties were brought together in the concept of "suggestion"—"the 'capacity to transform an idea directly and automatically into a sensation or movement'" (2006, 185). Soon thereafter, with the rise of drug-based therapies during the early to mid-twentieth century, the practice of giving patients chemically neutral pills became increasingly viewed by medical opinion at worst as a sham and at best as something with no physiological basis used to mollify "difficult" patients (ibid.). In the case of disulfiram, this epistemological ambiguity is compounded by the fact that unlike placebo analgesia or changes mediated by the immune system, the locus of disulfiram's nonspecific effect is particularly unclear. Sobriety that results from disulfiram therapy is a change in behavior that can be conceptualized as mediated by both conscious and unconscious mental processes.

9. The issue of compliance has been addressed by embedding disulfiram treatment into a number of institutional structures and coupling it with behavioral technologies in which patients' agency is closely delimited or curtailed—such as parole, probation, or dispensation of the drug at specialized clinics (White 1998, 227; Brewer, Meyers, and Johnsen 2000, 332–36; Steffen 2005). For this reason the treatment is depicted by critics as one that requires an unacceptable level of coercion or social control (Steffen 2005, 184–15).

10. Rozhnov directed the All-Union Psychotherapeutic Center and was head of the Department of Psychotherapy at the Central Institute of Advanced Medical Training (Babayan 1985). As was often the case in Soviet medicine, the most widely promoted therapies were also ones developed by persons at the top of their respective institutional hierarchies.

11. Rozhnov ascribes this argument to the Canadian researcher Hans Selye. In a thesis that Rozhnov explains influenced the development of emotional-stress psychotherapy, Selye argues that "stress" "may not mean only destruction, but also creation, be not only pathogenic but also sanogenic; in short, life itself is stress, while complete freedom from stress, according to Selye, is death" (Babayan 1985, 111).

12. This may be a misnaming of "Narkonon," the therapeutic and rehabilitation system developed by the Church of Scientology (Atak and Dvorkin 1996).

13. Most of the cases of patient deaths after disulfiram therapy involved commercial enterprises that offered the service of at-home disulfiram treatment. This procedure was sometimes carried out without checking the patient's current blood alcohol level, and the house-call teams often left immediately after completing the treatment.

14. Keenly aware of the negative connotations that the term "coding" has taken on, Grigoriev (2002) categorically rejects this appellation, arguing that the technique should be more accurately called decoding, in that the code refers to DNA and to the genetic predisposition to alcoholism. Grigoriev adds that Dovzhenko's method was important in the development of Russian narcology in that it made clear the necessity of cooperation between the church and medicine.

15. Another relatively common practice in Soviet psychiatry and narcology, the injection of sulfazine increased patients' body temperatures to 40°C and was used as a form of aversion therapy.

16. As Summerson Carr (2013) has argued, much of the literature on addiction therapeutics—and indeed much of the work in medical anthropology on therapeutics more generally—has focused on the production of neoliberal subjects. One important vein of research has developed a Foucauldian interpretation of addiction therapeutics and interventions as "technologies of the self" (Valverde 1998). According to many of these arguments, nineteenth-century US and British ideas of addictions as "diseases of the will"—translated in the twentieth century into "impairments of choice"—arose and continue to stand in a mutually constitutive relationship to free will or unfettered choice (Seddon 2007; Sedgwick 1993; Valverde 1998). To put it in very rough terms, the addict was seen as one who was unable to align his actions with his intentions because of a weakness or failure of the will, which was conceptualized as a human capacity alongside reason and emotion. As Eve Sedgwick pointed out in a highly influential essay, such formulations of addiction resonate deeply with the problematics of capitalism in its consumer phase, with its exhortations to the free, willing subject to compulsively consume (1993).

17. At its basis, the method involved putting the patient into a trance state (in the past Kalashnikov had used the mild hallucinogen ketamine, but after it became illegal, he had switched to a strong antihistamine) and showing her images on a computer interspersed with "subliminal suggestions." Using this method, Kalashnikov explained, "Alcohol is associated symbolically with something negative—like a sharp object, a nail, for instance."

18. Indeed, in Pelevin's novel *Chapaev i Pustota* (translated into English as *Buddha's Little Finger*), a psychiatrist refers to his mode of treatment, which involves putting patients into drug-induced trances, as the "Kanashnikov method." Veller, apparently a friend of Kalashnikov, writes about his practice in his book of stories, *Gonets iz Pize*.

19. Kalashnikov retells the story of the shaman in a 2001 newspaper article—taking some liberties with Levi-Strauss's original (Kalashnikov 2001).

5. Rehabilitation from Abroad

1. The issue of how to interpret the kind of movement that characterizes Nikolai's story—whether it is movement of people, money, or technologies—has been central to discussions among anthropologists for well over a decade. Most recently, debates about cultural homogenization and localization that took place under the rubrics of "transnationalism," "globalization," and the "glocal" have been joined by discussions of "global assemblages"—a term that seeks to acknowledge both the radically mobile character of certain elements (particularly tools of rationalization such as standards and software code) and the mutability and contingency of others (such as ethical orientations and personalistic relationships) (Ong and Collier 2005).

2. For example, Valverde and White-Mair argue that while "AA members are perpetually in recovery, always working on their souls . . . they do not imagine they will ever remake themselves from scratch, by contrast to the neoliberal illusion that the poor can become business executives by sheer willpower. AA goes so far as to challenge American individualism by regarding exaggerated views of one's power as part of the very illness of alcoholism" (1999, 401).

3. Although no surveys of AA in Russia have been conducted (and the informal nature of the organizations makes this a difficult proposition), by the time of my research, there were at least

ten AA groups in St. Petersburg with more than 150 members, at least thirty groups in Moscow, and according to some estimates, as many as three hundred groups throughout the Russian Federation (Critchlow 2000b). In addition to multiple groups in large cities such as Nizhni Novgorod and Kazan, AA members were active in small cities in European Russia such as Kostroma and Ivanovo. Other 12-step-based mutual-help groups, such as Narcotics Anonymous, and groups for codependent family members, such as Al-Anon, were also becoming increasingly popular in larger cities. In Moscow, a city then rife with casinos and automatic slot machines, Gamblers Anonymous groups were also being formed.

4. Valverde argues that the latter "fits the familiar Foucaultian pattern of identity-based governance" (1998, 140). The idea of an essentialized alcoholic identity is made clear in a frequently cited distinction between so-called dry drunks—people who have achieved sobriety yet continue to think and behave "alcoholically"—and those who have attained true sobriety or serenity and put grandiosity and resentments behind them (Kurtz 1979, 123). Thus while many of AA's techniques seem focused largely on behavior and its effects, eschewing a concern with the underlying roots of addiction, the emphasis on a complete and thoroughgoing change in self makes the program fully consonant with various stratigraphic conceptions of subjectivity—whether a Christian concern with the salvation of the soul or a depth psychology focus on insight or what Summerson Carr has called a linguistic "ideology of inner reference" (2006, 634).

5. Scholarly work on the practices of AA and other 12-step programs has closely examined how processes of self-transformation are linked to autobiographical narrative. Typically such narratives follow a script embedded in the AA literature: increasingly out-of-control drinking, losses and social isolation, hitting bottom, joining AA and recovery (Cain 1991; Hanninen and Koski-Jannes 1999; Humphreys 2000).

6. There are of course many varying interpretations of the processes central to healing and self-transformation in AA and other 12-step programs. For the purposes of this argument, it is worth noting that many participants—unlike the counselor mentioned above—may not view identification as an important element in the program, focusing instead on the values of humility or surrender or the modest techniques for living, such as "one day at a time" (Valverde 1998, 135–37; Wilcox 1998, 83–107). Others have interpreted the transformative aspects of AA in much more gradualistic terms as a spiritual awakening modeled on Protestant theology (Antze 1987, 173) or a radical epistemological shift away from a pathological Cartesian dualism (Bateson 1971).

7. Many researchers—including me—have dealt with this issue by attending open meetings and conducting in-depth conversations or interviews with group members outside the group setting (Mäkelä et al. 1996; Valverde 1998). David Rudy represented himself to the members of AA groups he attended for sixteen months not as an alcoholic but as a "sociologist interested in finding out about AA" (1986, 2), and he gradually progressed from being viewed as "a tolerated intruder, an outsider, to a near-member" (3). Members of the AA group Stanley Brandes studied in Mexico City allowed him to participate in meetings although he did not identify as an alcoholic, categorizing him as an "Admirer of Alcoholics Anonymous" (AAA) (2002, xv). On the other hand, Danny Wilcox was drawn to conduct an ethnography of AA only after a period of having experienced it as a recovering alcoholic (1998, 20–29).

8. Under Bantle's leadership, U.S. Tobacco had employed a number of advertising and sales-based strategies to successfully expand the market for smokeless tobacco from a core demographic of older blue-collar men to teenagers and athletes (Denny 1993; Wyckham 1999).

9. Several HOH counselors argued that the only reason people in the program relapsed was that they had failed to properly follow the practices outlined for them. One former counselor put it this way: "As Father Martin told us at Ashley [a rehab center in the United States], the program is not a salad bar [*shvedskii stol*]. You can't pick and choose what you want and leave the rest."

10. See Yurchak 2006 for an extended discussion of the Mit'ki.

11. This joke is somewhat lost in translation. The colloquial term for delirium tremens—*belaia goriachka*—literally means "white fever."

12. This sentiment pointed to something of a paradox at the heart of the Mit'ki's new project as spokesmen for AA. On the one hand, they were certainly doing the work of reducing a stigma attached to alcoholism. At the same time, it was never quite as simple as that—given the degree to which heavy drinking, alcoholism, and even mental illness have all been associated in a quasi-romantic myth about creativity in Russia (also a familiar theme in many European discursive traditions), the notion of the Mit'ki quitting the bottle could cut both ways. Indeed, while almost every educated person in St. Petersburg knew about the Mit'ki, many did not know about their new sober incarnation. When I told several friends about Shagin's involvement with the House of Hope, they immediately added that it made sense because his art was no longer interesting or compelling in the way it had been.

13. Though it was developed independently, this element of the Minnesota model shares many characteristics of the therapeutic community model developed in the United States and United Kingdom to address addiction and mental illness in the wake of deinstitutionalization (Cook 1988).

14. For example, even in his semiofficial history of AA, Ernest Kurtz notes that during the 1950s and '60s, "the impression of both sociologists and casual observers was that most regulars at meetings had hit the rocks of alcoholism from one of two related directions: the frustration of efforts at upward mobility—preeminently a lower middle class affliction; or the pains of perceived downward mobility" (1979, 133).

15. As one narcologist explained, "The most difficult thing was the acceptance of god, the higher power. And the idea that the higher power is not necessarily god was helpful. This was an epochal change for me as well, because I was raised in an entirely atheistic family. So I started to work out a philosophical background for the higher power for myself. It was not an easy process. The higher power is an all-human reason, it is nothingness. . . . Indeed, something has an influence on us, it depends what you call it."

16. The narcologist Alexander Sofronov made a related though somewhat different claim, arguing that the social and economic conditions of contemporary Russia were closer to that of the United States during the Depression, when AA was developed.

17. The insanity rule given in Chapter 21 of the Criminal Code of the Russian Federation (1997) reads: "A subject is not responsible for criminal offense, if at the time of commission of the socially dangerous act, he was in the state of insanity and was unable to appreciate the factual nature and social dangerousness of his act (or inaction) or control his actions as a result of chronic mental illness, temporary mental illness, mental deficiency or other pathological mental disturbance" (quoted in Bukhanovsky and Gleyzer 2001). Like many of the American insanity tests, this rule includes both a cognitive and a volitional aspect. The rule of nonculpability can be fulfilled by a subject who is either lacking in cognitive capacity to appreciate the factual nature and social dangerousness of his act or in volitional capacity to control his actions. Commentators have noted that this definition of insanity is in fact stricter than, for instance, the Model Penal Code's insanity test: whereas the Russian penal code requires that the person totally lack (cognitive or volitional) capacity, the American test requires only a "substantial" lack (Bukhanovsky and Gleyzer 2001). Both Russian and American systems also allow for temporary mental illnesses, which are conceived of as transitory states.

18. As David Joravsky suggests, in the vast majority of ordinary cases, the decision whether to track offenders into the psychiatric system for treatment or into the penal system for punishment was influenced more by the respective professional dispositions of forensic psychiatrists, legal officials, and political administrators. Throughout Soviet history, he argues, legal officials tended to be suspicious of the category of nonculpability, suspecting psychiatrists of "coddling criminals under the pretense of treating sick people" (1989, 416).

19. Those declared nonculpable also lost various rights accorded to defendants in criminal cases: they could not be party to legal documents, and they could be denied information regarding the charges filed against them (Smith and Oleszczuk 1996, 32–33). Critics further noted that the 1967 and 1970 codes regulating criminal commitment left the definition of "social danger" entirely open and that an earlier 1956 instruction on forensic psychiatry allowed (in exceptional cases) for examinations to be conducted in the absence of the patient. (The relevant documents were the "Instruction on Compulsory Treatment of the Mentally Ill Who Have Committed Socially Dangerous Acts" of February 14, 1967, and the Ministry of Public Health Instruction "Forensic Psychiatric Examination in the USSR" of October 27, 1970; see Smith and Oleszczuk 1996, 148, 151.) Add to this the fact that the Soviet legal system afforded defendants the right to a lawyer only *after* the psychiatric examination, and the lack of any clear provision for appeal of commitment, and a picture emerges of Soviet institutions that were structured so as to facilitate the overuse of nonculpability findings (Smith and Oleszczuk 1996).

20. Following the first prominent case of General Pyotr Grigorenko, there was a slew of public accusations, and eventually memoirs written by former political prisoners appeared on shelves in the United States and United Kingdom. While this entire discussion was heavily refracted through the murky glass of Cold War politics, the participants often had more at stake at home than they did across the ocean. In other words, the discussion of Soviet psychiatric abuses was not simply more fodder for ideological warfare and geopolitical realpolitik. It was that, to be sure, but more as well. For American and British participants in the discussion, Soviet psychiatry at times came to stand for everything about their *own* psychiatric institutions and practices that, depending on one's view, needed reform, revolution, or repeal (Belkin 1999).

21. Much discussion focused on the typology of schizophrenia developed by A.V. Snezhnevskii, the clinician who presided over Soviet psychiatry from the early 1950s to the mid-1980s in much the same way as Lysenko did over genetics. Snezhnevskii held schizophrenia to be a hereditary disease that developed into one of three courses or states—continuous, intermittent, or transitory. It was the last of these that provoked the most controversy, the idea being that although the patient's symptoms had disappeared, he was still a schizophrenic and could be diagnosed in the absence of any presenting symptoms (Joravsky 1989, 429–31). "Even as a result of complete recovery the organism does not return entirely to the condition that preceded the disease," explained Snezhnevskii (341). Though such criteria certainly led to more diagnoses of schizophrenia, the dominance of Snezhnevskii's school had much to do with developments unrelated to the political utility of their disease categories (420–38).

22. Both the last Soviet criminal code and the Russian criminal code of 1996 specifically address the issue of intoxication, the latter stating that "a person committing a crime in a state of intoxication, brought about by the use of alcohol, narcotics or other inebriating [*odurmanivaiushchikh*] substances, is subject to criminal responsibility" (Russian Criminal Codex 1996, pt. 1, chap. 4, art. 23, reprinted in Zharikov 1999, 389; on Soviet law, see Morozov and Kalashnik 1971). Nonculpability is, however, extended to those who commit crimes in a mental state characterized as a "psychosis"—including delirium tremens and "alcoholic paranoia," as well as the somewhat atypical case of pathological intoxication. In other words, psychosis is the descriptive category used to distinguish from all other drinking offenders those who fulfill the requirements of the nonculpability test mentioned above.

23. Such instrumental use of diagnoses validates the notion that however stigmatizing public identification as an addict may be in contemporary Russia, it is much less so than identification as a mentally ill person. Grigorii, a 12-step counselor who estimated that he had spent a total of four years in psychiatric hospitals during the Soviet period, said he saw the effects that the delegitimation of psychiatry had on his own patients' dispositions: "Everything having to do with psychiatry—I think that all of our patients have this problem—whenever there is this prefix *psych-* . . .

for me as a Soviet person, for a long time it was better to die than to become a mentally ill person [*psikh-bolnym*]."

24. As Cristiana Giordano has argued, the proliferation of such concepts risks "creating a surplus of characteristics linked to citizenship that may in the end void the term of its explicative power" (2008, 589).

Conclusion

1. I use the metaphor of translation here in the sense it has been developed in anthropology—to suggest a movement between two domains that can never be completely commensurable and that effects particular changes in each of the domains.

2. It should be clear that I am in no way suggesting a lack of medical multiplicity or hybridization of therapies or that all (or even most) physicians or patients devote themselves to certain therapies to the exclusion of others. This is the case in certain situations more than others: for instance, patients who have gone through the 12-step program tend to be at best dismissive of khimzashchita and kodirovanie. Doctors, activists, and counselors deeply involved in the 12-step movement were even less likely to give the favored narcological therapies any credit at all. These are, after all, people engaged in the work of building the therapeutic legitimacy of 12 steps. Physicians who had less of a direct stake in the success of Alcoholics or Narcotics Anonymous were often much more ecumenical. While some were certainly skeptical of AA and thought of it as undercutting their authority, other narcologists I spoke to were supportive of the 12-step programs as suitable for certain patients, though not for others.

Bibliography

A. B. 1991. "AA in the Soviet Union Resembles Early Days in US." *The Addiction Letter*, February 1991, 4.

Altschuler, Vladimir. 1994. *Patologicheskoe Vlechenic k Alkogolyu* [Pathological desire for alcohol]. Moscow: Meditsina.

Anderson, D. J., J. P. McGovern, and R. L. DuPont. 1999. "The Origins of the Minnesota Model of Addiction Treatment—A First Person Account." *Journal of Addictive Diseases* 18 (1): 107–14.

Andreev, Sergei. 2004. "Glavnyi Narkolog Ubival Kolleg?" [Did the head narcologist kill his colleagues?]. *Smena*, October 7. http://www.smena.ru/news/2004/10/07/3965.

Antze, P. 1987. "Symbolic Action in Alcoholics Anonymous." In *Constructive Drinking: Perspectives on Drink from Anthropology*, edited by Mary Douglas, 149–81. New York: Cambridge University Press.

Atlani, Laetitia, Michel Caraël, Jean-Baptiste Brunet, Timothy Frasca, and Nikolai Chaika. 2000. "Social Change and HIV in the Former USSR: The Making of a New Epidemic." *Social Science and Medicine* 50:1547–56.

Babayan, Edward A., and M. H. Gonopolsky. 1985. *Textbook on Alcoholism and Drug Abuse in the Soviet Union*. Translated by Vladimir N. Brobov. New York: International Universities Press.

Babayan, Edward A., and Yu. G. Shashina. 1985. *The Structure of Psychiatry in the Soviet Union*. Translated by Vladimir N. Brobov and Boris Meerovich. New York: International Universities Press.

Balabanova, Dina C., Jane Falkingham, and Martin McKee. 2003. "Winners and Losers: Expansion of Insurance Coverage in Russia in the 1990s." *American Journal of Public Health* 93 (12): 2124–30.

Bansovich, Elena. 2001. "Alkogolizm Mozhno Prosto Zagovorit'" [Alcoholism can be simply talked away]. *Kommersant-Daily*, August 15.

Barabash, Ekaterina. 2006. "Trebuyutsia Sotrudniki s Diagnozom 'Alkogolizm'" [Wanted: Workers with a diagnosis of "alcoholism"]. *Nezavisimaia Gazeta*, February 10.

Bateson, Gregory. 1972. "The Cybernetics of Self: A Theory of Alcoholism." In *Steps to an Ecology of Mind*. Northvale, NJ: Jason Aronson.

Beisenov, B. S. 1981. *Alkogolizm: Ugolovno-Pravovye i Kriminologicheskie Problemy.* [Alcoholism: Juridical and criminological problems]. Moscow: Iurid. Literatura.

Bekhterev (1897) 1998. *Suggestion and Its Role in Social Life*. Edited by Lloyd Strickland. Translated by T. Dobreva-Martinova. New Brunswick, NJ: Transaction Publishers.

Beliaev, V.P., and L.N. Lezhepetsova. 1977. "Opyt Organizatsii Narkologicheskoi Sluzhby V Leningrade" [The experience of organizing the narcological service in Leningrad]. In *Lechenie i Reabilitatsiia Bol'nykh Alkogolizma* [Treatment and rehabilitation for alcoholism patients], edited by I.V. Bokii and R.A. Zachepinskogo. Leningrad: Bekhterev Psychoneurological Institute.

Belkin, Gary. 1999. "Writing about Their Science: American Interest in Soviet Psychiatry during the Post-Stalin Cold War." *Perspectives in Biology and Medicine* 43 (1): 31–46.

Berdahl, Daphne. 1999. "'(N) Ostalgie' for the Present: Memory, Longing, and East German things." *Ethnos* 64 (2): 192–211.

Berliner, Joseph. 1957. *Factory and Manager in the USSR*. Cambridge, MA: Harvard University Press.

Bernstein, Anya. 2013. "An Inadvertent Sacrifice: Body Politics and Sovereign Power in the Pussy Riot Affair." *Critical Inquiry* 40 (1): 220–41.

Berridge, Virginia. 2013. *Demons: Our Changing Attitudes to Alcohol, Tobacco, and Drugs*. Oxford: Oxford University Press.

Bezrukova, Lyudmila. 2006. "Narkolog-Ubiitsa" [Narcologist-killer]. *Trud*, March 21. http://www.trud.ru/index.php/article/21-03-2006/102015_narkolog-ubijtsa.html.

Biehl, João. 2005. *Vita: Life in a Zone of Social Abandonment*. Berkeley: University of California Press.

——. 2007. "Pharmaceuticalization: AIDS Treatment and Global Health Politics." *Anthropological Quarterly* 80 (4): 1083.

Bloch, S., and P. Chodoff, eds. 1991. *Psychiatric Ethics*. Oxford: Oxford University Press.

Bondarev, Viktor G., and Ivan V. Karetnikov. 1991. *Kharakteristika Lits, Soderzhashchikhsia v Lechebno-Trudovykh Profilaktoriiakh: Po Materialam Spetsial'noi Perepisi 1989 Goda: Posobie* [Characteristics of persons contained in therapy centers: Based on the special 1989 census: A manual]. Moscow: Vsesoiuznyi Nauchno-Issledovatel'skij Institut MVD SSSR.

Boon, James A. 1982. *Other Tribes, Other Scribes: Symbolic Anthropology in the Comparative Study of Cultures, Histories, Religions, and Texts*. Cambridge: Cambridge University Press.

Borenstein, Eliot. 1999. "Suspending Disbelief: Cults and Postmodernism in Contemporary Russia." In *Consuming Russia: Popular Culture, Sex and Society since Gorbachev*, edited by Adele Marie Barker, 437–62. Durham, NC: Duke University Press.

Borovoy, Amy. 2001. "Recovering from Codependence in Japan." *American Ethnologist* 28 (1): 94–118.

Bourdieu, Pierre. 1986. "The Forms of Capital." In *Handbook of Theory and Research for the Sociology of Education*, edited by J. Richardson, translated by Richard Nice. New York: Greenwood Press.

Bourgois, Philippe. 2000. "Disciplining Addictions: The Bio-Politics of Methadone and Heroin in the United States." *Culture, Medicine and Psychiatry* 24 (2): 165–95.

Bourgois, Philippe, and Jeffrey Schonberg. 2009. *Righteous Dopefiend*. Berkeley: University of California Press.

Boyer, Dominic. 2005. "The Corporeality of Expertise." *Ethnos* 70 (2): 243–66.

———. 2006. "Conspiracy, History, and Therapy at a Berlin Stammtisch." *American Ethnologist* 33 (3): 327–39.

Boym, Svetlana. 1994. *Common Places: Mythologies of Everyday Life in Russia*. Cambridge, MA: Harvard University Press.

Brandes, Stanley H. 2002. *Staying Sober in Mexico City*. Austin: University of Texas Press.

Brewer, Colin, Robert Meyers, and Jon Johnsen. 2000. "Does Disulfiram Help to Prevent Relapse in Alcohol Abuse?" *CNS Drugs* 14 (5): 329–41.

Britton, Annie, and Martin McKee. 2000. "The Relation between Alcohol and Cardiovascular Disease in Eastern Europe: Explaining the Paradox." *Journal of Epidemiology and Community Health* 54 (5): 328–32.

Brodwin, Paul. 1996. *Medicine and Morality in Haiti: The Contest for Healing Power*. Cambridge: Cambridge University Press.

Brotherton, P. Sean. 2012. *Revolutionary Medicine: Health and the Body in Post-Soviet Cuba*. Durham, NC: Duke University Press.

Budartseva, Svetlana. 2002. "LTP Dlia Narkomana: Eshche Odna Tyurma ili Shans Vyzhit'?" [LTPs for drug addicts: Another prison or a chance to survive?]. *Kommersant-Vlast'* 32:52.

Bukhanovsky, Alexander O., and Roman Gleyzer. 2001. "Forensic Psychiatry in the Russian Criminal Justice System." *American Academy of Psychiatry and the Law Newsletter* 26 (3): 14–16.

Burke, Justin. 1990. "AA Marks Third Year in Soviet Union." *Christian Science Monitor*, November 20, 15.

Burroughs, William. 1957. "Letter from a Master Addict to Dangerous Drugs." *British Journal of Addiction* 53 (2): 119–32.

Butler, William. 2003. *HIV/AIDS and Drug Misuse in Russia: Harm Reduction Programmes and the Russian Legal System*. London: International Family Health.

Cain, Carole. 1991. "Personal Stories: Identity Acquisition and Self-Understanding in Alcoholics Anonymous." *Ethos* 19 (2): 210–53.

Calloway, Paul. 1992. *Soviet and Western Psychiatry: A Comparative Study*. Keighley, UK: Moor Press.

Campbell, Nancy D. 2007. *Discovering Addiction: The Science and Politics of Substance Abuse Research*. Ann Arbor: University of Michigan Press.

——. 2013. "Why Can't They Stop? A Highly Public Misunderstanding of Science." In *Addiction Trajectories*, edited by Eugene Raikhel and William Garriott, 238–63. Durham, NC: Duke University Press.

Canguilhem, Georges. (1966) 1989. *The Normal and the Pathological*. Reprint, New York: Zone Books.

Carr, E. Summerson. 2006. "'Secrets Keep You Sick': Metalinguistic Labor in a Drug Treatment Program for Homeless Women." *Language in Society* 35 (5): 631–53.

——. 2010. "Enactments of Expertise." *Annual Review of Anthropology* 39:17–32.

——. 2011. *Scripting Addiction: The Politics of Therapeutic Talk and American Sobriety*. Princeton: Princeton University Press.

——. 2013. "Signs of Sobriety: Rescripting American Addiction Counseling." In *Addiction Trajectories*, edited by Eugene Raikhel and William Garriott, 160–87. Durham, NC: Duke University Press.

Chepurnaya, O., and A. M. Etkind. 2006. "Instrumentalizatsiia Smerti: Uroki Antialkogol'noi Terapii" [The instrumentalization of death: Lessons of anti-alcohol therapy]. *Otechestvennyie Zapiski* 2 (27).

Chertok, Léon. 1981. *Sense and Nonsense in Psychotherapy: The Challenge of Hypnosis*. London: Pergamon Press.

Chertok, Léon, and Isabelle Stengers. 1992. *A Critique of Psychoanalytic Reason: Hypnosis as a Scientific Problem from Lavoisier to Lacan*. Stanford: Stanford University Press.

Chick, J., and C. Brewer. 1999. "National Differences in Disulfiram Prescribing." *Psychiatric Bulletin* 23 (6): 335.

Christian, David. 1990. *Living Water: Vodka and Russian Society on the Eve of Emancipation*. Oxford: Oxford University Press.

Cockerham, William. 1999. *Health and Social Change in Russia and Eastern Europe*. New York: Routledge.

——. 2000. "Health Lifestyles in Russia." *Social Science and Medicine* 51:1313–24.

Collier, Stephen J. 2011. *Post-Soviet Social: Neoliberalism, Social Modernity, Biopolitics*. Princeton: Princeton University Press.

Comaroff, Jean, and John L. Comaroff. 1999. "Occult Economies and the Violence of Abstraction: Notes from the South African Postcolony." *American Ethnologist* 26 (2): 279–303.

Connor, Walter D. 1972. *Deviance in Soviet Society: Crime, Delinquency, and Alcoholism*. New York: Columbia University Press.

Conrad, Peter. 1992. "Medicalization and Social Control." *Annual Review of Sociology* 18:209–32.

Conroy, Mary Schaeffer. 1990. "Abuse of Drugs Other Than Alcohol and Tobacco in the Soviet Union." *Europe-Asia Studies* 42 (3): 447–80.

Cook, Christopher C. H. 1988. "The Minnesota Model in the Management of Drug and Alcohol Dependency: Miracle, Method or Myth? Part 1, The Philosophy and the Programme." *Addiction* 83 (6).

Courtwright, David T. 2005. "Mr. Atod's Wild Ride: What Do Alcohol, Tobacco, and Other Drugs Have in Common?" *Social History of Alcohol and Drugs* 20 (1): 105–40.

Critchlow, Patricia. 2000a. "First Steps: AA and Alcoholism in Russia." *Current History* 99 (639): 345–49.

——. 2000b. "The Impact of Sociopolitical Change since 1991 on Alcohol Treatment in Russia." MA thesis, Harvard University.

Csordas, Thomas J. 1993. "Somatic Modes of Attention." *Cultural Anthropology* 8 (2): 135–56.

Demin, Andrei, and I. Demina. 1998. "Zdorovie Naseleniia i Alkogol'naia Epidemiia v Rossii: Lekarstvo ot Zhizni?" [The health of the population and the alcohol epidemic in Russia: A medicine for life?]. In *Alkogol' i Zdorovie* [Alcohol and health], edited by Andrei Demin. Moscow: Russian Association for Public Health.

Denny, Jeffrey. 1993. "The King of Snuff." *Common Cause Magazine* 19 (2): 20–27.

Dent, J. Y. 1949. "Apomorphine Treatment of Addiction." *British Journal of Addiction* 46 (1): 15–28.

Denzin, Norman K. 1987. *The Alcoholic Self.* New York: Sage.

Dmitrieva, T. B., A. L. Igonin, T. V. Klimenko, L. E. Pishchkova, and N. E. Kulagina. 2002. "Zavisimost' ot Psikhoaktivkikh Veshchestv" [Addiction to psychoactive substances]. *Narkologiia* 9:2–9.

Dovzhenko, Alexander R., A. F. Artemchuk, Z. N. Bolotova, T. M. Vorob'eva, Yu. A. Manuilenko, A. I. Minko, L. A. Kurilko, and V. A. Dovzhenko. 1988. "Stressopsikhoterapiia Bol'nikh Alkogolizmom v Ambulatornykh Usloviiakh" [Outpatient stress psychotherapy of patients with alcoholism]. *Zhurnal Nevropatologii i Psikhiatrii Imeni S. S. Korsakova* 88 (2): 94–97.

Dovzhenko, A. V. 1991. *Vozvrashchayu Vam Zhizn': Seans Nadezhdy* [I return your life: a séance of hope]. Minsk: A.V. Dovzhenko.

Dumit, Joseph. 2003. "Is It Me or My Brain? Depression and Neuroscientific Facts." *Journal of Medical Humanities* 24 (1–2): 35–47.

Dyleva, Evgeniia. 2004a. "Lechit' narkomanov? Net, 'mochit' narkologov!" [Treat drug addicts? No, "bloody" the narcologists!] *Peterburskii Chas Pik.* 10, March 4–10.

——. 2004b. "Vodka s Semenami Konopli Pressuet Molodezhnuiu Subkul'turu" [Vodka with cannabis seeds puts pressure on youth subculture]. *Peterburskii Chas Pik* 26 (336): 11.

Eberstadt, Nicholas. 1999. "Russia: Too Sick to Matter?" *Policy Review* 95:3–24.

Egorov, V. F. 1996. Eshche Raz ob Alkogol'no-Narkologicheskikh Problemakh" [Once more on alcohol and drug problems]. *Voprosy Narkologii* 1:66–70.

——. 1997. "O Sostoianii Narkologicheskoi Sluzhby v Possii i Problemakh Ee Sovershenstvovaniia" [On the state of the narcological service in Russia and problems of its improvement]. *Voprosy Narkologii* 1:9–18.

Egortsev, Aleksandr. 1997. *Totalitarnye Sekty—Svoboda ot Sovesti* [Totalitarian sects: Freedom from conscience]. Moscow: "Sector" Informational-Missionary Center.

Elizar'eva, T. 2002. "Russkii krest." *Vechernii Barnaul,* November 22.

Elkner, Julie. 2004. "*Dedovshchina* and the Committee of Soldiers' Mothers under Gorbachev." *Journal of Power Institutions in Post-Soviet Societies* 1:144–61.

Elovich, Richard. 2008. Behind Every Doctor Is a Policeman: Narcology, Drug Users and Civil Society in Uzbekistan. PhD diss., Columbia University.

Eneanya, Dennis I., Joseph R. Bianchine, Dumar O. Duran, and Brian D. Andresen. 1981. "The Actions and Metabolic Fate of Disulfiram." *Annual Reviews in Pharmacology and Toxicology* 21 (1): 575–96.

Entin, G.M. 1991. "Eshche Raz k Voprosu o Stresspsikhoterapii Alkogolizma po Metodu A.R. Dovzhenko" [More remarks on the problem of stress psychotherapy of alcoholism by the A. R. Dovzhenko method]. *Zhurnal Nevrologii i Psikhiatrii Imeni S. S. Korsakova* 91 (2): 132–33.

Entin, G.M., A. G. Gofman, A.V. Grazhenskii, E.N. Krylov, A. Yu. Magalif, I.A. Nosatovskii, and I.V. Yashkina. 1997. "O Sovremennom Sostaianii Narkologicheskoi Pomoshchi v Rossii" [On the contemporary state of narcological help in Russia]. *Voprosy Narkologii* 1:68–76.

Erofeev, Venedikt. (1970) 2000. *Moskva-Petushki.* Moscow: Vagruis.

Etkind, Alexander. 1997a. *Eros of the Impossible: The History of Psychoanalysis in Russia.* Boulder: Westview Press.

——. 1997b. "There Are No Naked Thoughts: Psychoanalysis, Psychotherapy and Medical Psychology in Russia. In *Psychology in Russia: Past, Present, Future,* edited by Elena Grigorenko, Patricia Ruzgis, and Robert Sternberg, 59–82. Hauppage, NY: Nova Publishers.

Falby, A. 2003. "The Modern Confessional: Anglo-American Religious Groups and the Emergence of Lay Psychotherapy." *Journal of the History of the Behavioral Sciences* 39 (3): 251–67.

Farquhar, Judith. 2002. *Appetites: Food and Sex in Post-Socialist China.* Durham, NC: Duke University Press.

Fassin, Didier. 2007. "Humanitarianism as a Politics of Life." *Public Culture* 19 (3): 499–520.

Favret-Saada, Jeanne. 1990. "About Participation." *Culture, Medicine and Psychiatry* 14 (2): 189–99.

Federal AIDS Center, Russian Federation. 2012. *HIV infection in the Russian Federation in 2012.* Moscow: Federal AIDS Center. http://hivrussia.ru/files/stat/sprav_22112012.doc.

Feklyunina, Valentina, and Stephen White. 2011. "Discourses of 'Krizis': Economic Crisis in Russia and Regime Legitimacy." *Journal of Communist Studies and Transition Politics* 27 (3–4): 385–406.

Field, Mark. 1967. *Soviet Socialized Medicine: An Introduction.* New York: Free Press.

——. 1991. "The Hybrid Profession: Soviet Medicine." In *Professions and the State: Expertise and Autonomy in the Soviet Union and Eastern Europe,* edited by A. Jones, 43–62. Philadelphia: Temple University Press.

Field, Mark, and Judyth Twigg. 2000. *Russia's Torn Safety Nets: Health and Social Welfare during the Transition.* New York: St. Martin's.

Finn, Peter. 2005. "Russia's 1-Step Program: Scaring Alcoholics Dry." *Washington Post,* October 2.

Fitzpatrick, Sheila. 1992. *The Cultural Front: Power and Culture in Revolutionary Russia.* Ithaca: Cornell University Press.

———. 1999. *Everyday Stalinism: Ordinary Life in Extraordinary Times: Soviet Russia in the 1930s*. New York: Oxford University Press.

Fleck, Ludwik. 1979. *Genesis and Development of a Scientific Fact*. Chicago: University of Chicago Press.

Fleming, Philip. 1996. "Drug and Alcohol User Treatment/Intervention Services in Russia—A Western Perspective." *Substance Use and Misuse* 31 (1): 103–14.

Fleming, Philip, Tim Bradbeer, and Anita Green. 2001. "Substance Misuse Problems in Russia: A Perspective from St. Petersburg." *Psychiatric Bulletin* 25:27–28.

Fleming, Philip, A. Meyroyan, and I. Klimova. 1994. "Alcohol Treatment Services in Russia: A Worsening Crisis." *Alcohol and Alcoholism* 29 (4): 357–62.

Fomenko, Ekaterina. 2002. "Anonimnye Alkogoliki Gordiatsia tem Chto Oni Alkogoliki" [Alcoholics Anonymous [members] are proud of the fact that they're alcoholics]. *Kommersant-Daily*, August 8.

Fomenkova, Anna. 2000. "Lovtsy Zabludshikh Dush . . . Ili Kak Sharlatany Vsekh Mastei Nazhivatyutsia na Chelovecheskoi Bede" [The catchers of lost souls . . . or how charlatans of all stripes make a living off of human misery]. *Slovo*, March 1.

Foucault, Michel. 1965. *Les Mots and Les Choses*. Paris: Editions Gallimard.

———. 1980. *The Politics of Health in the Eighteenth Century*. In *Power/Knowledge: Selected Interviews and Other Writings, 1972–1977*, edited by Colin Gordon, 166–82. New York: Pantheon Books.

———. 1988. *Technologies of the Self: A Seminar with Michel Foucault*. Edited by Luther H. Martin, Huck Gutman, and Patrick H. Hutton. Amherst: University of Massachusetts Press.

———. 2006. *Psychiatric Power: Lectures at the College de France, 1973–1974*. New York: Picador.

Friedman, Jack R. 2009. "The 'Social Case.'" *Medical Anthropology Quarterly* 23 (4): 375–96.

Fuller, Richard, and Enoch Gordis. 2004. "Does Disulfiram Have a Role in Alcohol Treatment Today?" *Addiction* 99:21–24.

Gafutulin, Nail. 2005. "Kollektivnoe samoubiistvo" [Collective suicide]. *Krasnaya zvezda*, 4 June.

Gal, Susan, and Gail Kligman. 2000. *The Politics of Gender after Socialism: A Comparative-Historical Essay*. Princeton: Princeton University Press.

Galina, I. V. 1968. *Alkolizm Razrushaet Sem'yu* [Alcoholism destroys the family]. Moscow: Meditsina.

Galkin, V. A. 1996. "Sovremenye Zadachi Narkologicheskoi Sluzhby" [Contemporary objectives of the narcological service]. *Voprosy Narkologii* 1:71–75.

———. 2004. "Narkologiia—Razdel Psikhiatrii ili Samostoiatel'naia Meditsinskaia Distsiplina?" [Narcology—A division of psychiatry or a self-sufficient medical discipline?] *Narkologiia* 1:67–68.

Garcia, Angela. 2010. *The Pastoral Clinic: Addiction and Dispossession along the Rio Grande*. Berkeley: University of California Press.

Gerasimova, Ol'ga Valentinovna, and Igor' Nikolaevich Zubov. 1991. *Sluzhba Meditsinskikh Vytrezvitelei: Uchebnoe Posobie* [Working in medical sobering-up stations:

A tutorial]. Moscow: Uchebno-metodicheskij Tsentr, Glavnoe Upravlenie Kadrov, MVD RF.

Gershon, Ilana. 2011. "Neoliberal Agency." *Current Anthropology* 52 (4): 537–55.

Gilinskii, Yakov, and Vladimir Zobnev. 1998. "The Drug Treatment System in Russia: Past and Present, Problems and Prospects." In *Drug Treatment Systems in an International Perspective: Drugs, Demons, and Delinquents*, edited by Harald Klingemann and Geoffrey Hung, 117–23. Thousand Oaks, CA: Sage.

Giordano, Cristiana. 2008. "Practices of Translation and the Making of Migrant Subjectivities in Contemporary Italy." *American Ethnologist* 35 (4): 588–606.

Goliusov, A. T., L. A. Dementyeva, N. N. Ladnaya, N. I. Briko, M. S. Tumanova, N. A. Korzhayeva, and M. V. Semenchenko. 2008. *Country Progress Report of the Russian Federation on the Implementation of the Declaration of Commitment on HIV/ AIDS*. Moscow: Federal Service for Surveillance of Consumer Rights Protection and Human Well-Being of the Russian Federation.

Good, Byron. 1994. "Medical Anthropology and the Problem of Belief." In *Medicine, Rationality, and Experience: An Anthropological Perspective*, 1–24. New York: Cambridge University Press.

Gordon, Harvey, and Clive Meux. 1994. "Forensic Psychiatry in Russia: A Renaissance?" *Journal of Forensic Psychiatry* 5 (3): 599–606.

Graham, Loren R. 1987. *Science, Philosophy, and Human Behavior in the Soviet Union*. New York: Columbia University Press.

Grigoriev, Grigorii. 2002. "Batyushka [Father]." *In Istselenie Slovom* [Healing with the word]. St. Petersburg: Alexander Nevskii Temperance Society.

Gronow, Jukka. 2003. *Caviar with Champagne: Common Luxury and the Ideals of the Good Life in Stalin's Russia*. Oxford: Berg.

Grossman, Gregory. 1977. "The Second Economy of the USSR." *Problems of Communism* 26 (5): 25–40.

Gusfield, Joseph R. 1996. *Contested Meanings: The Construction of Alcohol Problems*. Madison: University of Wisconsin Press.

Haaken, Janice. 1993. "From Al-Anon to ACOA: Codependence and the Reconstruction of Caregiving." *Signs* 18 (2): 321–45.

Hacking, Ian. 1986. "Making Up People." In *Reconstructing Individualism*, edited by Thomas C. Heller, Morton Sosna, and David E. Wellby, 161–71. Stanford: Stanford University Press.

———. 1992. "'Style' for Historians and Philosophers." *Studies in History and Philosophy of Science* 23:1–20.

———. 1995. "The Looping Effect of Human Kinds." In *Causal Cognition: An Interdisciplinary Approach,* edited by D. Sperber, David Premack, and Ann James Premack, 351–83. Oxford: Oxford University Press.

———. 2002. *Historical Ontology*. Cambridge, MA: Harvard University Press.

———. 2007. "Kinds of People: Moving Targets." *Proceedings of the British Academy* 151: 285–318.

Hald, J., and E. Jacobsen. 1948. "A Drug Sensitizing the Organism to Ethyl Alcohol." *Lancet* 2 (26): 1001–4.

Hanninen, V., and A. Koski-Jannes. 1999. "Narratives of Recovery from Addictive Behaviours." *Addiction* 94 (12): 1837–48.

Harrington, Anne. 2006. "The Many Meanings of the Placebo Effect: Where They Came From, Why They Matter." *BioSocieties* 1 (2): 181–93.

———. 2008. *The Cure Within: A History of Mind-Body Medicine*. New York: Norton.

Harris-Offutt, Rosalyn. 1995. "Inside Russia: A Look at Alcohol and Other Drug Use, Treatment Methodologies, and Effectiveness of Treatment." *Addictions Nursing* 7 (3): 73.

Healy, David. 1997. *The Antidepressant Era*. Cambridge, MA: Harvard University Press.

Heather, N. 1989. "Disulfiram Treatment for Alcoholism. *BMJ: British Medical Journal* 299 (6697): 471.

Herlihy, Patricia. 2002. *The Alcoholic Empire: Vodka and Politics in Late Imperial Russia*. New York: Oxford University Press.

Hessler, Julie. 2001. "Postwar Normalisation and Its Limits in the USSR: The Case of Trade." *Europe-Asia Studies* 53 (3): 445–71.

Hivon, Myriam. 1994. "Vodka: The 'Spirit' of Exchange." *Cambridge Anthropology* 17 (3): 1–18.

Hoffmann, David. 2003. *Stalinist Values: The Cultural Norms of Soviet Modernity, 1917–1941*. Ithaca: Cornell University Press.

Höjdestrand, Tova. 2009. *Needed by Nobody: Homelessness and Humanness in Post-Soviet Russia*. Ithaca: Cornell University Press.

Holt, E. 2010. "Russian Injected Drug Use Soars in Face of Political Inertia." *Lancet* 376: 13–14.

Honey, Larisa. 2006. "Transforming Selves and Society: Women, Spiritual Health, and Pluralism in Post-Soviet Moscow." PhD diss., CUNY Graduate Center.

Hopper, K., J. Jost, T. Hay, S. Welber, and G. Haugland. 1997. "Homelessness, Severe Mental Illness, and the Institutional Circuit." *Psychiatric Services* 48 (5): 659–65.

Hoskovec, J. 1967. "A Review of Some Major Works in Soviet Hypnotherapy." *International Journal of Clinical and Experimental Hypnosis* 15 (1): 1–10.

Humphrey, Caroline. 2002. *The Unmaking of Soviet Life: Everyday Economies after Socialism*. Ithaca: Cornell University Press.

Humphreys, Keith. 2000 "Community Narratives and Personal Stories in Alcoholics Anonymous." *Journal of Community Psychology* 28: 495–506.

Ialovoi, A. Ia. 1968. "Zamena Alkogol'no-Antabusnoi Probi Pri Lechenie Alkogolizma Platsebo" [Substitution of the alcohol-Antabuse test with a placebo in the treatment of alcoholism]. *Zhurnal Nevrologii i Psikhiatrii Imeni S.S. Korsakova* 68 (4): 593–96.

Illouz, Eva. 2008. *Saving the Modern Soul: Therapy, Emotions, and the Culture of Self-Help*. Berkeley: University of California Press.

Insel, Thomas R., and Remi Quirion. 2005. "Psychiatry as a Clinical Neuroscience Discipline." *JAMA* 294 (17): 2221–24.

Isaev, D., and V. Kagan. 1979. *Polovoe Vospitanie i Psikhogigiena Pola u Detei* [Sex education and the psychohygiene of sex among children]. Leningrad: Meditsina.

Ivanets, N. N. 2001. *Lektsii Po Narkologii* [Lectures on addiction medicine]. Moscow: Medica.

Ivanets, N. N., I. P. Anokhina, E. V. Borisova, and E. A. Kochkina. 2000. "The Modern Problem of Addiction in Russia: Status and Perspectives." *International Addiction* 1. http://www.ucalgary.ca/ucpress/journals/IA/modern_frame.html.

Ivanets, N. N., and Iu. V. Valentik. 1988. *Alkogolizm* [Alcoholism]. Moscow: Nauka.

Janousek, Jaromir, and Irina Sirotkina. 2003. "Psychology in Russia and Central and Eastern Europe." In *The Cambridge History of Science*. Vol. 7, *The Modern Social Sciences*, edited by Theodore Porter, 431–49. Cambridge: Cambridge University Press.

Jellinek, E. M. 1960. *The Disease Concept of Alcoholism*. New Haven, CT: Hillhouse Press.

Johnsen, J., and J. Morland. 1992. "Depot Preparations of Disulfiram: Experimental and Clinical Results." *Acta Psychiatrica Scandinavica* 86 (S369): 27–30.

Joravsky, David. 1989. *Russian Psychology, a Critical History*. London: Blackwell.

Kalashnikov, Boris. 2001. "Pochemu Ia Protiv Kodirovanie" [Why I am against coding]. *Duel*, http://www.duel.ru/200015/?15_6_4.

Kazakovtsev, B. A., Victor D. Styazhkin, and L. A. Tarasevich. 2002. "Psikhosotsial'naia Reabilitatsiia Patsientov s Sindromom Zavisimosti Nakhodiashchikhsia na Prinuditel'nom Lechenii v Psikhiatricheskom Stationare" [Psychosocial rehabilitation of patients with the addiction syndrome, receiving mandatory treatment in a psychiatric clinic]. *Narkologiya* 11:12–18.

Kenna, George, John E. McGeary, and Robert M. Swift. 2004. "Pharmacotherapy, Pharmacogenomics, and the Future of Alcohol Dependence Treatment, Part 1." *American Journal of Health-System Pharmacy* 61 (21): 2272–79.

Kharkhordin, Oleg. 1999. *The Collective and the Individual in Russia: A Study of Practices*. Berkeley: University of California Press.

Kirichenko, Vladimir F. 1967. *Ob Usilenii Bor'by s Khuliganstvom*. [On the strengthening of the battle with hooliganism]. Moscow: Znanie.

Kirman, Brian H. 1966. "Psychotherapy in the Soviet Union." In *Present-Day Russian Psychology: A Symposium by Seven Authors*, edited by Neil O'Connor, 39–62. New York: Pergamon Press.

Kirmayer, Laurence J. 1993. "Healing and the Invention of Metaphor: The Effectiveness of Symbols Revisited." *Culture, Medicine and Psychiatry* 17 (2): 161–95.

———. 2006. "Toward a Medicine of the Imagination." *New Literary History* 37 (3): 583–601.

———. 2007. "Psychotherapy and the Cultural Concept of the Person." *Transcultural Psychiatry* 44 (2): 232–57.

Kitanaka, Junko. 2012. *Depression in Japan: Psychiatric Cures for a Society in Distress* Princeton, NJ: Princeton University Press.

Kline, S. A., and E. Kingstone. 1977 "Disulfiram Implants: The Right Treatment but the Wrong Drug?" *Canadian Medical Association Journal* 116 (12): 1382–83.

Koch, Erin. 2013. *Free Market Tuberculosis: Managing Epidemics in Post-Soviet Georgia* Nashville: Vanderbilt University Press.

Kolomeiskaia, Inna. 1999. "Rossiiskikh P'ianets Zamorskie Stredstva ne Berut" [Foreign funding won't take Russian drunks]. *Segodnia*, August 12.

Kornai, Janos. 1992. *The Socialist System: The Political Economy of Communism*. Princeton: Princeton University Press.

Koselleck, Reinhart. 2006. "Crisis." *Journal of the History of Ideas* 67(2): 357–400.

Kotkin, Stephen. 1995. *Magnetic Mountain: Stalinism as a Civilization*. Berkeley: University of California Press.

Kozulin, Alexander. 1984. *Psychology in Utopia*. Cambridge, MA: MIT Press.

Kreisler, Harry, and Michael Marmot. 2002. "Redefining Public Health: Epidemiology and Social Stratification. Conversation with Sir Michael Marmot." Conversations with History. Institute of International Studies, University of California—Berkeley. http://globetrotter.berkeley.edu/people2/Marmot/marmot-con3.html.

Kurtz, Ernest. 1979. *Not-God: A History of Alcoholics Anonymous*. Minneapolis: Hazelden Foundation.

Lakoff, Andrew. 2006. *Pharmaceutical Reason: Knowledge and Value in Global Psychiatry*. Cambridge: Cambridge University Press.

Latypov, Alisher B. 2011. "The Soviet Doctor and the Treatment of Drug Addiction: 'A Difficult and Most Ungracious Task.'" *Harm Reduction Journal* 8 (1): 1–19.

Lauterbach, Wolf. 1984. *Soviet Psychotherapy*. London: Pergamon Press.

Ledeneva, Alena. 1998. *Russia's Economy of Favors: Blat, Networking, and Informal Exchange*. New York: Cambridge University Press.

Lemere, Fredrick. 1987. "Aversion Treatment of Alcoholism: Some Reminiscences." *British Journal of Addiction* 82:257–58.

Leon, David A., Laurent Chenet, Vladimir M. Shkolnikov, Sergei Zakharov, Judith Shapiro, Galina Rakhmanova, Sergei Vassin, and Martin McKee. 1997. "Huge Variation in Russian Mortality Rates 1984–94: Artefact, Alcohol, or What?" *Lancet* 350:383–88.

Leon, David A., Lyudmila Saburova, Susannah Tomkins, Evgueny Andreev, Nikolay Kiryanov, Martin McKee, and Vladimir M. Shkolnikov. 2007. "Hazardous Alcohol Drinking and Premature Mortality in Russia: A Population Based Case-Control Study." *Lancet* 369:2001–9.

Leshner, Alan I. 1997. "Addiction Is a Brain Disease, and It Matters." *Science* 278 (5335): 45.

Lévi-Strauss, Claude. 1963. *Structural Anthropology*. New York: Basic Books.

Levine, Misha Boris. 1999. "The 1985 Alcohol Reform in the USSR: A Case of Rejected Moral Reform." PhD diss., McMaster University.

Lincoln, W. Bruce. 2001. *Sunlight at Midnight: St. Petersburg and the Rise of Modern Russia*. Boulder: Basic Books.

Lindquist, Galina. 2005. *Conjuring Hope: Magic and Healing in Contemporary Russia*. New York: Berghahn Books.

Lipgart, N.K., A.V. Goloburda, and V. V. Ivanov. 1991. [Once more about A. R. Dobzhenko's method of stress psychotherapy in alcoholism]. *Zhurnal Nevrologii i Psikhiatrii Imeni S. S. Korsakova* 91 (6): 133–34.

Lock, Margaret, and Vinh-Kim Nguyen. 2010. *An Anthropology of Biomedicine*. Oxford: Wiley-Blackwell.

Lovell, Anne M. 2006. "Addiction Markets: The Case of High-Dose Buprenorphine in France." In *Global Pharmaceuticals: Ethics, Markets, Practices*, edited by Adriana

Petryna, Andrew Lakoff, and Arthur Kleinman, 136–70. Durham, NC: Duke University Press.

———. 2013. "Elusive Travelers: Russian Narcology, Transnational Toxicomanias, and the Great French Ecological Experiment." In *Addiction Trajectories*, edited by Eugene Raikhel and William Garriott, 126–59. Durham, NC: Duke University Press.

Lowie, Robert. 1948. *Social Organization*. New York: Rinehart.

Luhrmann, Tanya M. 2000. *Of Two Minds: The Growing Disorder in American Psychiatry*. New York: Knopf.

Mäkelä, Klaus. 1991. "Social and Cultural Preconditions of Alcoholics Anonymous (AA) and Factors Associated with the Strength of AA." *Addiction* 86 (11): 1405–13.

Mäkelä, Klaus, Ilkka Arminen, Kim Bloomfield, Irmgard Eisenbach-Stangl, Karin Helmersson Bergmark, Noriko Kurube, Nicoletta Mariolini et al. 1996. *Alcoholics Anonymous as a Mutual-Help Movement: A Study in Eight Societies*. Madison: University of Wisconsin Press.

Makinen, Ilkka Henrik, and Therese C. Reitan. 2006. "Continuity and Change in Russian Alcohol Consumption from the Tsars to Transition." *Social History* 31 (2): 160–79.

Malcolm, M. T., J. S. Madden, and A. E. Williams. 1974. "Disulfiram Implantation Critically Evaluated." *British Journal of Psychiatry* 125 (5): 485.

Mann, Karl. 2004. "Pharmacotherapy of Alcohol Dependence: A Review of the Clinical Data." *CNS Drugs* 18 (8): 485–504.

Marmot, Michael. 2004. *The Status Syndrome: How Social Standing Affects Our Health and Longevity*. New York: Times Books.

Marmot, Michael, Stephen Stansfeld, Chandra Patel, Fiona North, Jenny Head, Ian White, Eric Brunner, Amanda Feeney, and G. Davey Smith. 1991. "Health Inequalities among British Civil Servants: The Whitehall II Study." *Lancet* 337 (8754): 1387–93.

Martensen-Larsen, O. 1948. Treatment of Alcoholism with a Sensitizing Drug. *Lancet* 2 (6539): 1004.

Martin, Emily. 2000. Mind-Body Problems. *American Ethnologist* 27 (3): 569–590.

Matthews, Mervyn. 1993. *The Passport Society: Controlling Movement in Russia and the USSR*. Boulder: Westview Press.

Matza, Tomas. 2009. "Moscow's Echo: Technologies of the Self, Publics, and Politics on the Russian Talk Show." *Cultural Anthropology* 24 (3): 489–522.

———. 2012. "'Good Individualism'? Psychology, Ethics, and Neoliberalism in Postsocialist Russia." *American Ethnologist* 39: 804–18.

McKee, Martin, and David Leon. 2005. "Social Transition and Substance Abuse." *Addiction* 100:1205–9.

Mendelevich, V. D. 2004. [Contemporary Russian narcology: The paradoxicality of principles and imperfection of procedures]. http://www.narkotiki.ru/5_5801.htm.

———. 2013. "Psikhopatologicheskaia Doktrina v Otechestvennoi Narkologii i Problema Dokazatel'noi Meditsiny" [The psychopathological doctrine in domestic narcology and the problem of evidence-based medicine]. *Obozrenie Psikhiatrii i Meditsinskoi Psikhologii* 3:33–38.

Meyers, Todd. 2013. *The Clinic and Elsewhere: Addiction, Adolescents, and the Afterlife of Therapy*. Seattle: University of Washington Press.

Meylakhs, Peter. 2009. "Drugs and Symbolic Pollution: The Work of Cultural Logic in the Russian Press." *Cultural Sociology* 3(3): 377–95.

Miller, Martin. 1998. *Freud and the Bolsheviks: Psychoanalysis in Imperial Russia and the Soviet Union*. New Haven: Yale University Press.

Miroshnichenko, L. D., V. E. Pelipas, and N. N. Ivanets 2001. *Narkologicheskii Entsiklopedicheskii Slovar'* [Narcological encyclopedic dictionary]. Moscow: Anakharsis.

Moerman, Daniel. 2002. *Meaning, Medicine, and the Placebo Effect*. New York: Cambridge University Press.

Morozov, G., and Ia. Kalashnik. 1971. *Forensic Psychiatry*. New York: International Universities Press.

Narcology Research Institute. 2012. Plan for the Modernization of the Narcology Service of the Russian Federation by 2016. Moscow: Narcology Research Institute. http://www.nncn.ru/modernization.htm.

Nemtsov, A. 2011. *A Contemporary History of Alcohol in Russia*. Stokholm: Södertörns högskola.

Nguyen, Vinh-Kim. 2005. "Antiretroviral Globalism, Biopolitics, and Therapeutic Citizenship." In *Global Assemblages: Technology, Politics, and Ethics as Anthropological Problems*, edited by Stephen Collier and Aihwa Ong. Oxford: Blackwell.

———. 2009. "Government-by-Exception: Enrolment and Experimentality in Mass HIV Treatment Programmes in Africa." *Social Theory & Health* 7 (3): 196–217.

Nikitinskii, Leonid. 2004. "Mitki bez Portveina" [Mitki without port wine]. *Novaia Gazeta*, July 8.

Notzon, Francis, Yuri Komarov, Sergei Ermakov, Christopher Sempos, James Marks, and Elena Sempos. 1998. "Causes of Declining Life Expectancy in Russia." *JAMA* 279:793–800.

Ong, Aihwa. 1988. "The Production of Possession: Spirits and the Multinational Corporation in Malaysia." *American Ethnologist* 15 (1): 28–42.

Orlov, Arkadii. "Kurort Za Reshetkoi" [A resort behind bars]. *Smena*. http://www.smena.ru/Arc/22948-Log.html.

Oushakine, Serguei. 2007. "Vitality Rediscovered: Theorizing Post-Soviet Ethnicity in Russian Social Sciences." *Studies in East European Thought* 59 (3): 171–93.

Paoli, Letizia. 2002. "The Development of an Illegal Market: Drug Consumption and Trade in Post-Soviet Russia." *British Journal of Criminology* 42:21–39.

Parfitt, Tom. 2006. "Putin Urged to Address 'Russia's Curse.'" *Lancet* 367 (9506): 197–98.

Parry, Jonathan P., and Maurice Bloch. 1989. *Money and the Morality of Exchange*. Cambridge: Cambridge University Press.

Parsons, Michelle. 2014. *Dying Unneeded: The Cultural Context of the Russian Mortality Crisis*. Nashville: Vanderbilt University Press.

Patico, Jennifer. 2002. "Chocolate and Cognac: Gifts and the Recognition of Social Worlds in Post-Soviet Russia." *Ethnos* 67 (3): 285–94.

Pavlov, Ivan P. 1994. "Relations between Excitation and Inhibition: Delimitation between Excitation and Inhibition, Experimental Neuroses in Dogs." In *Psychopathology and Psychiatry*. New York: Transaction Publishers.

Pelkmans, Mathijs, and Rhys Machold. 2011. "Conspiracy Theories and Their Truth Trajectories." *Focaal* 59:66–80.

Pesmen, Dale. 2000. *Russia and Soul: An Exploration*. Ithaca: Cornell University Press.

Petersen, Alan, and Robin Bunton, eds. 1997. *Foucault, Health and Medicine*. London: Routledge.

Petryna, Adriana. 2002. *Life Exposed: Biological Citizens after Chernobyl*. Princeton: Princeton University Press.

——. 2007. "Experimentality: On the Global Mobility and Regulation of Human Subjects Research." *PoLAR: Political and Legal Anthropology Review* 30 (2): 288–304.

Phillips, Laura. 2000. *Bolsheviks and the Bottle: Drink and Worker Culture in St. Petersburg, 1900–1929*. DeKalb: Northern Illinois University Press.

Phillips, Sarah D., 2010. *Disability and Mobile Citizenship in Postsocialist Ukraine*. Bloomington: Indiana University Press.

Platonov, K. I. 1959. *The Word as a Physiological and Therapeutic Factor: The Theory and Practice of Psychotherapy according to I. P. Pavlov*. Moscow: Foreign Languages Publishing House.

Popov, V. P. 1995. "Pasportnaia Sistema v SSSR (1932–1976)" [Passport system in the USSR (1932–1976)]. *Sotsiologicheskie Issledovania* 8:3–14.

Pozdniaev, Mikhail. 2005. "Profilaktika Za Kolyuchei Provoloki" [Therapy behind barbed wire]. *Novye Izvestiia*, December 1.

Pridemore, William Alex. 2002. "Vodka and Violence: Alcohol Consumption and Homicide Rates in Russia." *American Journal of Public Health* 92 (12): 1921–30.

Rabinow, Paul, 1992. "Artificiality and Enlightenment: From Sociobiology to Biosociality." In *Zone 6: Incorporations*, edited by Jonathan Crary. Cambridge, MA: MIT Press.

——. 2003. *Anthropos Today: Reflections on Modern Equipment*. Princeton: Princeton University Press.

Raikhel, Eugene, and William Garriott. 2013. "Tracing New Paths in the Anthropology of Addiction." In *Addiction Trajectories*, edited by Eugene Raikhel and William Garriott, 1–35. Durham, NC: Duke University Press.

Ries, Nancy. 1997. *Russian Talk: Culture and Conversation during Perestroika*. Ithaca: Cornell University Press.

Rimke, Heidi Marie. 2000. "Governing Citizens through Self-Help Literature." *Cultural Studies* 14 (1): 61–78.

Rivkin-Fish, Michele. 2003. "Anthropology, Demography, and the Search for a Critical Analysis of Fertility: Insights from Russia." *American Anthropologist* 105 (2): 289–301.

——. 2005. *Women's Health in Post-Soviet Russia: The Politics of Intervention*. Bloomington: Indiana University Press.

Rogers, Douglas. 2005. "Moonshine, Money, and the Politics of Liquidity in Rural Russia." *American Ethnologist* 32 (1): 63–81.

Roitman, Janet. 2011. "Crisis." *Political Concepts: A Critical Lexicon*, 1. http://www.politicalconcepts.org/issue1/crisis/.

——. 2014. *Anti-crisis*. Durham, NC: Duke University Press.

Rose, Nikolas. 1996. *Inventing Ourselves: Psychology, Power and Personhood*. Cambridge: Cambridge University Press.

——. 2007. *The Politics of Life Itself: Biomedicine, Power, and Subjectivity in the Twenty-First Century*. Princeton: Princeton University Press.

Rozhnov, V. E. 1977. *Proroki i Chudotvortsy: Etiudy o Mistitsizme* [Prophets and miracle workers: Studies on mysticism]. Moscow: Politizdat.

——. 1989. "Emotsional'no-Stressovaia Psikhoterapiia" [Emotional-stress psychotherapy]. *Zhurnal Nevrologii i Psikhiatrii Imeni S. S. Korsakova* 89 (1): 58–62.

Rozhnov, V. E., and M. E. Burno. 1987. "Sistema Emotsional'no-Stressovoi Psikhoterapii Bol'nykh Alkogolizmom," [A system of emotional-stress psychotherapy for alcoholism patients]. Moscow: Sovetskaia Meditsina.

Rozhnov, V. E., and M. Rozhnova. 1987. *Gipnoz ot Drevnosti do Nashikh Dnei* [Hypnosis from ancient times to today]. Moscow: Sovietskaja Rossiia.

Rudy, J. 1986. *Becoming Alcoholic: Alcoholics Anonymous and the Reality of Alcoholism*. Carbondale: Southern Illinois University Press.Ryan, Michael. 1978. *The Organization of Soviet Medical Care*. Oxford: Blackwell.

——. 1990. *Doctors and the State in the Soviet Union*. New York: St. Martin's.

Salmi, Anna-Maria. 2003. "Health in Exchange: Teachers, Doctors, and the Strength of Informal Practices in Russia." *Culture, Medicine and Psychiatry* 27 (2): 109–30.

Sampson, Steven. 1987. "The Second Economy in Eastern Europe and the Soviet Union." *Annals of the American Academy of Political and Social Science* 493:120 36.

Saris, A. Jamie. 2008. "An Uncertain Dominion: Irish Psychiatry, Methadone, and the Treatment of Opiate Abuse." *Culture, Medicine and Psychiatry* 32 (2): 259–77.

Schecter, Kate. 2000. "The Politics of Health Care in Russia: The Feminization of Medicine and Other Obstacles to Professionalism." In *Russia's Torn Safety Nets: Health and Social Welfare during the Transition*, edited by Mark Field and Judyth Twigg, 83–99. New York: St. Martin's.

Schüll, Natasha Dow. 2012. *Addiction by Design: Machine Gambling in Las Vegas*. Princeton: Princeton University Press.

Scott, James C. 1998. *Seeing Like a State: How Certain Schemes to Improve the Human Condition Have Failed*. New Haven: Yale University Press.

Seddon, Toby. 2007. "Drugs and Freedom." *Addiction Research and Theory* 15 (4): 333–42.

Sedgwick, Eve Kosofsky. 1993. "Epidemics of the Will." In *Tendencies*, 130–42. Durham, NC: Duke University Press.

Segal, Boris. 1975. "The Theoretical Bases of Soviet Psychotherapy." *American Journal of Psychotherapy* 29 (4): 503–23.

——. 1990. *The Drunken Society: Alcohol Abuse and Alcoholism in the Soviet Union: A Comparative Study*. New York: Hippocrene Books.

Sereiskii, M. Ia. 1952. "Lechenie Khronicheskogo Alkogolizma Tiuramom [*Treatment of chronic alcoholism with tiuram*]. *Zhurnal Nevropatologii i Psikhiatrii Imeni S. S. Korsakova* 52(4): 51–57.

Shagin, Dmitrii. 1999. *Bezzavetnye Geroi* [Selfless heroes]. St. Petersburg: Obraztsovaja tipografia.

Shearer, David. 2004. "Elements Near and Alien: Passportization, Policing, and Identity in the Stalinist State, 1932–1952." *Journal of Modern History* 76:835–81.

Sheiman, I. 1994. "Forming the System of Health Insurance in the Russian Federation." *Social Science and Medicine* 39:1425–32.

Shevchenko, Olga. 2009. *Crisis and the Everyday in Postsocialist Moscow*. Bloomington: Indiana University Press.

Shlapentokh, Vladimir. 2005. "Russia's Demographic Decline and the Public Reaction." *Europe-Asia Studies* 57 (7): 951–68.

Simpura Jussi, and Boris M. Levin, eds. 1997. *Demystifying Russian Drinking: Comparative Studies from the 1990s*. Helsinki: Stakes.

Sirotkina, Irina. 2002. *Diagnosing Literary Genius: A Cultural History of Psychiatry in Russia*. Baltimore, MD: Johns Hopkins University Press.

Skultans, Vieda. 1997. "A Historical Disorder: Neurasthenia and the Testimony of Lives in Latvia." *Anthropology & Medicine* 4:7–24.

———. 2003. "From Damaged Nerves to Masked Depression: Inevitability and Hope in Latvian Psychiatric Narratives." *Social Science and Medicine* 56 (12): 2421–31.

———. 2005. "Varieties of Deception and Distrust: Moral Dilemmas in the Ethnography of Psychiatry." *Health* 9 (4): 491–512.

Slaby, Jan, and Suparna Choudhury. 2012. "Proposal for a Critical Neuroscience." In *Critical Neuroscience: A Handbook of the Social and Cultural Contexts of Neuroscience*, edited by Suparna Choudhury and Jan Slaby, 29–51. Chichester, UK: Wiley-Blackwell.

Slobodianik, A.P. 1963. *Psikhoterapiia, Vnushenie, Gipnoz* [Psychotherapy, suggestion, hypnosis]. Kiev: Gos. Med. Izd. USSR.

Sluchevsky, I.F., and A.A. Friken. 1933 "Lechenie Khronicheskogo Alkogolizma Apomorfinom" [On the treatment of chronic alcoholism with apomorphine]. *Sovetskaja Vrachebnaja Gazeta* 12:557–561.

Smith, Roger. 1992. *Inhibition: History and Meaning in the Sciences of Mind and Brain*. Berkeley: University of California Press.

Smith. Theresa C., and Thomas Oleszczuk. 1996. *No Asylum: State Psychiatric Repression in the Former USSR*. London: Macmillan.

Sofronov, Alexander G. 2003. "Aktual'nye Problemy Razvitiia Otechestvennoi Narkologii" [Issues in the development of a domestic narcology]. *Narkologiia* 3:2–6.

Solnick, Steven L. 1998. *Stealing the State: Control and Collapse in Soviet Institutions*. Cambridge, MA: Harvard University Press.

Solomon, Peter. 1978. *Soviet Criminologists and Criminal Policy: Specialists in Policy-Making*. London: Macmillan.

Solomon, Susan Gross. 1989. "David and Goliath in Soviet Public Health: The Rivalry of Social Hygienists and Psychiatrists for Authority over the Bytovoi Alcoholic." *Soviet Studies* 41 (2): 254–75.

———. 1990. "Social Hygiene and Soviet Public Health, 1921–1930." In *Health and Society in Revolutionary Russia*, edited by Susan Gross Solomon and John F. Hutchinson, 175–99. Bloomington: Indiana University Press.

Spicer, Jerry. 1993. *The Minnesota Model: The Evolution of the Multidisciplinary Approach to Addiction Recovery*. Center City, MN: Hazelden Educational Materials.

Stuckler, David, Lawrence King, and Martin McKee. 2009. "Mass Privatisation and the Post-Communist Mortality Crisis: A Cross-National Analysis." *Lancet* 373 (9661): 399–407.

Steffen, Viebeke. 2005. "Challenging Control: Antabuse Medication in Denmark." In *Managing Uncertainty: Ethnographic Studies of Illness, Risk and the Struggle for Control*, edited by H. Jessen, V. Steffen, and R. Jenkins. Copenhagen: University of Copenhagen/Museum Tusculanum Press.

Stephenson, Svetlana. 2006. Crossing the Line: Vagrancy, Homelessness and Social Displacement in Russia. Aldeshot, UK: Ashgate.

Strel'chuk, Ivan V. 1951. "Novyi Metod Lecheniia Alkogolikov Antabusom" [Treatment of alcoholics with Antabuse: Preliminary report]. *Nevropatologia i Psikhiatriia* 20 (1): 80–83.

———. 1952. Dal'neishie Nabliudeniia za Lecheniem Chronicheskogo Alkogolizma Antabusom (Tetraetiltiuramdisul'firadom) [Continued observations on the treatment of chronic alcoholism with Antabuse (Tetraethylthiuram disulfide)]. *Zhurnal Nevropatologii i Psikhiatrii Imeni S. S. Korsakova* 52 (4): 43–50.

———. 1954. *Alkogol': Vrag Cheloveka* [Alcohol: Enemy of humanity]. Moscow: Znanie.

Suh, J. J., H. M. Pettinati, K. M. Kampman, and C. P. O'Brien. 2006. "The Status of Disulfiram: A Half of a Century Later." *Journal of Clinical Psychopharmacology* 26 (3): 290.

Swora, M. G. 2002. "Narrating Community: The Creation of Social Structure in Alcoholics Anonymous through the Performance of Autobiography." *Narrative Inquiry* 11 (2): 363–84.

Takala, Irina. 2002. *Veselie Rusi: Istoriya Alkogol'noi Problemyi v Rossii* [Joyful Russians: The history of alcohol problems in Russia]. St. Petersburg: Zhurnal Neva.

Ticktin, Miriam. 2006. "Where Ethics and Politics Meet. *American Ethnologist* 33 (1): 33.

Tichtchenko, Pavel D., and Boris G. Yudin. 2000. "Toward a Bioethics in Post-Communist Russia." In *Cross-Cultural Perspectives in Medical Ethics*, edited by Robert M. Veatch, 220–33. Sudbury, MA: Jones & Bartlett.

Tkachevskii, Yu. M. 1974. *Pravovye Mery Bor'by s Pianstvom*. [Legal means in the fight against drunkenness]. Moscow: Moscow University Press.

———. 1990. *Pravovye Aspekty Bor'by s Narkomaniei i Alkogolizmom* [Legal aspects of the fight against drug addiction and alcoholism]. Moscow: Profizdat.

Todes, Daniel P. 1995. "Pavlov and the Bolsheviks." *History and Philosophy of the Life Sciences* 17 (3): 379–418.

———. 1997. "From the Machine to the Ghost Within: Pavlov's Transition from Digestive Physiology to Conditional Reflexes." *American Psychologist* 52 (9): 947–55.

———. 2002. *Pavlov's Physiology Factory: Experiment, Interpretation, Laboratory Enterprise*. Baltimore: Johns Hopkins University Press.

Todorova, Mariia Nikolaeva, and Zsuzsa Gille. 2010. Post Communist Nostalgia. Oxford: Berghahn Books.

Tomkins, S., L. Saburova, N. Kiryanov, E. Andreev, M. McKee, V. Shkolnikov, and D. A. Leon. 2007. "Prevalence and Socio-economic Distribution of Hazardous Patterns of Alcohol Drinking: Study of Alcohol Consumption in Men Aged 25–54 years in Izhevsk, Russia." *Addiction* 102 (4): 544–53.

Transchel, Kate. 2006. *Under the Influence: Working-Class Drinking, Temperance, and Cultural Revolution in Russia, 1895–1932.* Pittsburgh: University of Pittsburgh Press.

Treml, Vladimir. 1982. *Alcohol in the USSR: A Statistical Study.* Durham, NC: Duke University Press.

Tsyboulsky, Vadim B. 2001. "Patient's Rights in Russia." *European Journal of Health Law* 8 (3): 257–63.

Tumakova, Irina. 2004. "Na Finansovoi Igle" [Hooked on the financial needle]. *Izvestiia,* October 16, 5.

Twigg, Judyth. 1998. "Balancing the State and the Market: Russia's Adoption of Obligatory Medical Insurance." *Europe-Asia Studies* 50 (4): 583–602.

United Nations Office on Drugs and Crime (UNODC). 2011. *World Drug Report 2011.* Geneva: United Nations Publications, United Nations Office on Drugs and Crime.

Valentik, Yu. V. 2001. "Contemporary Methods of Psychotherapy for Patients Suffering from Dependence to Psychoactive Substances." In *Lektsii po Narkologii* [Lectures on addiction medicine], edited by N. N. Ivanets. Moscow: Medica.

Valsiner, Jaan. 2001. "From Energy to Collectivity: A Commentary on the Development of Bekhterev's Theoretical Views." In V. M. Bekhterev, *Collective Reflexology: The Complete Edition.* Edited by Lloyd H. Strickland. Translated by Eugenia Lockwood and Alisa Lockwood. New Brunswick, NJ: Transaction Publishers.

Valverde, Mariana. 1998. *Diseases of the Will: Alcohol and the Dilemmas of Freedom.* Cambridge: Cambridge University Press.

Valverde, Mariana, and Kimberley White-Mair. 1999. "'One Day at a Time' and Other Slogans for Everyday Life: The Ethical Practices of Alcoholics Anonymous." *Sociology* 33 (2): 393–410.

Van der Geest, Siaak, and Kaja Finkler. 2004. "Hospital Ethnography: Introduction." *Social Science & Medicine* 59:1995–2001.

Vasilyev, Pavel. 2012. "Medical Science, the State, and the Construction of the Juvenile Drug Addict in Early Soviet Russia." *Social Justice* 38 (4): 31–52.

Verdery, Katherine. 1996. *What Was Socialism, and What Comes Next?* Princeton: Princeton University Press.

Volkov, Vadim. 2002. *Violent Entrepreneurs: The Use of Force in the Making of Russian Capitalism.* Ithaca: Cornell University Press.

Voskresenskii, V. A. 1990. [Critical evaluation of ultra-rapid psychotherapy of alcoholism (concerning the article by A. R. Dovzhenko et al., "Ambulatory stress psychotherapy of alcoholics")]. *Zhurnal Nevrologii i Psikhiatrii Imeni S. S. Korsakova* 90:130–32.

Vrecko, Scott. 2006. "Folk Neurology and the Remaking of Identity." *Molecular Interventions* 6 (6): 300–303.

———. 2010. "Birth of a Brain Disease: Science, the State and Addiction Neuropolitics." *History of the Human Sciences* 23 (4): 52–67.

White, Stephen. 1996. *Russia Goes Dry: Alcohol, State and Society.* Cambridge: Cambridge University Press.

White, William L. 1998. *Slaying the Dragon: The History of Addiction Treatment and Recovery in America*. Bloomington, IL: Chestnut Health Systems/Lighthouse Institute.

Wilcox, Danny M. 1998. *Alcoholic Thinking: Language, Culture, and Belief in Alcoholics Anonymous*. New York: Praeger/Greenwood.

Williams, E. E. 1937. "Effects of Alcohol on Workers with Carbon Disulfide." *JAMA* 109:1472–73.

Windholz, George. 1997. "The 1950 Joint Scientific Session: Pavlovians as the Accusers and the Accused." *Journal of the History of the Behavioral Sciences* 33 (1): 61–81.

Wolff, Larry. 1994. *Inventing Eastern Europe: The Map of Civilization on the Mind of the Enlightenment*. Stanford: Stanford University Press.

Wortis, Joseph. 1950. *Soviet Psychiatry*. Baltimore: Williams & Wilkins.

Wyckham, Robert. 1999. "Smokeless Tobacco in Canada: Deterring Market Development." *Tobacco Control* 8:411–20.

Young, Allan. 1995. *The Harmony of Illusions: Inventing Post-Traumatic Stress Disorder*. Princeton: Princeton University Press.

———. 2000. "History, Hystery and Psychiatric Styles of Reasoning." In *Living and Working with the New Medical Technologies: Intersections of Inquiry*, edited by M. Lock, A. Young, and A. Cambrosio. Cambridge: Cambridge University Press.

Yurchak, Alexei. 1999. "Gagarin and the Rave Kids: Transforming Power, Identity and Aesthetics in Post-Soviet Nightlife." In *Consuming Russia: Popular Culture, Sex, and Society since Gorbachev*, edited by Adele Barker, 76–109. Durham, NC: Duke University Press.

———. 2006. *Everything Was Forever, Until It Was No More: The Last Soviet Generation*. Princeton: Princeton University Press.

Zajicek, Benjamin. 2009. *Scientific Psychiatry in Stalin's Soviet Union*. PhD diss., University of Chicago.

Zdravomyslova, Elena, and Anna Temkina. 2012. "The Crisis of Masculinity in Late Soviet Discourse." *Russian Studies in History* 51 (2): 13–34.

Zenevich, G. V. 1967. *Vrednaia Privychka ili Bolezn': O Vrede Alkogolizma* [Bad habit or illness: On the harmfulness of alcoholism]. Leningrad: Meditsina.

Zharikov, N. M. 1999. *Sudebnaia Psikhiatriia*. [Forensic psychiatry]. Moscow: Norma.

Zhislin, S. G. 1959. [Alcoholic abstinence syndrome]. *Zhurnal Nevrologii i Psikhiatrii Imeni S. S. Korsakova* 59 (6): 641–48.

Zhislin, S. G., and I. I. Lukomskii. 1963. "30 Let Uslovnoreflektornoi Terapii Alkogolizma" [30 years of conditioned-reflex therapy of alcoholism]. *Zhurnal Nevrologii i Psikhiatrii Imeni S. S. Korsakova* 63:1884.

Zigon, Jarrett. 2010. *"HIV Is God's Blessing": Rehabilitating Morality in Neoliberal Russia*. Berkeley: University of California Press.

Zola, Irving. K., 1972. "Medicine as an Institution of Social Control." *Sociological Review* 20 (4): 487–504.

INDEX

CPSIA information can be obtained at www.ICGtesting.com
Printed in the USA
BVOW04s1439061016

464305BV00001B/18/P

9 781501 703133